Serbian

An Essential Grammar

Serbian: An Essential Grammar is an up to date and practical reference guide to the most important aspects of Serbian as used by contemporary native speakers of the language.

This book presents an accessible description of the language, focusing on real, contemporary patterns of use. The *Grammar* aims to serve as a reference source for the learner and user of Serbian irrespective of level, by setting out the complexities of the language in short, readable sections.

It is ideal for independent study or for students in schools, colleges, universities and all types of adult classes.

Features of this *Grammar* include:

- use of Cyrillic and Latin script in plentiful examples throughout
- a cultural section on the language and its dialects
- clear and detailed explanations of simple and complex grammatical concepts
- detailed contents list and index for easy access to information.

Lila Hammond has been teaching Serbian both in Serbia and the UK for over twenty-five years and presently teaches at the Defence School of Languages, Beaconsfield, UK.

Routledge Essential Grammars

Essential Grammars are available for the following languages:

Chinese
Danish
Dutch
English
Finnish
Modern Greek
Modern Hebrew
Hungarian
Norwegian
Polish
Portuguese
Serbian
Spanish
Swedish
Thai
Urdu

Other titles of related interest published by Routledge:

Colloquial Croatian
Colloquial Serbian

Serbian

An Essential Grammar

 **Lila Hammond**

 Routledge
Taylor & Francis Group

LONDON AND NEW YORK

First published 2005
by Routledge
2 Park Square, Milton Park, Abingdon, Oxon OX14 4RN

Simultaneously published in the USA and Canada
by Routledge
270 Madison Ave, New York, NY 10016

Routledge is an imprint of the Taylor & Francis Group, an informa business

Reprinted 2006, 2007, 2008, 2009

© 2005 Lila Hammond

Typeset in 10/12pt Sabon
by Graphicraft Ltd, Hong Kong
Printed and bound in Great Britain
by the MPG Books Group

All rights reserved. No part of this book may be reprinted or reproduced or utilized in any form or by any electronic, mechanical, or other means, now known or hereafter invented, including photocopying and recording, or in any information storage or retrieval system, without permission in writing from the publishers.

British Library Cataloguing in Publication Data
A catalogue record for this book is available from the British Library

Library of Congress Cataloging in Publication Data
Hammond, Lila,
   Serbian : an essential grammar / Lila Hammond.
      p. cm. — (Routledge essential grammars)
    Includes bibliographical references and index.
      ISBN 0–415–28641–7 (pbk. : acid free) — ISBN 0–415–28640–9 (hardback : acid free)
   1. Serbian language—Textbooks for foreign speakers—English. 2. Serbian language—Grammar. I. Title. II. Series: Essential grammar.
   PG1239.5.E5H25 2005
   491.8′282421—dc22
                                                                                                    2004010094

ISBN 10: 0–415–28640–9 (hbk)
ISBN 10: 0–415–28641–7 (pbk)

ISBN 13: 978–0–415–28640–4 (hbk)
ISBN 13: 978–0–415–28641–1 (pbk)

Part III	Parts of speech		33
Chapter 6	**Verbs**		**35**
6.1	Infinitives – classification		37
6.2	Infinitive and present tense stems		39
	6.2.1	Type I conjugation	41
	6.2.2	Type II conjugation	42
	6.2.3	Type III conjugation	48
6.3	Types of verbs and aspects		50
	6.3.1	Transitive and intransitive verbs	50
	6.3.2	Imperfective and perfective verbs	51
6.4	Present tense		58
	6.4.1	Formation of the present tense and its use	58
	6.4.2	The negative present tense	63
	6.4.3	The interrogative present	63
	6.4.4	The negative interrogative present tense	64
6.5	Past tense (perfect tense)		64
	6.5.1	Formation of the perfect tense and its use	64
	6.5.2	The negative perfect tense	69
	6.5.3	The interrogative perfect tense	70
	6.5.4	The negative interrogative perfect tense	70
6.6	Future tense		71
	6.6.1	Formation of the future tense and its use	71
	6.6.2	The negative future	73
	6.6.3	The interrogative future	74
	6.6.4	The negative interrogative future	75
6.7	Aorist tense		75
	6.7.1	Formation of the aorist tense and its use	76
	6.7.2	The negative aorist	80
	6.7.3	The interrogative aorist	80
	6.7.4	The negative interrogative aorist	81
6.8	Future II		81
	6.8.1	Uses of future II	81
	6.8.2	Formation of the future II	82
6.9	The conditional		82
	6.9.1	Uses of the conditional	82
	6.9.2	Formation of the conditional	83
6.10	Imperative		87
	6.10.1	Use of the imperative	87
	6.10.2	Formation of the imperative	88
6.11	Reflexive verbs		90
6.12	Impersonal verbs		91

Contents

Preface xiii
Acknowledgements xiv

Part I The language and its dialects 1

Chapter 1 Cultural, literary and linguistic background 3

Chapter 2 Dialects 9

Part II Alphabet, pronunciation and stress 11

Chapter 3 Alphabet 13

Chapter 4 Pronunciation 17
    4.1 Consonants 19
        4.1.1 Voiced and unvoiced consonants 19
        4.1.2 Soft and hard consonants 20
        4.1.3 Consonantal assimilations 21
        4.1.4 Consonantal contractions 22
        4.1.5 Fleeting **a** 23
        4.1.6 Change of л/l to o 24
        4.1.7 J changes 25
        4.1.8 Effects of **e**/e and **и**/i on к/k, г/g and x/h 27
    4.2 Vowels 29
        4.2.1 Length and stress 29
        4.2.2 Vowel mutations 29

Chapter 5 Stress 31
    5.1 Word stress and tone 31
    5.2 Shift of stress 32
    5.3 Sentence stress 32

I dedicate this book to
Militca, Leo and Tara

	6.13	Auxiliary verbs	92
	6.14	Formation of the interrogative	93
	6.15	Formation of the negative	95
	6.16	Present perfective aspect of **бити**/**biti**	99
	6.17	**Ићи**/**ići** and its derivatives	99
	6.18	Modal verbs	101

Chapter 7 Nouns 105

	7.1	Types of nouns	105
	7.2	Gender of nouns	111
	7.3	Cases of nouns	112
		7.3.1 Nominative case	115
		7.3.2 Genitive case	117
		7.3.3 Dative case	126
		7.3.4 Accusative case	133
		7.3.5 Vocative case	140
		7.3.6 Instrumental case	142
		7.3.7 Locative case	146
	7.4	Declension of nouns	152
		7.4.1 Masculine and neuter nouns	153
		7.4.2 Feminine and masculine nouns ending in -a and the noun **мати**/**mati**	162
		7.4.3 Feminine nouns ending in a consonant, in -o, -ост/ost or -ад/ad, and the noun **кћи**/**kći**	168
		7.4.4 Declension of irregular nouns	173

Chapter 8 Pronouns 178

	8.1	Personal pronouns	180
		8.1.1 Declension of personal pronouns	181
		8.1.2 Stressed personal pronouns	183
		8.1.3 Unstressed personal pronouns	184
		8.1.4 Order of unstressed personal pronouns	185
	8.2	Reflexive pronouns	186
	8.3	Possessive pronouns	188
	8.4	Demonstrative pronouns	192
	8.5	Relative pronouns	195
	8.6	Interrogative pronouns	197
	8.7	Universal pronouns	199

Chapter 9 Adjectives 201

	9.1	Classification of adjectives	203
	9.2	Indefinite adjectives	205
	9.3	Definite adjectives	207

9.4	Possessive adjectives		210
9.5	Adjectival declension		212
9.6	Comparative adjectives		214
9.7	Superlative adjectives		216
9.8	Verbal adjectives		217
	9.8.1	The active past participle	217
	9.8.2	Formation of the active past participle	218
	9.8.3	The passive participle	220
	9.8.4	Formation of the passive past participle	220

Chapter 10 Adverbs — 223

10.1	Substantival (nominal) adverbs		224
10.2	Adjectival adverbs		226
10.3	Pronominal adverbs		226
10.4	Verbal adverbs		229
	10.4.1	The present verbal adverb	229
	10.4.2	The past verbal adverb	231

Chapter 11 Prepositions — 233

11.1	Simple prepositions	234
11.2	Compound prepositions	235
11.3	Accentuation	235
11.4	Prepositions through the cases	236

Chapter 12 Conjunctions — 240

12.1	Coordinating conjunctions	240
12.2	Subordinating conjunctions	243
12.3	Differences in usages of што/što and који/koji	246

Chapter 13 Enclitics — 249

13.1	Order and importance of enclitics	250

Chapter 14 Numerals — 255

14.1	Cardinal numbers and their declension		255
	14.1.1	Number one	258
	14.1.2	Numerals two, three, four and the numeral 'both'	260
	14.1.3	Numerals five, six, seven and onwards	263
14.2	Ordinal numbers and their declension		265
14.3	Fractions and decimal numbers		267
14.4	Collective numerals		268
14.5	Number nouns		269
14.6	Multiplicatives		270
14.7	Approximatives		270

14.8	Distributives	271
14.9	Frequentatives	271
14.10	Weights and measures	272
14.11	Age	273
14.12	Days, months and dates	274
14.13	Time	278
	14.13.1 Telling the time	278
	14.13.2 Time-related words and expressions	280

Chapter 15 Quantifiers — 282

15.1	Types of quantifiers	282
	15.1.1 Countable quantifiers	282
	15.1.2 Uncountable quantifiers	284
	15.1.3 Countable and uncountable quantifiers	285

Chapter 16 Determiners — 288

16.1	Possessive determiners	288
16.2	Demonstrative determiners	289
16.3	Indefinite determiners	290
16.4	Interrogative determiners	291
16.5	Negative determiners	291

Chapter 17 Particles, conjunctions and exclamations — 293

Part IV Sentence elements and structure — 297

Chapter 18 Sentences — 299

18.1	Elements of a sentence	299
18.2	Types of clauses	301

Chapter 19 Sentence structure — 303

19.1	Word order	303
19.2	Punctuation	303
19.3	Simple sentences	306
19.4	Complex sentences	306

Chapter 20 Word formation — 307

20.1	Prefixes	308
20.2	Suffixes	310
	20.2.1 Nouns	310
	20.2.2 Adjectives	314

Bibliography — 316
Index — 317

Preface

The purpose of this book is to offer the English-speaking student of Serbian a thorough and accessible overview of Serbian grammar.

Serbian is a complex and expressive language and the scope of this book is too narrow to allow for sufficient examples to facilitate a more profound comprehension and understanding of the language. It does however, strive to explain, as much as possible, the rules governing most linguistic and grammatical conditions and structures.

Serbian is not a language of simple constructions and straightforward expressions, and perhaps the most important piece of advice to the student would be to approach his or her study of this language with a curious and courageous mind.

It is a beautiful language and I compliment the student wishing to learn it.

Lila Hammond
London, 2005

Acknowledgements

I wish to express my gratitude to all the people who made writing this book possible. Amongst them are Verica Stevanović, Gordana Ilić, Miroslava Virijević, as well as Farret Abbas, Wayne Doran and Zlata Krivokuća, who were always at hand with their support and encouragement.

I also wish to thank my students, for their patience and perseverance in studying this language and in continually challenging me to improve my methods of explaining and defining it. I thank them especially for their determination in pursuing their studies during those difficult times, of which there were, and inevitably are, many. Seeing them develop into users and speakers of Serbian has been a great inspiration and reward for me as a teacher.

And finally, I wish to thank my editors, Sophie Oliver and James Folan for their patience, understanding, support and trust during the writing of this book.

Part I
The language and its dialects

Chapter 1
Cultural, literary and linguistic background

Serbian belongs to the Slavonic group of languages, which, along with the Romance and Germanic languages, is one of the three largest groups of the Indo-European family of languages.

The Slavonic group of languages includes Polish, Czech and Slovak (belonging to the western group of Slavonic languages), Ukrainian, Belarus and Russian (belonging to the eastern group of Slavonic languages) and Slovenian, Serbian, Croatian, Bosnian, Bulgarian and Macedonian (belonging to the southern group of Slavonic languages).

In the sixth and seventh centuries, various Slavonic tribes, some of which were to become the Serbian nation, migrated from the north – Russia, Byelorussia and the Ukraine, where they shared the land with the eastern Slavs – and travelled to the Balkan peninsula and the region of Pannonia. At the time Bulgaria and the Byzantine Empire both wanted to occupy this region. The Slavs, themselves pagans, were also caught between the Western, Catholic, and the Eastern, Orthodox religions. In the ninth century, Serbian rulers, struggling for power, converted to Christianity and were baptised by priests from the Byzantine Empire. Different tribes joined together under the common Christian religion.

In the twelfth century, the founder of the most significant medieval Serbian dynasty, Stefan Nemanja, expanded his lands to include Kosovo and, further, to what is now the Montenegrin coast. Appointing his middle son, Stefan Nemanjić, a son-in-law of the Byzantine imperial family, to replace him, Nemanja joined his youngest son, Sava, a monk in the Orthodox faith, to become a monk himself. Stefan Nemanjić managed, through clever running of the state, to fend off Serbia's enemies. He managed to maintain good relations with both the West and the East and in the thirteenth century he received a royal crown from the Pope, which gave him the title of Stevan Prvovenčani, the 'first-crowned king' of Serbia.

His father, Stefan Nemanja, and brother, Sava, built the monastery of Hilandar on Mount Athos in Greece, which became the most prestigious

1 Cultural background

school for Serbian monks. This monastery is of great importance in the development of the Serbian church and Serbian culture.

With the appointment of Sava (who was proclaimed a saint upon his death) as archbishop in Nicaea, the centre for Greeks in Asia Minor, the links between the Serbian nation and the Orthodox tradition were further strengthened. On Sava's instruction the Byzantine code of church laws and rules for use by the clergy, as well as many medical and scientific writings, were translated. He founded the first Serbian hospitals (in Hilandar and Studenica) and was the founder of Serbian literature, having written, with his brother Stefan Nemanjić, the first original Serbian literary work, the *Vitae of St Simeon* (The Life of Stefan Nemanja, their father and founder of the dynasty). (St Sava's remains were burnt by the Turks four centuries later in Belgrade, where the temple of St Sava now stands.)

Although Sava's brother, Stefan Nemanjić, had been crowned by the Pope, he was under the influence of his brother and father and wanted to unify the Serbian state under the Orthodox religion. The Nemanja dynasty gradually succeeded in uniting all the Serbian lands and gave to their country a strong and united church, the Serbian Orthodox Church. Culturally very active, the kingdom and church had their own Slavonic liturgy and language (based on Old Slavonic). The translation of important Byzantine scrolls, liturgies, church laws, literary and architectural works was pursued and highly respected.

The Nemanja dynasty continued to rule the state, and under the rule of Stefan Dušan (1331–1355), its boundaries expanded southward to include not only Macedonia and Albania, but regions of the Byzantine Empire too. It covered the area from the Sava and Danube rivers down to the Gulf of Corinth, and became the leading power of the Balkan peninsula. And as Dušan elevated the Serbian archbishopric to the level of a Patriarchate, he was crowned the 'Emperor of the Serbs and Greeks'.

Dušan ruled the state and set up all the major state systems and judiciary based on the Byzantine model. And since some of his territories were under the rule of custom and had never been under Byzantine law, he adopted an entire code of laws, under the name of *Dušan's Code*, in an attempt to unify the territories and bridge the gap between the impoverished and the wealthy.

And, as had the rulers before him, Dušan also emulated Byzantine architecture and art, and the many monasteries and churches built in the Serbian state at the time are examples of a distinct Serbian Byzantine style in both these fields.

The Serbs were eventually conquered by the Turks in the fifteenth century. An event in history that is taken to mark the fall of the great Serbian Empire was the battle at Kosovo Polje in 1389. The lands were divided between the Turkish warlords, who recognised each religious group as an administratively separate community, even though, in many ways, the Serbian nation was placed under pressure to abide by Muslim social order. From the middle of the fifteenth century to the beginning of the nineteenth century, during the Ottoman rule, great migrations of Serbs took place. Throughout this time, the Serbian Orthodox Church did much to give the Serbs a sense of unity and continuity. In two of the most important migrations that took place during this period the people were led by their patriarchs. When the Turkish government dissolved the Patriarchate of Peć in 1766, church authority was re-established with the Greek archbishops, thus gaining an international position. In 1832, the Serbian Church became autonomous. It did not unify into a Serbian Patriarchate until 1920 when the Serbs were united into one state.

After the elimination of the Patriarchate of Peć, the Turkish pashalic of Belgrade became the centre of Serbian culture and tradition. In 1804 the Serbs there rebelled against the janissaries and Turkish landowners. Led by Đorđe Petrović, known as Karađorđe, the rebels liberated the whole pashalic.

However, the war with the Turks continued, and in 1815 the new Serbian leader, Miloš Obrenović, signed a peace treaty with the Turks that brought an end to the struggle against the Turks in that area. The Serbs organised a state with a legal structure and a strong army, and, though still a client state of the Ottoman Empire, it had its autonomy.

The state expanded to include territories already liberated by Karađorđe.

While the Serbian people were fighting for an independent state from 1835 to 1878, their rulers were aware that they needed a massive action plan in order to recover their people and culture from the backwardness caused by centuries of slavery under the Turks. By the end of the 1830s the principality had its own constitution, followed by a *Civil Code* as Prince Miloš laid down the foundations of democracy by distributing land to the peasants. State management, culture and education were institutionalised, and in 1882, elementary education became obligatory. The Serbian Association of Scholars was founded as well as the National Museum and the Academy of Arts and Sciences. The Great School, founded in 1863, became a university in 1905. The economy and trade developed and the beginnings of industrialisation and banking also appeared. Talented people were sent to universities throughout Europe, returning as knowledgeable and well-educated Europeans. This striving for scientific and scholarly advancement continued later in the Republic of Yugoslavia. Among the scholars of these times was Nikola Tesla (the late nineteenth–early twentieth-century inventor in the field of electricity, a Serb originally from Croatia who later moved to the United States), and other experts in their field.

Cultural background

I Cultural background

In 1918 the Kingdom of the Serbs, Croats and Slovenes was created. From 1929 it was called Yugoslavia.

Yugoslavia emerged from the Second World War with a completely new social structure. Led by the president of the state, Josip Broz Tito, it was initially a 'people's republic' and then a 'socialist republic', consisting of six republics (Slovenia, Croatia, Bosnia-Herzegovina, Serbia, Montenegro and Macedonia) and two autonomous provinces, Vojvodina and Kosovo. In the Yugoslavia prior to the war, the Serb, Croat and Slovene people were free to express and share their culture and faith. Postwar Yugoslavia saw a suppression of freedom in culture, also open expression of religious practice was not looked upon favourably.

Following Tito's death in 1980 and under pressure from the autonomous provinces (particularly Kosovo, which sought to be granted the status of a republic) Yugoslavia began to disintegrate into its constituent republics. A bloody civil war broke out in 1991, and the country was divided into separate states, with many Serbs living outside Serbia and Montenegro, the two states which remained together.

The language of the Slavs who migrated to the Balkans in the sixth and seventh centuries also underwent changes. As the Slavonic tribes migrated, the language of the southern Slavs changed from that spoken by the eastern Slavs. Though the languages remained essentially similar, the differences became distinctive when the south Slavs reached the Balkans and the Pannonia region, at which time some tribes travelled southeast, while others moved southwest. The differences in the interrogative pronoun 'What?' is a handy label for laying down the basic differences in what were to become the different languages and dialects spoken in the region today. Those who travelled southwest used кај/kaj or ча/ča to say 'What?' Those Slavs travelling southeast used the interrogative што-шта/što-šta.

When in the ninth century the Moravian ruler asked the Byzantine Emperor to send missionaries to convert the Slavs of the region to the Christian faith, the latter responded by sending the brothers Constantine (later called Cyril when he became a monk) and Methodius. They were asked to translate, on the basis of their knowledge of the Slavonic language spoken by a Macedonian tribe in the Salonika area, the most important Byzantine religious books. The language had no written form and the brothers had to invent one. The language which they created and translated into, Old Church Slavonic, was the first of the Slavonic languages to be used in literary and liturgical spheres.

In order to translate the works, the brothers used the Greek alphabet as the basis on which they invented letters to represent the sounds of the Slavonic language. Glagolitic, the alphabet invented by Cyril, had forty letters, a letter for each of the sounds. This alphabet was soon replaced by the Cyrillic alphabet, consisting of the Greek alphabet of the period with fourteen letters added. In cultural terms, the invention of the alphabet was of great significance.

Cultural background

Slavic monasteries on Athos were among the main centres of translation. Translation constantly developed and enriched the literary Serbian Church Slavonic as many Slavic authors developed and practised the art of creating new words to express the abstract concepts they were translating into literary works.

Church Slavonic, with its local variants, facilitated further dissemination of the Orthodox faith. The works translated from Greek were quickly shared by all the countries of the Orthodox Slavic world and the languages of these countries, particularly Russian Church Slavonic, had a strong influence on Serbian Church Slavonic at the end of the eighteenth century.

During the rule of Karađorđe, many educated Serbs from Austria moved into Serbia. Among them was Dositej Obradović, a great scholar who spoke Latin, Greek, German, French, Italian and Russian. As soon as he heard of the liberation from the Turks, he returned to Serbia and met with Karađorđe. He believed that people had to be educated and enlightened. As Church Slavonic, which was interspersed with Russian, was too far removed from the living language of the people (most of whom were not able to understand the texts) Dositej wanted to bridge the gap between this church language and the people's language. Having been exposed to the European Enlightenment, he insisted that the written language be understood by everybody, including the uneducated. Soon the Russian literary language was no longer used by Serbian authors and Church Slavonic was used only in theological and liturgical books. Dositej became the minister of culture and fought to have schools built and for both men and women to attend.

The great Serbian philologist Vuk Karadžić (1787–1864) played a crucial role in the development of the alphabet. He travelled around the country, collecting folk stories and sayings, and incorporated this spoken language into the written literary form. He attempted to create a completely phonetic alphabet, where one sound of the spoken language was represented by one symbol in the written form. With this in mind, he discarded some symbols he felt did not correspond to a particular sound, and introduced six new ones, in accordance with the principle, 'a letter for every sound':

Ђ Љ Њ Ћ Џ Ј

đ lj nj ć dž j

In 1818 he wrote the Serbian dictionary in the language spoken by the people. However, Karadžić's own language was of the Ijekavian dialect, spoken in western Serbia, Bosnia and Herzegovina,

I Cultural background

and Montenegro and among Serbs in Croatia and Dalmatia. The literary language until then was the Ekavian Štokavian dialect, spoken in the northeastern regions, as that was where the most significant cultural, political and economic centres of the Serbs were located. The Serbs from these areas were not prepared to give up their Ekavian for an Ijekavian dialect, and Serbia and Vojvodina retained their dialect. The Croats and Muslims of Bosnia-Herzegovina, on the other hand, accepted his reforms completely, as did the Serbs living in Montenegro.

In spite of these differences, Karadžić's reforms paved the way for a spontaneous development of the literary language through its relationship with the spoken word. The language expanded as new words were created from existing roots and nuances of meaning acquired. Words of Latin and Greek origin were adopted as the Serbian language became increasingly cosmopolitan. During the twentieth century, many French and English words were also adopted.

In the meantime, the Croats, who had during the fourteenth century, while under the influence of the western world and Catholicism, adopted the Latin alphabet, had in the nineteenth century, added letters for palatal and palatalised consonants from Czech and Polish. Now this alphabet, too, was phonetic (with the exception of **lj, nj** and **dž**, where two letters represent one sound).

By the nineteenth century, realising that their languages had a lot in common, the Croats and Serbs unified their languages under the name of Serbo-Croatian. However, wanting secession from Yugoslavia, during the twentieth century, Croatian linguists began to emphasise the differences between the languages, proclaiming Croatian as a separate language. New words were coined to prove that differences existed. With the break-up of Yugoslavia at the end of the twentieth century came the fragmentation of the unified language, Serbo-Croatian. The Croatian language quickly developed as a separate language in relation to Serbian, with new words speedily introduced to mark its differences. Serbian, on the other hand, remained unchanged.

Chapter 2
Dialects

Three distinctive dialects are spoken in the various regions of former Yugoslavia. The dialects refer to the different ways the word 'what' is spoken:

1   кајкавски/kajkavski – the Kajkavian dialect – кај/kaj (what)
    This dialect is mostly spoken in Slavonia and northwestern Croatia and near the Slovenian border where it closely resembles the Slovenian language.
2   чакавски/čakavski – the Čakavian dialect – ча/ča (what)
    This dialect is spoken in northern parts of Croatia and Istria, and along the Adriatic coast and its islands.
3   штокавски/štokavski – the Štokavian dialect – што/što or шта/šta (what)
    This is the most widely spoken dialect in the region. It is spoken by all Serbs, Croats, Bosnians and Montenegrins, except in those regions already mentioned.

The Štokavian dialect has three sub-dialects that developed from three different pronunciations of the Old Slavonic **jat**, the long vowel ě (distinct from the ordinary vowel e, which still exists as the e sound).
   The three sub-dialects are:

1   икавски/ikavski (Ikavian)
    Spoken in western Vojvodina, western Bosnia and Herzegovina, western Croatia and northwestern parts of the Adriatic.
2   ијекавски/ijekavski (Ijekavian)
    Spoken in western Serbia, Croatia, Montenegro, the southern Adriatic coast and eastern Bosnia. The Croatian and Bosnian languages are of the Ijekavian dialect, written in the Latin alphabet.
3   екавски/ekavski (Ekavian)
    Spoken in Serbia and Vojvodina, this is the dialect of the Serbian language which generally uses the Cyrillic alphabet.

2 Dialects

The vowel ě is pronounced as follows in each dialect:

Ikavian – **и/i**

| **млико** | **mliko** | milk |
| **вриме** | **vrime** | time |

Ijekavian – **je, иje/ije**

| **млијеко** | **mlijeko** | milk |
| **вријеме** | **vrijeme** | time |

Ekavian – **e/e**

| **млеко** | **mleko** | milk |
| **време** | **vreme** | time |

The above differences in pronunciation apply only to words where the original **jat** sound existed and not whenever the vowel **e** appears. The word **пет/pet** (five), for example, is pronounced the same in all three sub-dialects.

Part II
Alphabet, pronunciation and stress

Chapter 3
Alphabet

The Cyrillic alphabet, **ћирилица**/ćirilica, and the Latin alphabet, **латиница**/latinica, are the two alphabets in use in Serbian. They both contain the same thirty letters, though not in the same order.

The Cyrillic alphabet, **ћирилица**/ćirilica, is based on Greek and was adopted by the Serbs during the Byzantine era. The Latin alphabet, **латиница**/latinica, adopted by the Serbs living in the western parts of the country, in what was to become Croatia, in the fourteenth century, is the same as the one used in English, with the addition of five new letters and eight new sounds.

3 Alphabet

The Cyrillic alphabet:

		Italics	Latin equivalent	
А	а	*А, а*	A	Assam
Б	б	*Б, б*	B	bench
В	в	*В, в*	V	victim
Г	г	*Г, г*	G	good
Д	д	*Д, д*	D	desk
Ђ	ђ	*Ђ, ђ*	Đ	due
Е	е	*Е, е*	E	let
Ж	ж	*Ж, ж*	Ž	pleasure
З	з	*З, з*	Z	Zen
И	и	*И, и*	I	he
Ј	ј	*Ј, ј*	J	yoyo
К	к	*К, к*	K	club
Л	л	*Л, л*	L	liver
Љ	љ	*Љ, љ*	Lj	million
М	м	*М, м*	M	man
Н	н	*Н, н*	N	no
Њ	њ	*Њ, њ*	Nj	minion
О	о	*О, о*	O	operate
П	п	*П, п*	P	pen
Р	р	*Р, р*	R	Ferrero
С	с	*С, с*	S	stop
Т	т	*Т, т*	T	top
Ћ	ћ	*Ћ, ћ*	Ć	tube
У	у	*У, у*	U	room
Ф	ф	*Ф, ф*	F	futon
Х	х	*Х, х*	H	Henry
Ц	ц	*Ц, ц*	C	lots
Ч	ч	*Ч, ч*	Č	chocolate
Џ	џ	*Џ, џ*	Dž	juke-box
Ш	ш	*Ш, ш*	Š	shoulder

Note: There are two possible forms of Cyrillic **г** (the letter g) – one with a crossbar, one without. There are also two possible forms of Cyrillic **д** (the letter d) – one with a 'tail' going up: *ð*, and one with a 'tail' going down: *g*.

Alphabet

Аа Бб Вв Гг Дд
Ђђ Ее Жж Зз Ии
Јј Кк Лл Љљ Мм
Нн Њњ Оо Пп Рр
Сс Тт Ћћ Уу Фф
Хх Цц Чч Џџ Шш

Нашао сам пса.

Нашао сам пса./Našao sam psa.

I found the dog.

It is important that the cursive or hand-written Cyrillic form is learnt properly. The letters are distinctive in form, and each is connected to another in an elaborate manner. Note the crossbar above **Г** (**G**), **П** (**P**), **Т** (**T**). A horizontal bar is often written under **Ш** (**Š**) as well.

3 Alphabet

The Latin alphabet:

		Cyrillic equivalent	
A	a	А	Assam
B	b	Б	bench
C	c	Ц	lots
Č	č	Ч	chocolate
Ć	ć	Ћ	tube
D	d	Д	desk
Dž	dž	Џ	juke-box
Đ	đ	Ђ	due
E	e	Е	let
F	f	Ф	futon
G	g	Г	good
H	h	Х	Henry
I	i	И	He
J	j	Ј	yoyo
K	k	К	club
L	l	Л	liver
Lj	lj	Љ	million
M	m	М	man
N	n	Н	no
Nj	nj	Њ	minion
O	o	О	operate
P	p	П	pen
R	r	Р	Ferrero
S	s	С	stop
Š	š	Ш	shoulder
T	t	Т	top
U	u	У	room
V	v	В	victim
Z	z	З	Zen
Ž	ž	Ж	pleasure

Note: The hand-written forms of the Latin letters, with the addition of **Ž ž**, **Đ đ**, **Ć ć**, **Č č** and **Š š**, are the same as those used in English. The English letters **q**, **w**, **x** and **y** do not exist in the Serbian alphabet.

Chapter 4
Pronunciation

Every letter is pronounced.

Consonants are pronounced similarly to English, with the following exceptions:

1 The four consonants written as in English but with only one pronunciation as compared to several in English, are:

ц/c is never pronounced as in 'carry' but always as in 'Tzar'

г/g is never pronounced as in 'giant', but always as in 'good'

j is never pronounced as in 'jade' but always as in 'yes'

с/s is never pronounced as in 'season' or 'shower', but always as in 'see'

2 The eight consonants which do not appear in English are:

ђ	đ	*d*ue
ж	ž	plea*s*ure
љ	lj	mi*lli*on
		(The two sounds which form this letter are pronounced simultaneously, and not separately.)
њ	nj	mi*ni*on
		(The two sounds which form this letter are pronounced simultaneously, and not separately.)
ћ	ć	*ch*ase
ч	č	*ch*ocolate
џ	dž	*j*uke-box
ш	š	*ch*ampagne

3. The *dental* sounds, where the tongue is pressed against the back of the teeth, are т/t, д/d, з/z, с/s, ц/c, р/r, л/l and н/n.

4. The letter т/t is dropped before the letter ц/c – отац/otac (nominative) – оца/ocà (genitive). Both т/t and д/d are usually dropped when they occur between two consonants of which the first may be с/s, ш/š, з/z, ж/ž, followed by б/b, к/k, л/l, љ/lj, м/m, н/n or њ/nj.

болестан (m) – **болесна** (f)   **bolestan** (m) – **bolesna** (f)   ill

жалостан (m) – **жалосна** (f)   **žalostan** (m) – **žalosna** (f)   sad

5. The consonant р/r can occur:

- on its own: оркестар/orkestar (orchestra), осигурати/osigurati (to insure), Оливера/Olivera (female name, Olivera);
- before or after another consonant: наградити/nagraditi (to award), преглед/pregled (review, examination);
- between two consonants: мртав/mrtav (dead), пргав/prgav (short-tempered), etc., where it acts as a vowel.

6. The following are some of the consonant clusters that can stand together at the end of a word in modern Serbian. The first four of these are considered in traditional Serbian to be the only consonant clusters with which a word can end:

-ст	**-st**	храст/hrast	oak
-шт	**-št**	плашт/plašt	sheet
-зд	**-zd**	грозд/grozd	grape
-жд	**-žd**	вожд/vožd	duke
-рк	**-rk**	парк/park	park
-нц	**-nc**	принц/princ	prince
-нт	**-nt**	матурант/maturant	graduate
-ск	**-sk**	диск/disk	disc

7. All vowels are pronounced:

а	**a**	Ass*a*m
е	**e**	s*e*t
и	**i**	sh*e*
о	**o**	*o*ccult
у	**u**	r*oo*m

4.1 Consonants

Consonants are divided into two basic categories depending on the degree of obstruction or restriction in the airflow during articulation of the consonant within the mouth cavity:

(a) Obstruent consonants – formed with restricted air flow:

all consonants excluding those under (b)

(b) Resonant consonants – formed with the air flowing uninterruptedly from the vocal cords to the mouth or nose in a continuous sound, similar to vowels:

в/v, р/r, j/j, л/l, љ/lj, н/n, њ/nj, м/m

Further classification is based on the movement of the lips or the position of the tongue inside the mouth in relation to the teeth and the palate when air flows into the mouth and through the throat:

1. Labial consonants: б/b, п/p, ф/f are formed with the lips pressed against each other or the upper teeth pressed against the lower lip.
2. Dental consonants: д/d, т/t, з/z, с/s, ц/c, н/n, р/r, л/l are formed with the tongue pressing against the teeth.
3. Palatal consonants: ђ/đ, ћ/ć, ч/č, џ/dž, ж/ž, ш/š are formed with the tongue pressed against the palate.
4. Velar consonants: г/g, к/k, х/h are formed with the tongue pressed further back against the palate, creating a more guttural sound.

The twenty-five consonants are classified in the following groups:

1. Voiced and unvoiced.
2. Soft (palatal and palatalised) and hard (non-palatal and non-palatalised).

Not all consonants can stand next to each other and there are certain rules applicable to the clustering of consonants. In such instances, either consonants mutate or a fleeting **a** is introduced to separate them. Mutation of consonants occurs through consonantal assimilation or contraction.

4.1.1 Voiced and unvoiced consonants

When in pronouncing a consonant, the vocal cords are tense and vibrating, the consonant is said to be *voiced*. When the vocal cords are relaxed and are not vibrating, the consonant is said to be *unvoiced* or *voiceless*. Of the twenty-five consonants, fourteen form pairs in which the only difference between the two consonants forming the pair is that one is voiced and the other is not.

1   Voiced consonants: б/b г/g д/d ђ/đ ж/ž з/z џ/dž
2   Unvoiced (voiceless) consonants: п/p к/k т/t ћ/ć ш/š с/s ч/č

A *voiced obstruent* consonant cannot stand in front of an unvoiced consonant in one word. Should this occur, the voiced consonant is replaced by its unvoiced partner:

сладак (m) – **слатка** (f)   **sladak** (m) – **slatka** (f)   sweet

тежак (m) – **тешка** (f)   **težak** (m) – **teška** (f)   heavy

Equally, an unvoiced consonant cannot stand in front of a voiced obstruent consonant in one word. When it does, the unvoiced consonant is replaced by its voiced partner:

сват – свадба   **svat – svadba**   wedding guest – a wedding

Thus, when a group, or cluster, of two or more of the fourteen consonants above come together in one word, the last consonant determines whether the cluster becomes voiced or voiceless.

There are exceptions to this rule. The letter д/d does not change to its unvoiced partner т/t in spelling, though it does in pronunciation when standing before a с/s or a ш/š, with words prefixed with над/nad-, од/od-, пред/pred-, под/pod-, etc., or with the suffixes -ски/ski or -ство/stvo:

одштета	**odšteta**	compensation
градски	**gradski**	city
председник	**predsednik**	president

Of the remaining consonants, seven are voiced and have no unvoiced partner:

ј/j   л/l   љ/lj   р/r   м/m   н/n   њ/nj

while three are unvoiced:

х/h   ф/f   ц/c

4.1.2 | Soft and hard consonants

The distinction between soft and hard consonants is whether or not in the formation of the consonant the tongue is raised to the palate.

Those consonants during the formation of which the tongue is raised to the palate:

ц/c ч/č ћ/ć џ/dž ш/š ж/ž j/j

are referred to as *palatal* consonants and are said to be *soft*.

Although the consonant ц/c is not pronounced as soft, it acts as a soft consonant in declensional endings.

The *dental* consonants т/t, д/d, н/n and л/l, which although *hard* consonants as they are formed with the tongue pressing against the teeth, are softened when the letter j, formed with the tongue pressing against the palate, is added to them and the two are spoken simultaneously. These consonants then become palatalised:

ћ/ć ђ/dj њ/nj љ/lj

All the remaining consonants are said to be hard.

4.1.3 Consonantal assimilations

Consonantal assimilation occurs when, in specific linguistic conditions, certain consonants regularly replace certain other consonants. This can occur in the following conditions:

1 When two or more consonants from the group of voiced and unvoiced consonants come together, the whole cluster will be either voiced or unvoiced, in agreement with the last consonant. (See Section 4.1.1 Voiced and unvoiced consonants.) The alternations that occur are as follows:

п/p	alternates with	б/b
т/t		д/d
к/k		г/g
с/s		з/z
ш/š		ж/ž
ћ/ć		ђ/đ
ч/č		џ/dž

2 When the hard consonants с/s or з/z occur before the soft consonants љ/lj and њ/nj, they are replaced by their own palatal (softened) equivalent (see Section 4.1.2 Soft and hard consonants):

мрзети – мржња   mrzeti – mržnja   to hate – hatred
мислити – мишљење   misliti – mišljenje   to think – opinion

3   When the letter б/b is preceded by н/n, the latter often changes to м/m:

ста*н* – ста*м*бен   sta*n* – sta*m*ben   flat – residential

4.1.4 Consonantal contractions

Consonantal contractions are applied when, in forming a word out of two words or adding a prefix to a word, double consonants occur. In Serbian one word (with certain exceptions) cannot contain double consonants:

| пе*т* – пе*т* + десе*т* – пе*д*есет | pe*t* – pe*t* + dese*t* – pe*d*eset | five – five + ten – fifty |
| бе*з* – бе*з* + *з*вучан – бе*з*вучан | be*z* – be*z* + *z*vučan – be*z*vučan | without – without + sound – soundless |

This rule also applies to words with a fleeting a: when a fleeting a drops out, т/t (or д/d) and ц/c can come together, becoming just ц/c:

| отац – отaца – ц = тс – оттца – оца (gen.) | otac – otaca – c = ts – ottca – oca (gen.) | father |
| судац – судaца – ц = тс – судца – суца (gen.) | sudac – sudaca – c = ts – sudca – suca (gen.) | judge |

It does not, however, apply to adjectives in the superlative beginning with j, in which case the double j remains:

| на*јј*ачи | na*jj*ači | strongest |
| на*јј*ужнији | na*jj*užniji | southernmost |

Consonantal contractions also occur with consonants т/t and д/d, which are usually dropped when they occur between any of the following two consonants, of which the first may be с/s, ш/š, з/z, ж/ž followed by б/b, к/k, л/l, љ/lj, м/m, н/n or њ/nj:

| час*т*ан (m) – часна (f) | čas*t*an (m) – časna (f) | honourable |
| жалос*т*ан (m) – жалосна (f) | žalos*t*an (m) – žalosna (f) | sad |

This rule does not apply to words ending in the suffixes -ство/stvo or -штво/štvo:

| становништво | stanoviništvo | population |
| мноштво | mnoštvo | multitude |

4.1.5 Fleeting a

Although many consonant clusters do occur at the end of a word – бицикл/bicikl (bicycle), филм/film (film), диск/disk (disc), дигирент/dirigent (conductor), etc. – the following consonant clusters are traditionally considered to be the only clusters that can occur at the end of a word:

-ст   -st

-шт   -št

-зд   -zd

-жд   -žd

A word ending in any other combination of consonants will generally have a fleeting a inserted before the final consonant.

This insertion of the fleeting a occurs in the nominative singular and genitive plural of many nouns:

ловац	lovac	hunter (m nom. sg.)
девојка	devojka	young girl (f nom. sg.)
ловца	lovca	hunter (m gen. sg.)
ловаца	lovaca	hunters (m gen. pl.)
девојка	devojka	young girl (f nom. sg.)
девојака	devojaka	young girls (f gen. pl.)

as well as in the formation of various tenses, including the past tense masculine singular participle ending -ao:

1	рек + л	rek + l	(he) said (see Section 4.1.6 Change of л/l to о)
2	рекал	rekal	
3	рекао	rekao	

1	плак + л	plak + l	(he) cried (see Section 4.1.6 Change of л/l to о)
2	плакал	plakal	
3	плакао	plakao	

The fleeting a occurs in the prepositions с/s (with) in the instrumental, and (off) in the genitive case, and к/k (towards) in the dative case, where the preposition с/s has to have the form ca/sa before a word beginning with с/s, з/z, ш/š or ж/ž, and the preposition к/k has to have the form ка/ka before a word beginning к/k or г/g, to avoid double consonants occurring:

4 Pronunciation

са сином	*sa* sinom	with (my) son
са шунком	*sa* šunkom	with ham
ка Крагујевцу	*ka* Kragujevcu	towards Kragujevac
ка кући	*ka* kući	towards (the) house

4.1.6 Change of л/l to o

The letter л/l changes to o at the end of a word in the following instances:

1. All masculine singular active past participle endings:

чекати/čekati (to wait)					
радити/raditi (to work)					
Masculine		Neuter		Feminine	
чекао	čekao	чекало	čeka*lo*	чекала	čeka*la*
радио	radio	радило	radi*lo*	радила	radi*la*

2. A few adjectives in the masculine singular:

топло/toplo (warm) (neuter form)					
дебело/debelo – (fat) (neuter form)					
Masculine		Neuter		Feminine	
топао	topao	топло	top*lo*	топла	top*la*
дебео	debeo	дебело	debe*lo*	дебела	debe*la*

3. Masculine nouns **угао/ugao, део/deo, сто/sto, во/vo** and the feminine noun **со/so** end in o in the nominative singular, while the letter л/l appears in the nominative plural and other cases:

угао (nom. sg.)	ugao (nom. sg.)	corner
углови (nom. pl.)	ug*lo*vi (nom. pl.)	
угла (gen. sg.)	ug*la* (gen. sg.)	

сто (nom. sg.)	sto (nom. sg.)	table
столови (nom. pl.)	stolovi (nom. pl.)	
стола (gen. sg.)	stola (gen. sg.)	
део (nom. sg.)	deo (nom. sg.)	part
делови (nom. pl.)	delovi (nom. pl.)	
дела (gen. sg.)	dela (gen. sg.)	
во (nom. sg.)	vo (nom. sg.)	ox
волови (nom. pl.)	volovi (nom. pl.)	
вола (gen. sg.)	vola (gen. sg.)	
со (nom. sg.)	so (nom. sg.)	salt
соли (nom. pl.)	soli (nom. pl.)	
соли (gen. sg.)	soli (gen. sg.)	

When a masculine noun ends in **-ao**, this is usually an example of fleeting **a** (as in **угао/ugao**, all of the other forms of which have **угл/ugl** – see above). There are also examples of masculine nouns ending in -eo in the nominative singular which have **ел/el** in all the forms, such as **део/deo** (see above).

4   Nouns ending in the suffix **-лац/lac**, where the л/l is retained in the nominative singular and genitive plural but is replaced by **o** in all other instances, as л/l changes to **o** at the end of a syllable which precedes a syllable beginning with **ц/c**:

гледалац (nom. sg.)	gledalac (nom. sg.)	member of the
гледалаца (gen. pl.)	gledalaca (gen. pl.)	audience, viewer
гледаоцу (dat. sg.)	gledaocu (dat. sg.)	
мислилац (nom. sg.)	mislilac (nom. sg.)	thinker
мислилаца (gen. sg.)	mislilaca (gen. sg.)	
мислиоце (acc. pl.)	mislioce (acc. pl.)	

When the л/l is not final, it is not replaced by the **o**:

чекала   čekala   (she) waited

топла   topla   warm (f)

4.1.7 | J changes

The letter **j** and its effect on other consonants is of particular importance in Serbian. The letter **j** is a soft sounding consonant. In the past whenever this letter followed another consonant, certain changes occurred.

Many of these changes have been retained and are part of the language today.

The letter j is used in forming the following:

1. The comparative of adjectives (see Section 9.6 Comparative adjectives):

   сладак – слађи   **sladak – slađi**   sweet – sweeter

2. The past passive participle of verbs (see Section 9.8 Verbal adjectives):

   носити – ношен   **nositi – nošen**   to carry – carried
   с + j = ш   **s + j = š**

   ослободити –   **osloboditi –**   to liberate – liberated
   ослобођен   **oslobođen**
   д + j = ђ   **d + j = đ**

3. Nouns formed from verbal adjectives and other nouns ending with the suffixes -je and -ja:

   ослобођен –   **oslobođen –**   liberated – liberation
   ослобођење   **oslobođenje**

   кап – капља   **kap – kaplja**   a drop

4. The instrumental singular ending of feminine nouns ending in -jy/ju:

   љубав –   **ljubav –**   love – with love
   с љубављу   **s ljubavlju**

The following are the effects of the letter j on other consonants:

д/d	+ j	changes to	ђ/đ
т/t	+ j		ћ/ć
л/l	+ j		љ/lj
н/n	+ j		њ/nj
з/z	+ j		ж/ž
с/s	+ j		ш/š
п/p	+ j		пљ/plj
б/b	+ j		бљ/blj
в/v	+ j		вљ/vlj
м/m	+ j		мљ/mlj

к/k	+ j	changes to	ч/č
х/h	+ j		ш/š
г/g	+ j		ж/ž
ст/st	+ j		шћ/šć
зд/zd	+ j		жд/žd

There are, however, some nouns and adjectives in which j does not affect the preceding **с/s** or **з/z** consonant:

коза – козји koza – kozji goat – goat's (concerning a goat)

клас – класје klas – klasje ear of grain – ears of grain

4.1.8 Effects of e/e and и/i on к/k, г/g and х/h

The following consonant replacements:

к/k to	ч/č
г/g	ж/ž
х/h	ш/š

occur before the letter **е** in the vocative case:

војник – војниче	vojnik – vojniče	soldier
Бог – Боже	Bog – Bože	God
дух – душе	duh – duše	ghost

or before the -e- endings in the present tense:

пећи	peći	to bake
пек + е =	pek + e =	stem + present tense -e- ending
печем	pečem	1st p.sg.
		but
пеку	peku	stem + 3rd p.pl. -у/u ending
вући	vući	to pull
вук + е =	vuk + e =	stem + present tense -e- ending
вучем	vučem	1st p.sg.
		but
вуку	vuku	stem + 3rd p.pl. -у/u ending

4 Pronunciation

стрићи	strići	to shear
стриг + е =	strig + e =	stem + present tense -e- ending
стажем	strižem	1st p.sg.
		but
стригу	strigu	stem + 3rd p.pl. -у/u ending

The following consonant replacements:

к/k to ц/c
г/g   з/z
х/h   c/s

occur before the letter и/i in the following instances:

1. In the plural declension of masculine and neuter nouns in all cases except masculine genitive and accusative and neuter nominative, genitive and accusative:

војник – војници	vojnik – vojnici	soldier
бубрег – бубрези	bubreg – bubrezi	kidney
дух – дуси	duh – dusi	ghost

2. In the singular declension of feminine nouns ending in these consonants in the dative and locative cases:

рука – руци	ruka – ruci	arm
нога – нози	noga – nozi	leg

   There are, however, many exceptions to this rule, where the final consonant does not change:

бака – баки	baka – baki	grandmother
Анка – Анки	Anka – Anki	Anka (woman's name)
Олга – Олги	Olga – Olgi	Olga (woman's name)
Београђанка – Београђанки	Beograđanka – Beograđanki	a woman from Belgrade
Босанка – Босанки	Bosanka – Bosanki	a Bosnian woman
фризерка – фризерки	frizerka – frizerki	a hairdresser (other female occupational names also do not change)
патка – патки	patka – patki	a duck

3   In the imperative:

    секу – сеци!   seku – seci!   cut!

4.2 Vowels

In addition to the five vowels:

a   e   и/i   o   y/u

the letter **p/r** in Serbian behaves as a sixth vowel sound when it is found placed between two consonants:

хрт   **hrt**   greyhound

трг   **trg**   market square

The pronunciation of vowels in Serbian always remains constant, regardless of the letters preceding or following them, and it is important that vowels are pronounced correctly because of the different vowel endings, all of which denote a particular meaning:

честитамо   **čestitamo**   we congratulate

честитате   **čestitate**   you (pl.) congratulate

4.2.1 Length and stress

Depending on its pronunciation, a vowel may be either long or short. In Serbian, all vowels may be both. The distinction is important in words only differentiated by the length of the vowel:

грâд   **grâd**   city

град   **grad**   hail

4.2.2 Vowel mutations

Vowel mutations generally occur with soft consonants, where the vowels o and e interchange. These changes are evident in the following instances:

1   With possessive adjectives, the **-ов/ov** ending is replaced by an **-ев/ev** ending when the preceding consonant is soft:

    човеков сат   **čovekov sat**   a man's watch

    водичев ауто   **vodičev auto**   a guide's car

2   The suffix **-овати/ovati** changes in some instances to **-евати/evati** when the preceding consonant is soft:

бичевати   bičevati   to whip

бичовати   bičovati   (though this form is also possible)

3   In the instrumental case, where masculine and neuter singular nouns generally take the **-ом/om** ending, after a soft consonant the ending changes to **-ем/em**, except with most foreign words, where the **-ом/om** ending remains in use:

са мајмуном   **sa majmunom**   with a monkey

са слонићем   **sa slonićem**   with a little elephant

са Рађом   **sa Radžom**   with Raj

Chapter 5
Stress

A word is pronounced with an accent (stress) on one of its vowels. This accent may have a rising pitch or a falling pitch, which may be on a long vowel or on a short vowel.

There are thus four possibilities:

1   a long rising stress;
2   a long falling stress;
3   a short rising stress;
4   a short falling stress.

Words are generally written with an accent mark only to indicate instances where the choice of accent makes the difference between one word and another.

5.1 Word stress and tone

The general rule regarding stress is that it can fall on any syllable except the last, although there are exceptions to the rule, e.g. **матурант/ maturant** (a high school graduate), where the stress falls on the final syllable.

In a word of two syllables, the stress will fall on the first syllable:

| кола | kola | car |
| пиво | pivo | beer |

In a three-syllable word, it will fall on either the first or the second syllable:

Милија	Milija	Milija (man's name)
судија	sudija	judge
сладолед	sladoled	ice-cream

5 Stress

In the common speech of Belgrade, where the stressed syllable of a word distinguishes long vs short, unstressed syllables have almost exclusively short vowels in them, with the long vowel generally carrying the stress. In more classical pronunciations, and certainly in the speech of people from Bosnia, there can be several long vowels in the same word even when they are not the stressed vowel.

5.2 Shift of stress

A shift of stress may occur when a *proclitic* (e.g. a preposition) precedes a word only if the first syllable of the word has a falling stress. The stress will then shift onto the last syllable of the previous word, the proclitic. The stress on the proclitic then becomes a short falling or rising stress.

Ишли су *ка* кући. **Išli su *ka* kući.** They went towards the house.

If the word following the proclitic has a rising stress on the first syllable, this rule does not apply.

5.3 Sentence stress

Although each word has its own particular stress and tone, generally speaking, the more important a word is in the sentence, the heavier its stress will be. This explains why one word may seem to be changing stress depending on the context and its importance in it.

Part III

Parts of speech

Chapter 6
Verbs

Verbs are words used to indicate the following:

1 that someone or something is at a particular moment in time carrying out a certain action:

| **Милена** *фарба* **косу.** | **Milena** *farba* **kosu.** | Milena *is dyeing* her hair. |

2 that something is happening:

| *Наоблачило се.* | *Naoblačilo se.* | Clouds *have gathered*. |

3 that someone or something is in a certain condition or state:

| **Свако јутро** *спавам* **до 8 сати.** | **Svako jutro** *spavam* **do 8 sati.** | Every morning I *sleep* until 8 o'clock. |

Depending on the type and nature of the activity, verbs can be divided into:

1 Transitive verbs – verbs which can take a direct object:

| **Ана** *је понела* **торбу са собом.** | **Ana** *je ponela* **torbu sa sobom.** | Anna *took* her bag with her. |

2 Intransitive verbs – verbs which do not take a direct object:

| **Сви смо заједно** *отишли* **у биоскоп.** | **Svi smo zajedno** *otišli* **u bioskop.** | We *went* all together to the cinema. |

Depending on the duration of the action which a verb denotes, verbs can have two aspects:

1 Imperfective verbs indicate a lasting action in the past, the present or the future:

6 Verbs

На мору *се* **купамо** свакoг дана.	**Na moru** *se* **kupamo** svakog dana.	At the seaside *we* bathe (ourselves) every day.
купати	kupati	to bathe (imperfective)
На мору *ћемо се* **купати** свакoг дана.	**Na moru** *ćemo se* **kupati** svakog dana.	At the seaside *we will* bathe every day.

2 Perfective verbs indicate a past complete action or a future complete action:

Окупао се пре изласка.	*Okupao se* pre izlaska.	He had a bath before going out.
окупати	okupati	to bathe (perfective)
Окупаће се пре изласка.	*Okupaće se* pre izlaska.	He will have a bath before going out.

A verb consists of two parts: a stem and an ending. Each verb has two stems, an *infinitive stem* and a *present tense stem*. With some verbs the two stems are identical, but with most they differ. All the verbal forms are formed from these two stems, reflecting their conjugation and tense.

Verbs are given in the dictionary in the infinitive. The infinitive of a verb does not reflect *number*, *person* or *gender*. In English, the infinitive consists of two words: the word 'to' plus the verb itself: 'to buy, to drive, to read', etc. This is not the case in Serbian where the infinitive consists of the stem of the verb, to which one of several endings is added: **купити**/kup*iti* (to buy), **доћи**/do*ći* (to come), **трести**/tre*sti* (to shake).

There are three main types of conjugations, depending on the infinitive ending. In addition to the above, the time of the action, whether it took place in the past or present, or is to take place some time in the future, is indicated by the *tense* of the verb. Tenses covered in this book include the perfect (past) tense, the present tense, the future tense, future II and the aorist tense. The present and aorist consist of a single verb; the remaining tenses are compound tenses, formed from the main verb and an auxiliary verb.

Он *воли* фудбал.	On *voli* fudbal.	He *likes* football. (present)
Волео је позориште.	*Voleo je* pozorište.	He *liked* the theatre. (past)

Serbian verbs conjugate. This means they change form depending on the person or persons performing the action, and sometimes on the gender, if it is expressed by the verb. A verb conjugation consists of a singular and a plural form, referred to as *number*, of the 1st person (I), 2nd person (you) and 3rd person (he, she, or it) in the singular, and in the plural, 1st person (we), 2nd person (you) and 3rd person (they). This is referred to as *person* and is reflected in the ending added to the basic stem of the verb. In most compound tenses, verbs also reflect whether the doer of the action is of masculine, feminine or neuter gender. This is referred to as *gender*.

Infinitives – classification

| **Идем на море сутра.** | **Id*em* na more sutra.** | *I'm* going to the coast tomorrow. (1st p.sg.) |
| **Би*ле* су у биоскопу са нама.** | **Bi*le* su u bioskopu sa nama.** | *They* were at the cinema with us. (f pl.) |

When two verbs are found in a sentence, one of which is a *modal* verb (can, may, should, need to, ought to, have to, be able to), expressing an attitude, judgement, interpretation or feeling, the two verbs are linked together with the conjunction да/da (that/to) or by means of putting the second verb into the infinitive (see Section 6.1 Infinitives – classification):

| *Треба да идемо* на скијање зими. | *Treba da idemo* na skijanje zimi. | *We should go* skiing in the winter. |

6.1 Infinitives – classification

The infinitive is the simplest form of a verb. It is the form under which a verb is listed in a dictionary. This form does not give information on the number or persons performing the action denoted by the verb nor is it part of a tense (except in the future tense).

In English the infinitive of a verb is preceded by the word 'to': 'to eat, to sleep, to go', etc., while in Serbian the infinitive consists of only one word **јести/jesti** (to eat), **спавати/spavati** (to sleep), **ићи/ići** (to go).

The infinitive form of a verb can be used in the following instances:

(a) With modal verbs – verbs which cannot stand on their own but precede another verb (can, may, might, must, should, need to, ought to, have to, be able to) (see Section 6.18 Modal verbs):

　I　**Морате** *пожурити.*　**Morate** *požuriti.*　You must *hurry.*

2   **Треба** *веровати.*   **Treba** *verovati.*   One needs *to believe.*

In (1) the modal verb **морати/morati** (must) has been conjugated in the 2nd person plural – 'you' – and is followed by the infinitive. In (2) the modal verb **требати/trebati** (need to) has been conjugated in the 3rd person singular, and as the verb in the infinitive following it does not give further information on the person performing the action, in English the subject is given as 'one'.

(b) In forming the future tense (see Section 6.6 Future tense):

1   **Радници ће радити.**   **Radnici će raditi.**   The workers will work.

2   **Киша ће падати.**   **Kiša će padati.**   Rain will fall.

All verbs in Serbian have an infinitive form. The infinitive form falls into one of three main types depending on its endings. The infinitive endings will determine how a verb conjugates through the tenses. Generally, a verb's present tense type will depend on its infinitive ending. It is necessary to learn the infinitive of a verb as well as its endings.

The infinitive is essentially formed from the infinitive stem with the addition of -ти/ti or -ћи/ći. Due to consonantal and other assimilations that occurred in the past, we have the following infinitive endings:

When following a vowel:

-ти/ti	прљати	prljati	to dirty
	гледати	gledati	to watch
-ћи/ći	ићи	ići	to go

When following a consonant:

-ивати/ivati*	избацивати	izbacivati	to throw out
-овати/ovati*	образовати	obrazovati	to educate
-авати/avati*	обећавати	obećavati	to promise

When following either a vowel or a consonant:

-сти/sti	јести	jesti	to eat
	гристи	gristi	to bite
	грепсти	grepsti	to scratch

* The endings **-ивати/ivati**, **-овати/ovati**, **-авати/avati** are in fact suffixes used to make a verb out of another verb. Strictly speaking, the suffixes are **-ива/iva**, **-ова/ova**, **-ава/ava**, and **-ти/ti** is the ending that nearly all verbs take to form their infinitives (see Section 6.3.2 Imperfective and perfective verbs).

Some verbs have dual infinitive endings:

дићи – дигнути	dići – dignuti	to raise
подићи – подигнути	podići – podignuti	to raise
маћи – макнути	maći – maknuti	to remove
таћи – такнути	taći – taknuti	to touch
избећи – избегнути	izbeći – izbegnuti	to avoid
истаћи – истакнути	istaći – istaknuti	to emphasise
навићи – навикнути	navići – naviknuti	to get used to
означавати – означивати	označavati – označivati	to mark
омогућавати – омогућивати	omogućavati – omogućivati	to enable

Infinitive and present tense stems

Depending on the infinitive ending, there are three main types of conjugation:

1. Type I conjugation – infinitives ending in: **-ати/ati**, with all endings containing the vowel a.
2. Type II conjugation – infinitives ending in: **-ати/ati, -ти/ti, -овати/ovati, -ивати/ivati, -ути/uti, -ети/eti, -сти/sti, -ћи/ći**, with the present tense ending containing the vowel e.
3. Type III conjugation – infinitives ending in: **-ити/iti, -ети/eti, -ати/ati**, with most endings containing the vowel и/i.

6.2 Infinitive and present tense stems

The infinitive stem is formed in the following manner:

1. In verbs which have a vowel preceding the **-ти/ti** ending, the ending is dropped:

Infinitive	Infinitive stem	Infinitive	Infinitive stem	
певати	пева	**pevati**	peva	to sing
чекати	чека	**čekati**	čeka	to wait

2   In verbs ending in **-сти/sti** and **-ћи/ći**, in the aorist tense (see Section 6.7 Aorist tense), the 1st person singular ending **-ox/oh** is dropped:

Infinitive	Aorist	Infinitive stem	Infinitive	Aorist	Infinitive stem	
	1st p.sg			1st p.sg		
сести	седох	сед	sesti	sedox	sed	to sit
доћи	дођох	doђ	doći	dođoh	dod́	to come

The present tense stem is formed by dropping the personal ending from the 1st person singular:

Present tense	Present tense stem	Present tense	Present tense stem
1st p.sg.		1st p.sg.	
певам	пева	pevam	peva
дођем	дође	dođem	dođe

While with some verbs, the infinitive stem and the present tense stem are the same, with most verbs these two stems will differ:

Infinitive	Infinitive stem	Present tense	Present tense stem
		1st p.sg.	
ћутати	ћута	ћутим	ћути
ćutati	ćuta	ćutim	ćuti
пећи	пек	печем	пече
peći	pek	pečem	peče

It is recommended that both the infinitive and the present tense 1st person singular form of the verb be learnt.

6.2.1 | Type I conjugation

Infinitive and present tense stems

This conjugation applies to verbs in which the infinitive always ends in **-ати/ati**. The endings of these verbs contain the vowel a:

Conjugation of **знати/znati** (to know) present tense

sg.	1st p.	ja	зн*ам*	ja	zn*am*	I know
	2nd p.	ти	зн*аш*	ti	zn*aš*	you know
	3rd p.	он/она/оно	зн*а*	on/ona/ono	zn*a*	he/she/it knows
pl.	1st p.	ми	зн*амо*	mi	zn*amo*	we know
	2nd p.	ви	зн*ате*	vi	zn*ate*	you know
	3rd p.	они оне она	зн*ају*	oni one ona	zn*aju*	they know

In the 3rd person plural these verbs take the ending **-ју/ju**.
The following verbs conjugate in this way:

треб*ати* – треб*ам*	treb*ati* – treb*am*	to need – I need
треб*ају*	treb*aju*	3rd p.pl.
треб*ао*/треб*ала*/треб*ало*	treb*ao*/treb*ala*/treb*alo*	past tense (masc./fem./neut.)
мор*ати* – мор*ам*	mor*ati* – mor*am*	to have to – I have to
мор*ају*	mor*aju*	3rd p.pl.
мор*ао*	mor*ao*	past tense
им*ати* – им*ам*	im*ati* – im*am*	to have – I have
им*ају*	im*aju*	3rd p.pl.
им*ао*	im*ao*	past tense
нем*ати* – нем*ам*	nem*ati* – nem*am*	not to have – I don't have
нем*ају*	nem*aju*	3rd p.pl.
нем*ао*	nem*ao*	past tense

6.2.2 Type II conjugation

This conjugation applies to verbs with infinitive endings in **-ати/ati, -ити/iti, -овати/ovati, -евати/evati, -ивати/ivati, -ути/uti, -ети/eti, -сти/sti, -ћи/ći**. In this conjugation, the present tense ending contains the vowel e.

This conjugation also contains all the verbs which have a modified stem in the present tense:

Conjugation of **викнути/viknuti** (to shout) present tense

sg.	1st p.	ја	викн*ем*	ja	vikn*em*	I shout
	2nd p.	ти	викн*еш*	ti	vikn*eš*	you shout
	3rd p.	он/она/оно	викн*е*	on/ona/ono	vikn*e*	he/she/it shouts
pl.	1st p.	ми	викн*емо*	mi	vikn*emo*	we shout
	2nd p.	ви	викн*ете*	vi	vikn*ete*	you shout
	3rd p.	они/оне/она	викн*у*	oni/one/ona	vikn*u*	they shout

In the 3rd person plural these verbs take the ending **-у/u**, except for some verbs with the infinitive ending in **-ети/eti**.

1. In verbs with the infinitive ending in **-овати/ovati, -евати/evati, -ивати/ivati**, the first two letters of the infinitive endings change to **-уј/uj**, followed by the present tense ending:

Conjugation of **радовати/radovati** (to rejoice) present tense

sg.	1st p.	ја	раду*ј*ем	ja	raduj*em*	I rejoice
	2nd p.	ти	раду*ј*еш	ti	raduj*eš*	you rejoice
	3rd p.	он/она/оно	раду*ј*е	on/ona/ono	raduj*e*	he/she/it rejoice
pl.	1st p.	ми	раду*ј*емо	mi	raduj*emo*	we rejoice
	2nd p.	ви	раду*ј*ете	vi	raduj*ete*	you rejoice
	3rd p.	они/оне/она	раду*ј*у	oni/one/ona	raduj*u*	they rejoice

2. When one of the following consonants precedes the infinitive ending -ати/ati (excluding those belonging to Type 1 conjugation), it changes to a soft consonant:

к/k – ч/č   г/g – ж/ž   с/s – ш/š
х/h – ш/š   т/t – ћ/ć   з/z – ж/ž

Infinitive and present tense stems

Conjugation of **писати/pisati** (to write) present tense

sg.	1st p.	ја	пишем	ja	pišem	I write
	2nd p.	ти	пишеш	ti	pišeš	you write
	3rd p.	он/она/оно	пише	on/ona/ono	piše	he/she/it writes
pl.	1st p.	ми	пишемо	mi	pišemo	we write
	2nd p.	ви	пишете	vi	pišete	you write
	3rd p.	они	пишу	oni	pišu	they write
		оне		one		
		она		ona		

Sometimes a vowel is inserted into the stem:

Conjugation of **прати/prati** (to wash) present tense

sg.	1st p.	ја	перем	ja	perem	I wash
	2nd p.	ти	переш	ti	pereš	you wash
	3rd p.	он/она/оно	пере	on/ona/ono	pere	he/she/it washes
pl.	1st p.	ми	перемо	mi	peremo	we wash
	2nd p.	ви	перете	vi	perete	you wash
	3rd p.	они	перу	oni	peru	they wash
		оне		one		
		она		ona		

6 Verbs

The following verbs belong to this group:

стиз*ати* – стиж*ем*	stiz*ati* – stiž*em*	to arrive – I arrive
стиж*у*	stiž*u*	3rd p.pl.
стиз*ао*, стиз*ала*, стиз*ало*	stiz*ao*, stiz*alo*, stiz*ala*	past tense (masc./fem./neut.)
(по)стиз*ан*	(po)stiz*an*	passive participle
помаг*ати* – помаж*ем*	pomag*ati* – pomaž*em*	to help – I help
помаж*у*	pomaž*u*	3rd p.pl.
помаг*ао*	pomag*ao*	past tense
(пот)помаг*ан*	(pot)pomag*an*	passive participle
крет*ати* – крећ*ем*	kret*ati* – kreć*em*	to set off, move – I set off
крећ*у*	kreć*u*	3rd p.pl.
крет*ао*	kret*ao*	past tense
(по)крет*ан*	(po)kret*an*	passive participle
јах*ати* – јаш*ем*	jah*ati* – jaš*em*	to ride – I ride
јаш*у*	jaš*u*	3rd p.pl.
јах*ао*	jah*ao*	past tense
јах*ан*	jah*an*	passive participle
вик*ати* – вич*ем*	vik*ati* – vič*em*	to shout – I shout
вич*у*	vič*u*	3rd p.pl.
вик*ао*	vik*ao*	past tense
(из)вик*ан*	(iz)vik*an*	passive participle
диз*ати* – диж*ем*	diz*ati* – diž*em*	to lift – I lift
диж*у*	diž*u*	3rd p.pl.
диз*ао*	diz*ao*	past tense
диз*ан*	diz*an*	passive participle
бр*ати* – бер*ем*	br*ati* – ber*em*	to pick – I pick
бер*у*	ber*u*	3rd p.pl.
бр*ао*	br*ao*	past tense
бр*ан*	br*an*	passive participle

Note: When a prefix-less verb does not form a passive participle, the passive participles are cited from a prefix-bearing verb.

3   Some verbs in this conjugation with an **-ети/eti** ending in the infinitive have an **-ejy/eju** ending in the 3rd person plural:

доспети – доспеју	dospeti – dospeju	to reach/arrive
уметти – умеју	umeti – umeju	to know how to
успети – успеју	uspeti – uspeju	to succeed
смети – смеју	smeti – smeju	to dare/be allowed to

4   A vowel may be inserted in the present tense stem of verbs with an infinitive ending in **-рети/reti** and **-лети/leti**:

млети – мељем	mleti – meljem	to grind
мељу	melju	3rd p.pl.
млео	mleo	past tense
(из)мељен	(iz)meljen	passive participle

5   Some verbs with an infinitive ending in **-ети/eti** or **-ати/ati** may have an **м/m** or **н/n** inserted in the present tense stem:

почети – почнем	početi – počnem	to begin
престати – престанем	prestati – prestanem	to stop
узети – узмем	uzeti – uzmem	to take/get

6   Verbs ending in **-нути/nuti** lose the **у/u**:

метнути – метнем	metnuti – metnem	to put/place
погинути – погинем	poginuti – poginem	to die
кренути – кренем	krenuti – krenem	to set off/move

7   Some verbs with an infinitive ending in **-сти/sti** may have a **т/t** or **д/d**, often with an **н/n** inserted in the present tense stem:

јести – једем	jesti – jedem	to eat
срести – сретнем	sresti – sretnem	to meet
сести – седнем	sesti – sednem	to sit
пасти – паднем	pasti – padnem	to fall
украсти – украдем	ukrasti – ukradem	to steal
плести – плетем	plesti – pletem	to knit

Infinitive and present tense stems

8 Some verbs with infinitives in -сти/sti and -ети/eti may also have с/s, з/z, п/p or б/b inserted in the present tense stem:

превести – превезем	prevesti – prevezem	to transport
превезу	prevezu	3rd p.pl.
превезао	prevezao	past tense
превежен	prevežen	passive participle
однети – однесем	odneti – odnesem	to carry away
однесу	odnesu	3rd p.pl.
однео	odneo	past tense
однет	odnet	passive participle

9 Some verbs with infinitives ending in -ти/ti are also in this conjugation. With those verbs, a j is inserted before the e ending of the present tense stem and in the formation of the passive participle:

убити – убијем	ubiti – ubijem	to kill
убију	ubiju	3rd p.pl.
убио	ubio	past tense
убијен	ubijen	passive participle
пити – пијем	piti – pijem	to gain
пију	piju	3rd p.pl.
пио	pio	past tense
(по)пијен	(po)pijen	passive participle
добити – добијем	dobiti – dobijem	to gain
добију	dobiju	3rd p.pl.
добио	dobio	past tense
добијен	dobijen	passive participle

Some verbs that insert this j have a в/v in the passive participle:

чути – чујем	čuti – čujem	to hear
чују	čuju	3rd p.pl.
чуо	čuo	past tense
чувен	čuven	passive participle

10 Verbs with infinitives ending in **-ћи/-ći**. The **-ћи/-ći** ending of these verbs was derived from the addition of the **-ти/ti** ending to one of the following consonants: к/k, г/g, д/d or х/h (к/k + т/t = ћ/ć, г/g + т/t = ћ/ć, etc.). Having undergone an assimilation in the formation of the infinitive, the original consonants reappear in the present tense stem of the verb.

Infinitive and present tense stems

In the perfect (past) tense masculine singular, an **a** is inserted before the past participle ending, while the **к/k** and **г/g** are retained:

моћи – мог + ти –	moći – mog + ti –	to be able to
могу	mogu	1st p.sg.
могао	mogao	past tense (masc.)

When **к/k** and **г/g** appear before an e they are usually followed by an **н/n**:

рећи – рек + ти –	reći – rek + ti –	to say/tell
рекнем	reknem	1st p.sg.
рекао	rekao	past tense

стићи – стиг + ти –	stići – stig + ti –	to arrive
стигнем	stignem	1st p.sg.
стигао	stigao	past tense

помоћи – помог + ти –	pomoći – pomog + ti –	to help
помогнем	pomognem	1st p.sg.
помогао	pomogao	past tense

However, these consonants may still undergo further changes when conjugated either in the present tense or in the other tenses:

(a) When preceding an e:

к/k – ч/č

рећи – рекнем –	reći – reknem –	to say
речен	rečen	passive participle

(b) When preceding an и/i:

к/k – ц/c

г/g – з/z

47

вӯћи – вӯк + ти – вӯци!	vući – vuk + ti – vuci!	to pull imperative
лећи – легнем – лези!	leći – legnem – lezi!	to lie down imperative
помоћи – помогнем – помози!	pomoći – pomognem – pomozi!	to help imperative

6.2.3 Type III conjugation

This conjugation applies to verbs in which the infinitive ends in **-ити/iti**, as well as in **-ети**/eti and **-ати**/ati. The endings of these verbs contain the vowel **и/i** in the present tense:

Conjugation of **говорити/govoriti** (to speak) present tense					
sg.	1st p.	ја	говорим	ja	govorim	I speak
	2nd p.	ти	говориш	ti	govoriš	you speak
	3rd p.	он/она/оно	говори	on/ona/ono	govori	he/she/it speaks
pl.	1st p.	ми	говоримо	mi	govorimo	we speak
	2nd p.	ви	говорите	vi	govorite	you speak
	3rd p.	они оне она	говоре	oni one ona	govore	they speak

In the 3rd person plural these verbs take the ending -e.

The following are some verbs with an **-ити**/iti ending in this conjugation:

учити – учим – уче	učiti – učim – uče	to study 3rd p.pl.
учио	učio	past tense (m)
учен	učen	passive participle
хвалити – хвалим – хвале	hvaliti – hvalim – hvale	to praise 3rd p.pl.

хвал*ио*	hval*io*	past tense (m)	Infinitive and present tense stems
хваљ*ен*	hvalj*en*	passive participle	

плаш*ити* – плаш*им* – плаш*е*	plaš*iti* – plaš*im* – plaš*e*	to scare 3rd p.pl.
плаш*ио*	plaš*io*	past tense (m)
плаш*ен*	plaš*en*	passive participle
рад*ити* – рад*им* – рад*е*	rad*iti* – rad*im* – rad*e*	to work/do 3rd p.pl.
рад*ио*	rad*io*	past tense (m)
рађ*ен*	rađ*en*	passive participle

The following are some verbs with an **-ети**/**eti** ending in this conjugation:

жел*ети* – жел*им* – жел*е*	žel*eti* – žel*im* – žel*e*	to desire 3rd p.pl.
жел*ео*	žel*eo*	past tense (m)
жељ*ен*	želj*en*	passive participle
жив*ети* – жив*им* – жив*е*	živ*eti* – živ*im* – živ*e*	to live 3rd p.pl.
жив*ео*	živ*eo*	past tense (m)
(пре)живљ*ен*	(pre)življ*en*	passive participle
мрз*ети* – мрз*им* – мрз*е*	mrz*eti* – mrz*im* – mrz*e*	to hate 3rd p.pl.
мрз*ео*	mrz*eo*	past tense (m)
(о)мрж*ен*	(o)mrž*en*	passive participle

The following are some verbs with an **-ати**/**ati** ending in this conjugation:

број*ати* – број*им* – број*е*	broj*ati* – broj*im* – broj*e*	to count 3rd p.pl.
број*ао*	broj*ao*	past tense (m)
(од)број*ан*	(od)broj*an*	passive participle

трчати – трчим –	trčati – trčim –	to run
трче	trče	3rd p.pl.
трчао	trčao	past tense (m)
(пре)трчан	(pre)trčan	passive participle
држати – држим –	držati – držim –	to hold
држе	drže	3rd p.pl.
држао	držao	past tense (m)
држан	držan	passive participle
постојати – постојим –	postojati – postojim –	to exist
постоје	postoje	3rd p.pl.
постојао	postojao	past tense (m)

Note: When a prefix-less verb does not form a passive participle, the passive participles are cited from a prefix-bearing verb.

6.3 Types of verbs and aspects

6.3.1 Transitive and intransitive verbs

The following types of verbs exist, depending on the type and nature of the activity:

1 Transitive verbs take a direct object:

Милош *је купио* телевизор.	Miloš *je kupio* televizor.	Miloš *bought* a TV.

2 Intransitive verbs do not take a direct object:

Сваког дана *устајемо* у исто време.	Svakog dana *ustajemo* u isto vreme.	Every day we *get up* at the same time.

3 Some verbs may be used both transitively and intransitively:

Он *гледа* кроз прозор.	On *gleda* kroz prozor.	He *is looking* through the window.
Пас *гледа* мачку.	Pas *gleda* mačku.	The dog *is looking at* the cat.

| Не волим брзо да *једем*. | Ne volim brzo da *jedem*. | I don't like to *eat* quickly. |
| Не *једем* хлеб са месом. | Ne *jedem* hleb sa mesom. | I don't *eat* bread with meat. |

6.3.2 Imperfective and perfective verbs

Most Serbian verbs have two aspects, each reflecting the duration of the action or state described by the verb. One verb in the pair reflects the imperfective aspect and the other the perfective. The imperfective verb has its own infinitive, set of tenses and participles, and so does the perfective verb.

1 The imperfective aspect indicates that the action or state expressed by the verb may be of unlimited duration, may still be in progress, or may be a repetitive, habitual action.

| *Пијем* пиво без пене. | *Pijem* pivo bez pene. | I *drink* beer without a head (froth). |
| *Редовно читам* новине. | *Redovno čitam* novine. | I *read* the papers regularly. |

There are two kinds of imperfective verbs:

(a) Durative verbs – the action of these verbs is continuous and uninterrupted with no foreseen completion:

| Петар *пише* писмо својој мајци. | Petar *piše* pismo svojoj majci. | Peter *is writing* a letter to his mother. |

(b) Iterative or frequentative verbs – the action of these verbs is interrupted or repeated frequently or at regular intervals:

| Ана *узима* лек на сваки сат. | Ana *uzima* lek na svaki sat. | Anna *takes* her medicine every hour. |

Imperfective verbs are generally used in the present tense. They can also be used in the past tense if the action lasted for a longer period of time or was repetitive.

Imperfective verbs are sometimes formed by the addition of a suffix to a perfective verb, or an infix to the infinitive stem:

(a) With the infix **и/i**:

| *Perfective* | позвати – позов*ем* | pozvati – pozov*em* | to invite |

Types of verbs and aspects

Imperfective позивати – позивам	pozivati – pozivam	to call

(b) With the suffix **-ва/va**:

Perfective дати – дам	dati – dam	to give
Imperfective давати – дајем	davati – dajem	

(c) With the suffix **-ава/ava**:

Perfective извинити (се) – извиним (се)	izviniti (se) – izvinim (se)	to apologise
Imperfective извињавати (се) – извињавам (се)	izvinjavati (se) – izvinjavam (se)	

Before this suffix, the following hard consonants soften:

б/b –	бљ/blj
н/n –	њ/nj
сн/sn –	шњ/šnj
ст/st –	шт/št
т/t –	ћ/ć
д/d –	ђ/đ
л/l –	љ/lj
м/m –	мљ/mlj
п/p –	пљ/plj
сл/sl –	шљ/šlj
в/v –	вљ/vlj
зн/zn –	жњ/žnj
с/s –	ш/š
з/z –	ж/ž

If the perfective verb ends in **-ати/ati**, there is no consonant softening.

(d) With the suffix **-ива/iva** added to an **-ити/iti** verb:

Perfective средити – средим	srediti – sredim	to tidy up, organise

Imperfective	сређивати – сређујем	sređivati – sređujem	
Perfective	обогатити – обогатим	obogatiti – obogatim	to enrich
Imperfective	обогаћивати – обогаћујем	obogaćivati – obogaćujem	

Before this suffix, the following hard consonants soften:

т/t –	ћ/ć
д/d –	ђ/đ
л/l –	љ/lj
м/m –	мљ/mlj
п/p –	пљ/plj
сл/sl –	шљ/šlj
в/v –	вљ/vlj
зн/zn –	жњ/žnj
с/s –	ш/š
з/z –	ж/ž
ст/st –	шћ/šć
зд/zd –	жд/žd
ф/f –	фљ/flj

(e) With the suffix -ja/ja:

Perfective	убити – убијем	ubiti – ubijem	to kill
Imperfective	убијати – убијам	ubijati – ubijam	
Perfective	састати се – састанемо се	sastati se – sastanemo se	to meet, get together
Imperfective	састајати се – састајемо се	sastajati – sastajemo se	(1st p.pl)

(f) With the suffix -ова/ova:

Perfective	купити – купим	kupiti – kupim	to buy
Imperfective	куповати – купујем	kupovati – kupujem	

6 Verbs

Some imperfective forms are created from perfective verbs, where the vowel before the infinitive ending changes to -a-. In these cases, the following root consonants soften:

т/t – ћ/ć

ст/st – шт/št

в/v – вљ/vlj

д/d – ђ/đ

з/z – ж/ž

в/v – вљ/vlj

Perfective	снимити – снимим	snimiti – snimim	to record
Imperfective	снимати – снимам	snimati – snimam	
Perfective	наместити – наместим	namestiti – namestim	to fix, set up
Imperfective	намештати – намештам	nameštati – nameštam	to furnish, set up

Some imperfective forms end in -ати/ati while the perfective form ends in -нути/nuti:

Perfective	кренути – кренем	krenuti – krenem	to move, set off
Imperfective	кретати – крећем	kretati – krećem	
Perfective	гурнути – гурнем	gurnuti – gurnem	to push
Imperfective	гурати – гурам	gurati – guram	
Perfective	затегнути – затегнем	zategnuti – zategnem	to tighten
Imperfective	затезати – затежем	zatezati – zatežem	

Stems ending in hard consonants soften.

Some imperfective forms end in -ати/ati or -ити/iti while the basic perfective form ends in -ети/eti, -сти/sti or -ћи/ći. These perfective forms may have a stem ending in any one of the following consonants which disappear in the perfective infinitive but reappear in the present tense of the perfective and imperfective forms, including the imperfective infinitive: -м/m, -н/n, -т/t, -д/d, -к/k, -х/h.

Perfective	заузети – заузмем	zauzeti – zauzmem	to occupy
Imperfective	заузимати – заузимам	zauzimati – zauzimam	to be in the process of occupying
Perfective	сести – седнем	sesti – sednem	to sit
Imperfective	седати – седам	sedati – sedam	to be in the process of sitting

Types of verbs and aspects

2   The perfective aspect indicates that the action or state expressed by the verb is completed or of limited duration and is perceived as a completed whole. Perfective verbs are generally used in the past tense or the future tense (or the infinitive):

Попила сам чашу коњака пре јела.	*Popila* sam čašu konjaka pre jela.	I *drank* a glass of cognac before my meal.
Прочитала сам добру књигу прошле недеље.	*Pročitala* sam dobru knjigu prošle nedelje.	I *read* a good book last week.
Добро је *попити* чашу млека пре спавања.	Dobro je *popiti* čašu mleka pre spavanja.	It's good *to drink* a glass of milk before going to sleep.

Perfective verbs cannot be used in the present tense to express present action, but only to describe a subject's desire in the present to carry out an action that is to be completed in the future. In the present tense they are used after the conjunctions да/da (that/to), што/što (that/to), ако/ako (if) and кад/kad (when):

Хоћу да прочитам ту књигу.	*Hoću da pročitam* tu knjigu.	I want to read that book.

These verbs can be used after the same conjunctions in the past and future tenses as well:

Окренуо се да погледа шта се догодило.	*Okrenuo se da pogleda* šta se dogodilo.	He turned around to take a look at what happened.
Зажалиће што су отишли с њим.	*Zažaliće* što otišli s njim.	They will regret that they had gone with him.

6 Verbs

Perfective verbs are sometimes formed by adding a prefix (most of which are prepositional) to an imperfective verb, which becomes the basic verb, while the newly formed verb becomes a compound verb:

Imperfective	јести – једем	jesti – jedem	to be eating
Perfective	појести – поједем	pojesti – pojedem	to complete eating
Imperfective	бринути – бринем	brinuti – brinem	to worry, be concerned
Perfective	забринути – забринем	zabrinuti – zabrinem	to start worrying
Imperfective	ћутати – ћутим	ćutati – ćutim	to be silent
Perfective	ућутати – ућутим	ućutati – ućutim	to become silent

Every verb with a prefix added to it will become a new verb, which might then have a new, corresponding imperfective partner, in which case these two verbs become an aspectual pair. Thus, although there already exists the original imperfective verb to which the prefix had been added, the resulting prefixed perfective and its new aspectual partner may be independent of the original verb:

Imperfective	ставити	staviti	to put, place
Perfective	поставити	postaviti	to lay out
Imperfective	постављати	postavljati	to be laying out

Some prefixes may change the meaning of the verb:

Imperfective	писати – пишем	pisati – pišem	to write
Perfective	пописати – попишем	popisati – popišem	to list, make an inventory
Imperfective	пописивати – пописујем	popisivati – popisujem	
Perfective	записати – запишем	zapisati – zapišem	to note down
Imperfective	записивати – записујем	zapisivati – zapisujem	
Perfective	преписати – препишем	prepišem – prepišem	to copy

Imperfective	преписивати – преписујем	prepis*i*vati – prepis*uje*m	

Certain compound verbs have different stems for each aspect. Amongst these are the derivaties of **ићи/ići** (to go):

Perfective	доћи – дођем	doći – dođem	to come
Imperfective	долазити – долазим	dolaziti – dolazim	
Perfective	отићи – одем/отидем	otići – odem/ otidem	to go
Imperfective	одлазити – одлазим	odlaziti – odlazim	
Perfective	изаћи – изађем	izaći – izađem	to go/ come out
Imperfective	излазити – излазим	izlaziti – izlazim	

and the aspectual pairs of imperfectives ending in **-лагати/lagati** and perfectives ending in **-ложити/ložiti**:

Perfective	сложити – сложим	sl*o*žiti – sl*o*žim	to fold
Imperfective	слагати – слажем	sl*a*gati – sl*a*žem	
Perfective	предложити – предложим	pred*lo*žiti – pred*lo*žim	to suggest
Imperfective	предлагати – предлажем	pred*la*gati – pred*la*žem	

Some verbs have one form that can express both aspects depending on the context:

видети	videti	to see
чути	čuti	to hear
доручковти	doručkovati	to have breakfast
ручати	ručati	to have lunch
вечерати	večerati	to have supper
ићи	ići	to go
контролисати	kontrolisati	to control
телефонирати	telefonirati	to telephone

Types of verbs and aspects

While others express only the imperfective aspect:

бити	biti	to be
имати	imati	to have
држати	držati	to hold
морати	morati	must
становати	stanovati	to live, dwell

Some verbs could be said to form an aspectual pair with a completely different verb where they have become a pair only through their meaning:

| Perfective | рећи/казати – кажем | reći/kazati – kažem | to say/tell |
| Imperfective | говорити – говорим | govoriti – govorim | to speak |

6.4 Present tense

6.4.1 Formation of the present tense and its use

The present tense indicates that the action is being carried out at the present time. There is only one present tense in Serbian and it is formed with imperfective and perfective verbs, though with the latter it is used almost exclusively after the conjunctions да/da, што/što, ако/ako, кад/kad, to make a sort of subjunctive (see Section 6.3 Types of verbs and aspects).

The present tense is formed by the addition of personal endings to the present tense stem. Personal endings reveal what person and number is performing the action of the verb:

Present tense personal endings				
sg.	1st p.	I	-м	-m
	2nd p.	you	-ш	-š
	3rd p.	he/she/it	–	–
pl.	1st p.	we	-мо	-mo
	2nd p.	you	-те	-te
	3rd p.	they	-е/-у/-jу	-e/-u/-ju

The vowel preceding these endings belongs to one of three conjugations. Each conjugation differs slightly, and this is reflected in the final endings of each verb (see Sections 6.2.1–3 for types of conjugations). The personal endings for 1st person singular and plural, and 2nd person singular and plural remain unchanged in all the conjugations. The 3rd person singular and plural endings may differ with each conjugation:

Present tense

1   Endings for verbs in Type I conjugation, infinitives ending in **-ати/ati**, with all endings containing **a**:

Type I conjugation present tense personal endings				
sg.	1st p.	I	**-ам**	**-am**
	2nd p.	you	**-аш**	**-aš**
	3rd p.	he/she/it	**-а**	**-a**
pl.	1st p.	we	**-амо**	**-amo**
	2nd p.	you	**-ате**	**-ate**
	3rd p.	they	**-ају**	**-aju**

Verbs with the vowel **a** preceding any personal ending will have a **-ју/ju** ending in the 3rd person plural:

Infinitive	Present tense stem	Present tense	
		1st p.sg.	3rd p.pl.
причати	прича-	причам	причају
pričati	priča-	pričam	pričaju
читати	чита-	читам	читају
čitati	čita-	čitam	čitaju

2   Endings for verbs in Type II conjugation, infinitives ending in **-ати/ati, -ти/ti, -овати/ovati, -ивати/ivati, -ути/uti, -ети/eti, -сти/sti, -ћи/ći**, with all endings containing **e**:

Type II conjugation present tense personal endings				
sg.	1st p.	I	-ем	-em
	2nd p.	you	-еш	-eš
	3rd p.	he/she/it	-е	-e
pl.	1st p.	we	-емо	-emo
	2nd p.	you	-ете	-ete
	3rd p.	they	-у (ејy)	-u (eju)

Verbs with the vowel **e** preceding any personal ending will have an **-y/u** ending in the 3rd person plural:

Infinitive	Present tense stem	Present tense	
		1st p.sg.	3rd p.pl.
казати (з – ж)	**каже-**	**кажем**	**кажу**
kazati	**kaže-**	**kažem**	**kažu**
прати	**пере-**	**перем**	**перу**
prati	**pere-**	**perem**	**peru**
умети	**уме-**	**умем**	**умеjу**
umeti	**ume-**	**umem**	**umeju**

3 Endings for verbs in Type III conjugation, infinitives ending in **-ати/ati, -ити/iti, -ети/eti**, with all endings containing **и/i**:

Type III conjugation present tense personal endings				
sg.	1st p.	I	-им	-im
	2nd p.	you	-иш	-iš
	3rd p.	he/she/it	-и	-i
pl.	1st p.	we	-имо	-imo
	2nd p.	you	-ите	-ite
	3rd p.	they	-е	-e

Verbs with the vowel и/i preceding any personal ending will have an -e ending in the 3rd person plural:

Infinitive	Present tense stem	Present tense	
		1st p.sg.	3rd p.pl.
радити	ради-	радим	раде
raditi	radi	radim	rade
живети	живи-	живим	живе
živeti	živi	živim	žive

It is worth learning the combination of vowels preceding the personal endings for the 1st person singular and the 3rd person plural for all three types of conjugations as each is typical of its group:

а/у	читам, читају	a/u	čitam, čitaju
е/у	умем, умеју	e/u	umem, umeju
и/е	живим, живе	i/e	živim, žive

The verb **бити/biti** (to be) has two forms in the present tense:

1 A short form:

Present tense short form of **бити/biti** (to be)				
sg.	1st p.	I am	ја сам	ja sam
	2nd p.	you are	ти си	ti si
	3rd p.	he/she/it is	он/она/оно је	on/ona/ono je
pl.	1st p.	we are	ми смо	mi smo
	2nd p.	you are	ви сте	vi ste
	3rd p.	they are	они/оне/она су	oni/one/ona su

This is the more frequently used form. When the subject is known, or has already been mentioned in a preceding sentence, the personal pronoun is generally omitted. It can be omitted because the verbal endings will, in most instances, indicate person and number, while any nouns or adjectives referring to the subject will also indicate gender. The personal pronoun may in those instances be included for emphasis:

Она је моја сестра.	*Ona je* moja sestra.	*She is* my sister.
Врло *је* лепа.	Vrlo *je* lepa.	She *is* very pretty.

2   A long form:

Present tense long form of **бити/biti** (to be)				
sg.	1st p.	I am	јесам	jesam
	2nd p.	you are	јеси	jesi
	3rd p.	he/she/it is	јест(е)*	jest(e)*
pl.	1st p.	we are	јесмо	jesmo
	2nd p.	you are	јесте	jeste
	3rd p.	they are	јесу	jesu

* 3rd p. sg. is also used to mean 'yes' јесте/jeste.

This form is quite restricted in its use and is generally only used when the verb occurs as the first word of a sentence or phrase, often in posing a question, when it is followed by the interrogative enclitic ли/li. It is also used in response to a question, often on its own, denoting an affirmative response:

Јеси ли била на пијаци данас? – *Јесам.*	*Jesi* li bila na pijaci danas? – *Jesam.*	*Have you* been to the market today? – Yes, I have.
Јесмо ли се договорили? – *Јесмо.*	*Jesmo* li se dogovorili? – *Jesmo.*	*Have we* reached an agreement? – Yes, we have.

When the 3rd person singular is followed by the interrogative enclitic ли/li, it has a different form: **је ли**/**je li**. The **je** here looks like the enclitic form of 'to be', but is not in fact an enclitic.

Although the personal pronoun is generally omitted with the long form, as it is already included in its formation, it can also be used:

Ми нисмо Енглези, али *они јесу*.	Mi nismo Englezi, ali *oni jesu*.	We're not English, but *they are*.

6.4.2 The negative present tense

The negative form of the present tense is formed by placing the negative particle **не/ne** before the verb. The two words are written separately. The only exceptions to this rule are the negative forms of the verbs **бити/biti** (to be), **имати/imati** (to have) and **хтети/hteti** (to want), where the two are written together.

Present tense

Negative form of **бити/biti** (to be)				
sg.	1st p.	нисам	nisam	I am not
	2nd p.	ниси	nisi	you are not
	3rd p.	није	nije	he/she/it is not
pl.	1st p.	нисмо	nismo	we are not
	2nd p.	нисте	niste	you are not
	3rd p.	нису	nisu	they are not

Не идем у град.   *Ne idem u grad.*   I'm not going to town.
Ja нисам инжењер.   *Ja nisam inženjer.*   I'm not an engineer.

Negative form of **имати/imati** (to have)				
sg.	1st p.	немам	nemam	I have not
	2nd p.	немаш	nemaš	you have not
	3rd p.	нема	nema	he/she/it has not
pl.	1st p.	немамо	nemamo	we have not
	2nd p.	немате	nemate	you have not
	3rd p.	немају	nemaju	they have not

For negative forms of **хтети/hteti**, see Section 6.6 Future tense.

6.4.3 The interrogative present

The following are ways in which to ask a question in the present tense:

(a) By beginning the sentence with the verb, followed by the interrogative particle **ли/li**:

  Волите ли пасуљ?   *Volite li pasulj?*   Do you like beans?

(b) By beginning the sentence with да ли/da li followed by the verb:

Да ли волите пасуљ?   *Da li volite pasulj?*   Do you like beans?

(c) By beginning the sentence with je, followed by the interrogative particle ли/li and the verb:

Је ли волите пасуљ?   *Je li volite pasulj?*   Do you like beans?

6.4.4 The negative interrogative present tense

This is formed by placing зар/zar before the negative form of the verb:

Зар не идемо у град?   *Zar ne idemo u grad?*   Are we not going to town?

Зар нисте инжењер?   *Zar niste inženjer?*   Are you not an engineer?

6.5 Past tense (perfect tense)

The main past tense in use today is the perfect tense. The imperfect and the pluperfect tenses are rarely in use in the spoken language and are not included in this book, while the aorist is covered in Section 6.7 Aorist tense.

The perfect tense corresponds to all the English past tenses: the simple past (I spoke), the continuous past (I was speaking), the habitual past (I used to speak) and the pluperfect (I had spoken).

6.5.1 Formation of the perfect tense and its use

The perfect tense is a compound tense formed using the short form* of the present tense of the verb **бити/biti**, which reflects person and number and which becomes the auxiliary verb to the main verb and acts as an enclitic:

Present tense short form of **бити/biti** (to be)				
sg.	1st p.	I am	сам	sam
	2nd p.	you are	си	si
	3rd p.	he/she/it is	је	je
pl.	1st p.	we are	смо	smo
	2nd p.	you are	сте	ste
	3rd p.	they are	су	su

* The long form can also be used in forming the past tense, when used for emphasis.

and the main verb which has a past adjectival participle ending (see Section 9.8 Verbal adjectives) (also referred to as the indeclinable active past participle, the past participle, etc.) which agrees with the gender of the subject. Thus, this tense shows person, number and gender.

The formation of the past adjectival participle will depend on the infinitive ending of the verb concerned. Generally, it is formed by replacing the **-ти/ti** infinitive ending of the verb with an **-о/o** or **-л/l** to which the corresponding gender and number ending is added. The masculine singular ending is **-о/o**, the feminine singular ending is **-ла/la**, and the neuter singular ending is **-ло/lo**. The plural endings are **-ли/li** (masculine), **-ле/le** (feminine) and **-ла/la** (neuter):

Past (perfect) tense

Singular			Plural		
Masculine	Feminine	Neuter	Masculine	Feminine	Neuter
-о/o	**-ла/la**	**-ло/lo**	**-ли/li**	**-ле/le**	**-ла/la**

Thus, the perfect tense, i.e. past tense, of the verb **почети/početi** (to start) would be:

sg.	1st p.	Ja сам почео/почела	or	Почео/почела сам
		Ja sam počeo/počela		Počeo/Počela sam
	2nd p.	Ти си почео/почела		Почео/почела си
		Ti si počeo/počela		Počeo/počela si
	3rd p.	Он је почео/On je počeo		Почео је/Počeo je
		Она је почела/Ona je počela		Почела је/Počela je
		Оно је почело/Ono je počelo		Почело је/Počelo je
pl.	1st p.	Ми смо почели/Mi smo počeli		Почели смо/Počeli smo (m)
		Ми смо почеле/Mi smo počele		Почеле смо/Počele smo (f)

6 Verbs

pl.	2nd p.	Ви сте почели/ Vi ste počeli		Почели сте/ Počeli ste (m)	
		Ви сте почеле/ Vi ste počele		Почеле сте/ Počele ste (f)	
	3rd p.	Они су почели/ Oni su počeli		Почели су/ Počeli su (m)	
		Оне су почеле/ One su počele		Почеле су/ Počele su (f)	
		Она су почела/ Ona su počela		Почела су/ Počela su (n)	

The verb **бити/biti** (to be) has its own past tense, made with an auxiliary and a participle, like any other verb. (Since the past adjectival participle denotes gender and number, the subject, especially if a pronoun, is often omitted.)

Perfect (past) tense of **бити/biti** (to be)

sg.	1st p.	Ја сам био/ била Ja sam bio/ bila	or	Био/ била сам Bio/ bila sam	I — have been/ was
	2nd p.	Ти си био/ била Ti si bio/bila		Био/ била си Bio/bila si	You — have been/ were
	3rd p.	Он је био/ On je bio		Био је/ Bio je	He — has been/ was
		Она је била/ Ona je bila		Била је/ Bila je	She — has been/ was
		Оно је било/ Ono je bilo		Било је/ Bilo je	It — has been/ was
pl.	1st p.	Ми смо били/ Mi smo bili		Били смо/ Bili smo	We (m) — have been/ were
		Ми смо биле/ Mi smo bile		Биле смо/ Bile smo	We (f) — have been/ were
	2nd p.	Ви сте били/ Vi ste bili		Били сте/ Bili ste	You (m) — have been/ were

		Ви сте биле/ **Vi ste bile**	Биле сте/ **Bile ste**	You (f)	have been/ were	Past (perfect) tense
pl.	3rd p.	Они су били/ **Oni su bili**	Били су/ **Bili su**	They (m)	have been/ were	
		Оне су биле/ **One su bile**	Биле су/ **Bile su**	They (f)	have been/ were	
		Она су била/ **Ona su bila**	Била су/ **Bila su**	They (n)	have been/ were	

Био сам у биоскопу.	*Bio sam* u bioskopu.	I (m) *was* at the cinema.
Деца *су била* у школи.	Deca *su bila* u školi.	The children *have been* to school.
Почела сам да једем.	*Počela sam* da jedem.	I (f) *have started* to eat.
Ви *сте почели* да радите.	*Vi ste počeli* da radite.	You (pl.) *have started* to work.

The auxiliary verb **бити/biti** must always be used in forming the perfect tense. It acts as an enclitic and must take second place, in accordance with the word order rule (see Section 13.1 Order and importance of enclitics).

Below are examples of verbs in the perfect tense which have endings other than -ти/ti in the infinitive.

The stems of infinitives ending in -ћи/ći are either with -к/k or with -г/g. In both cases, the past adjectival participle ending is added directly to the -к/k or -г/g stem, with the fleeting **a** inserted before the participle in the masculine singular. Where there is a -сти/sti infinitive ending, the stem and ending need to be looked at and learnt separately.

(плести, **plesti**)	(плетем, **pletem**)	плео/**pleo** плела/**plela**	to knit
(провести, **provesti**)	(проведем, **provedem**)	провео/**proveo** провела/**provela**	to spend
(срести, **sresti**)	(сретнем, **sretnem**)	срео/**sreo** срела/**srela**	to meet
(помоћи, **pomoći**)	(помогнем, **pomognem**)	помогао/**pomogao*** помогла/**pomogla**	to help

(рећи, reći)	(рекнем, reknem)	рекао/rekao* рекла/rekla	to say
(моћи, moći)	(могу, mogu)	могао/mogao* могла/mogla	to be able to

* Note the fleeting **a** in the masculine singular between the -к/k or -г/g and the past adjectival participle ending -о/o, alternating with the -л/l in the past adjectival participle feminine and neuter singular and plural endings.

Среле су се у граду.	Srele su se u gradu.	They (*f, pl.*) *met* in town.
Одмах *си* им помогла.	Odmah *si* im pomogla.	You (*f*) immediately *helped* them.
Ја *сам* му рекао.	Ja *sam* mu rekao.	I (*m*) *told* him.

With ићи/ići and its derivatives (доћи/doći, наћи/naći, изаћи/izaći, поћи/poći, отићи/otići, проћи/proći, ући/ući, etc.) the present tense -д/d or -ћ/đ is replaced with -ш/š to which the past adjectival participle endings are added (see Section 6.17 Ићи/ići and its derivatives):

(ићи, ići)	(идем, idem)	ишао/išao (m) ишла/išla (f)	to go
(доћи/doći)	дођем/dođem	дошао/došao* дошла/došla	to come
(наћи/naći)	нађем/nađem	нашао/našao* нашла/našla	to find
(изаћи/izaći)	нзађем/izađem	изашао/izašao* нзашла/izašla	to exit
(поћи/poći)	пођем/pođem	пошао/pošao* пошла/pošla	to set off
(отићи/otići)	отиђем/одем otiđem/odem	отишао/otišao* отишла/otišla	to leave
(проћи/proći)	прођем/prođem	прошао/prošao* прошла/prošla	to pass
(ући/ući)	уђем/uđem	ушао/ušao* ушла/ušla	to enter

* Note the fleeting **a** in the masculine singular between the -ш/š and the past adjectival participle ending -о/o, alternating with the -л/l in the past adjectival participle feminine and neuter singular and plural endings.

			Past (perfect) tense
Дошао сам код бабе у посету.	Došao sam kod babe u posetu.	I (m) came to visit my grandmother.	
Дечаци *су* нашли новчаник у парку.	Dečaci *su* našli novčanik u parku.	The boys *found* a wallet in the park.	
Ти *си* отишла у школу са мојом сестром.	Ti *si* otišla u školu sa mojom sestrom.	You (f) *went* to school with my sister.	

If there are two or more subjects and they are of different gender, the past adjectival participle ending added to the main verb will be in the masculine plural:

Он и она *су* се срели у парку.	On i ona *su* se sreli u parku.	He and she *met* in the park.
Драган и Наташа *су* отишли на море.	Dragan i Nataša *su otišli* na more.	Dragan and Nataša *have gone* to the coast.

6.5.2 | The negative perfect tense

The negative form of the perfect tense is formed using the negative form of the verb **бити/biti**, followed by the main verb with its active past participle ending. The negative forms are not enclitics.

Negative form of **бити/biti** (to be)				
sg.	1st p.	нисам	nisam	(I) am/have not
	2nd p.	ниси	nisi	(you) are/have not
	3rd p.	није	nije	(he/she/it) is/has not
pl.	1st p.	нисмо	nismo	(we) are/have not
	2nd p.	нисте	niste	(you) are/have not
	3rd p.	нису	nisu	(they) are/have not

Нису ишли заједно у биоскоп.	*Nisu* išli zajedno u bioskop.	They *didn't go* together to the cinema.
Гојко *није* могао да дође.	Gojko *nije* mogao da dođe.	Gojko *couldn't come*.
Није било довољно шећера у кафи.	*Nije* bilo dovoljno šećera u kafi.	*There wasn't* enough sugar in the coffee.

The negative form can also be preceded by **још/još** (still, as yet) for emphasis:

Још им *ниси* помогла.	*Još* im *nisi* pomogla.	You *still haven't* helped them.
Ја *још* ништа *нисам* рекао.*	Ja *još* ništa *nisam* rekao.*	I *still haven't* said anything.* (nothing)

* Note the double negative. (See Section 6.15 Formation of the negative.)

6.5.3 The interrogative perfect tense

In addition to using interrogative (question) words (why, how, where, when, etc.):

Зашто ниси гледао куда идеш?	Zašto nisi gledao kuda ideš?	Why didn't you *look* where you were going?

the interrogative form of the past tense is used in forming a yes/no type question when using either one of the two interrogative constructions:

1 By conjugating the long form of **бити + ли/biti + li**:

Је ли разговарала са наставницом?	*Je li* razgovarala sa nastavnicom?	Has she *spoken* to the teacher?
Јесмо ли се договорили?	*Jesmo li* se dogovorili?	Have we *agreed*?
Јесте ли се поздравили?	*Jeste li* se pozdravili?	Did you say your goodbyes (hellos)?
Јесу ли вам дали новац за карте?	*Jesu li* vam dali novac za karte?	Did they *give* you the money for the tickets?

2 By beginning the question with **да/da** followed by interrogative enclitic **ли/li** and the short form of **бити/biti**:

Да ли си се јавила мами?	*Da li si* se javila mami?	Did you *call* your mother?
Да ли је био код лекара?	*Da li je* bio kod lekara?	Has he *been* to the doctor?
Да ли су вам дали новац за карте?	*Da li su* vam dali novac za karte?	Did they *give* you the money for the tickets?

6.5.4 The negative interrogative perfect tense

The interrogative form of the negative perfect tense is created by using the word **зар/zar** at the beginning of the sentence, followed by the negative form of the auxiliary verb. Although neither functions as an enclitic, the word order must be followed where enclitics appear:

Зар није био код лекара?	*Zar nije bio kod lekara?*	Has he *not been* to the doctor?
Зар се нисмо договорили?	*Zar se nismo dogovorili?*	Have we *not agreed*?
Зар се нисте поздравили?	*Zar se niste pozdravili?*	Did you *not say* your goodbyes (hellos)?

6.6 Future tense

6.6.1 Formation of the future tense and its use

The future tense is used to express an action which is to take place some time in the future. Like the past tense, it is a compound tense, formed from two verbs: the short form of the present tense of the verb **хтети/hteti** (to want) (which then acts as an auxiliary verb and takes on the meaning 'will') and the main verb in its infinitive form. As in the past tense, the auxiliary verb is an enclitic and as such must follow the word order (see Chapter 13 Enclitics).

Present tense short form of **хтети/hteti** (to want)				
sg.	1st p.	ћу	ću	I will
	2nd p.	ћеш	ćeš	you will
	3rd p.	ће	će	he/she/it will
pl.	1st p.	ћемо	ćemo	we will
	2nd p.	ћете	ćete	you will
	3rd p.	ће	će	they will

Although it does not indicate gender, the auxiliary verb indicates both person and number. This will often lead to the omission of the subject, especially if it is a pronoun:

Вечерас ћу доћи у Лондон.	*Večeras ću doći u London.*	Tonight *I will come* to London.
Сутра ћемо звати шефа.	*Sutra ćemo zvati šefa.*	Tomorrow *we will call* the boss.

Мајка ће знати да си дошао.	**Majka će znati da si došao.**	Mother *will know* that you have come.

Only when at the beginning of a sentence or clause can the future tense also be formed by placing the infinitive first and annexing the auxiliary verb to it. In order to do this, the infinitive ending is replaced by the auxiliary, thus forming one word. This applies to infinitives ending in -ти/ti:

звати – зва + ћу	zva-ti – zva + ću	to call – I will call
знати – зна + ћу	zna-ti – zna + ću	to know – I will know
Зваћемо сестру сутра.	**Zvaćemo sestru sutra.**	We *will call* (our) sister tomorrow.
Знаће мајка да си дошао.	**Znaće majka da si došao.**	Mother *will know* that you have come.

With infinitives ending in -сти/sti, the **с/s** becomes **ш/š**, before the auxiliary is added to the verb:

Ја ћу јести у ресторану.	**Ja ću jesti u restoranu.**	I will eat in the restaurant.
Јешћу у ресторану.	**Ješću u restoranu.**	I will eat in the restaurant.

With infinitives ending in **-ћи/ći**, the two words remain separate and the auxiliary takes second place:

доћи	doći	to come
ићи	ići	to go
Доћи ћу у Лондон вечерас.	**Doći ću u London večeras.**	I *will come* to London tonight.
Ићи ћеш сада на спавање.	**Ići ćeš sada na spavanje.**	You *will go* to sleep now.

When sentences begin with a group of words acting as a unit and independent of the main sentence, the infinitive of the main verb will follow this unit and act as the first word in the word order. The auxiliary will either follow it as an enclitic (with verbs ending in **-ћи/ći**) or be attached to it, having replaced the infinitive ending **-ти/ti**:

У девет сати ићи ћеш на спавање.	**U devet sati ići ćeš na na spavanje.**	At nine o'clock *you will go* to sleep.
Кад прође киша, сијаће сунце.	**Kad prođe kiša, sijaće sunce.**	When the rain stops, the sun *will shine*.

The future tense can also be formed by using the auxiliary of the verb **хтети/hteti** and connecting it to the main verb in the present tense with the conjunction **да/da**:

Future tense

Ја ћу да дођем у Лондон вечерас.	**Ja ću da dođem u** London večeras.	**I will come** to London tonight.
Ти ћеш да идеш сада на спавање.	**Ti ćeš da ideš** sada na spavanje.	**You will go** to sleep now.

When this construction of the future tense is used in the affirmative, the subject, even if a pronoun, is often, though not always, included:

Он ће да дође код мене вечерас.	**On će da dođe** kod mene večeras.	**He will come** to my place tonight.
Вечерас **ће да дође** код мене.	Večeras **će da dođe** kod mene.	Tonight (he) **will come** to my place.

6.6.2 | The negative future

When a negative is formed in the future tense, the auxiliary verb **хтети/hteti** is negated:

Negative form of **хтети/hteti** (to want)				
sg.	1st p.	нећу	neću	I will not
	2nd p.	нећеш	nećeš	you will not
	3rd p.	неће	neće	he/she/it will not
pl.	1st p.	нећемо	nećemo	we will not
	2nd p.	нећете	nećete	you will not
	3rd p.	неће	neće	they will not

This negative form of the short form of **хтети/hteti** is not an enclitic and can therefore stand in first position.

When forming the negative of **хтети/hteti** (**нећу/neću**), it is important to note that only the short form (and *never* the long form) is negated, and so **не хоћу/ne hoću** would never be used.

Ја нећу да дођем у Лондон вечерас.	**Ja neću da dođem** u London večeras.	**I will not come** to London tonight.
Ти нећеш да идеш сада на спавање.	**Ti nećeš da ideš** sada na spavanje.	**You will not go** to sleep now.

6.6.3 The interrogative future

The interrogative future expressed with affirmative meaning can be formed in two ways.

1. The first form includes the auxiliary verb and either the infinitive or the present tense of the main verb. In either case, the conjunction да/da followed by the interrogative enclitic ли/li is placed before the main verb:

Да ли ћеш ићи сада на спавање?	*Da li ćeš ići sada na spavanje?*	Will you go to sleep now?
Да ли ће Ана певати?	*Da li će Ana pevati?*	Will Anna sing?

When the main verb is in the present tense, another conjunction да/da precedes it:

Да ли ћеш да идеш сада на спавање?	*Da li ćeš da ideš sada na spavanje?*	Will you go to sleep now?
Да ли ће Ана да пева?	*Da li će Ana da peva?*	Will Anna sing?

2. The second form of the interrogative future includes the long form of the verb хтети/hteti which replaces the conjunction да/da, and is also followed by the interrogative enclitic ли/li to which is added either the infinitive or the present tense of the main verb:

Хоћеш ли ићи сада на спавање?	*Hoćeš li ići sada na spavanje?*	Will you go to sleep now?
Хоће ли Партизан играти овог месеца?	*Hoće li Partizan igrati ovog meseca?*	Will Partisan play this month?

When the main verb is in the present tense, the conjunction да/da precedes it:

Хоћеш ли да идеш сада на спавање?	*Hoćeš li da ideš sada na spavanje?*	Will you go to sleep now?
Хоће ли Партизан да игра овог месеца?	*Hoće li Partizan da igra ovog meseca?*	Will Partisan play this month?

Since, in addition to its role as an auxiliary verb in the creation of the future tense, the verb хтети/hteti, when used in its long form, i.e. хоћу/hoću, хоћеш/hočeš, etc., means 'to want':

Хоћу да идем у Лондон сутра.	**Hoću da idem u London sutra.**	I *want to go* to London tomorrow.

as contrasted with:

Ићи ћу у Лондон сутра.	**Ići ću u London sutra.**	I *will go* to London tomorrow.

this might cause confusion in the formation of the interrogative when using the long form as it might not be clear whether the question refers to a future action or to a person's willingness to perform that action. The future reference may thus be inferred more easily in the interrogative with the use of the infinitive of the main verb rather than the present tense:

Хоће ли играти наша екипа?	**Hoće li igrati naša ekipa?**	*Will* our team *play*?
Хоће ли да игра наша екипа?	**Hoće li da igra naša ekipa?**	*Does* our team *want to play*?

However, this is not always a reliable method of understanding intention and it would be best to draw the meaning from the context itself.

6.6.4 The negative interrogative future

The negative interrogative is expressed with the use of the word **зар/zar** before the auxiliary verb:

Зар нећеш ићи сада на спавање?	**Zar nećeš ići sada na spavanje?**	*Will* you *not go* to sleep now?
Зар неће да игра наша екипа овог месеца?	**Zar neće da igra naša ekipa ovog meseca?**	*Will* our team *not play* this month?

Here also, there might be some ambiguity in the meaning with regard to the future of the action or the willingness of the subject to perform it, and again the meaning should be drawn from the context.

6.7 Aorist tense

In the spoken language, this tense is generally replaced by the perfect tense (the past tense). It is still, however, in use in the written form of the language, mainly for stylistic reasons.

6.7.1 Formation of the aorist tense and its use

The aorist tense is used in the following instances:

1. To indicate an action or situation which was carried out or completed immediately prior to this moment in which it is described:

   Ево га, *стиже*. **Evo ga, *stiže*.** Here he is, *he has arrived.*

   Само што се вратисмо! **Samo što se vratismo!** We've only just *got back!*

2. To indicate an action or situation which occurred in the past. Though not necessarily completed, this action was terminated at a specific time in the past. It is often used in a narrative sense:

   Хтедох **да му платим али ми није дао.** ***Htedoh*** **da mu platim ali mi nije dao.** *I wanted* to pay him but he didn't let me.

   Коначно *написах* писмо брату. **Konačno *napisah* pismo bratu.** I've finally *written* a letter to my brother.

3. To indicate an action or situation which will be carried out in the immediate future:

   Сачекај нас, *одосмо* по кључеве. **Sačekaj nas, *odosmo* po ključeve.** Wait for us, *we're off* to get the keys.

The aorist form of the verb **бити/biti** (to be) is equivalent to the English 'would':

Aorist tense of **бити/biti** (to be)			
sg.	1st p.	(ја) бих	(ja) bih	I would
	2nd p.	(ти) би	(ti) bi	you would
	3rd p.	(он/а/о)би	(on/a/o) bi	he/she/it would
pl.	1st p.	(ми) бисмо	(mi) bismo	we would
	2nd p.	(ви) бисте	(vi) biste	you would
	3rd p.	(они) бише	(oni) biše	they would

For further use, see Section 6.9 The conditional.

Aorist tense

As the aorist is used to express terminated and/or completed actions, it is generally formed from perfective verbs by the addition of the following endings, indicating person and number:

(a)	**-ти/ti** infinitives			(b)	**-сти/sti** or **-ћи/ći** infinitives	
sg.	1st p.	**-x**	**-h**	sg.	1st p.	**-ox**	**-oh**
	2nd p.	–	–		2nd p.	**-e**	**-e**
	3rd p.	–	–		3rd p.	**-e**	**-e**
pl.	1st p.	**-смо**	**-smo**	pl.	1st p.	**-осмо**	**-osmo**
	2nd p.	**-сте**	**-ste**		2nd p.	**-осте**	**-oste**
	3rd p.	**-ше**	**-še**		3rd p.	**-оше**	**-oše**

Endings in (a) replace the **-ти/ti** endings of the infinitives and follow the vowel:

			To take	To return	To write
Infinitive			узети	вратити	написати
			uzeti	vratiti	napisati
			узе-*ти*	врати-*ти*	написа-*ти*
			uze-*ti*	vrati-*ti*	napisa-*ti*
sg.	1st p.	(ја)	узе**х**	врати**х**	написа**х**
		(ja)	uze**h**	vrati**h**	napisa**h**
	2nd p.	(ти)	узе	врати	написа
		(ti)	uze	vrati	napisa
	3rd p.	(он/она/оно)	узе	врати	написа
		(on/ona/ono)	uze	vrati	napisa
pl.	1st p.	(ми)	узе**смо**	врати**смо**	паписа**смо**
		(mi)	uze**smo**	vrati**smo**	napisa**smo**
	2nd p.	(ви)	узе**сте**	врати**сте**	написа**сте**
		(vi)	uze**ste**	vrati**ste**	napisa**ste**
	3rd p.	(они/one/она)	узе**ше**	врати**ше**	паписа**ше**
		(oni/one/ona)	uze**še**	vrati**še**	napisa**še**

Endings in (b) are added to the original stem of the infinitive (before assimilation occurred from **-ти/ti** to **-ћи/ći** as well as to **-сти/sti** endings). These endings follow the consonant:

			To be able to	To say/tell	To leave	To scratch
	Infinitive		моћи	рећи	поћи	загрепсти
			moći	reći	poći	zagrepsti
			мог-ти	рек-ти	по-ид-ти	загреб-ти
			mog-ti	rek-ti	po-id-ti	zagreb-ti
sg.	1st p.	(ja)	могох	рекох	пођох	загребох
		(ja)	mogoh	rekoh	pođoh	zagreboh
	2nd p.	(ти)	може	рече	пође	загребе
		(ti)	može	reče	pođe	zagrebe
	3rd p.	(он/она/оно)	може	рече	пође	загребе
		(on/ona/ono)	može	reče	pođe	zagrebe
pl.	1st p.	(ми)	могосмо	рекосмо	пођосмо	загребосмо
		(mi)	mogosmo	rekosmo	pođosmo	zagrebosmo
	2nd p.	(ви)	могосте	рекосте	пођосте	загребосте
		(vi)	mogoste	rekoste	pođoste	zagreboste
	3rd p.	(они/оне/она)	могоше	рекоше	пођоше	загребоше
		(oni/one/ona)	mogoše	rekoše	pođoše	zagreboše

In the 2nd and 3rd person singular, sound changes occur in some of the verbs before the ending -e:

-**к/k** changes to **-ч/č**

-**г/g** changes to **-ж/ž**

-**х/h** changes to **-ш/š**

A few verbs, although ending in **-ти/ti**, have dual aorist forms, with and without an added д/d:

		To want		To know		To have	
Infinitive		хтети	хтед-ти	знати	знад-ти	имати	имад-ти
		hteti	hted-ti	znati	znad-ti	imati	imad-ti
sg. 1st p.	(ja)	хтех	хтедох	знах	знадох	имах	имадох
		hteh	htedoh	znah	znadoh	imah	imadoh
2nd p.	(ти)	хте	хтеде	зна	знаде	има	имаде
		hte	htede	zna	znade	ima	imade
3rd p.	(он/она/ оно)	хте	хтеде	зна	знаде	има	имаде
		hte	htede	zna	znade	ima	imade
pl. 1st p.	(ми)	хтесмо	хтедосмо	знасмо	знадосмо	имасмо	имадосмо
		htesmo	htedosmo	znasmo	znadosmo	imasmo	imadosmo
2nd p.	(ви)	хтесте	хтедосте	знасте	знадосте	имасте	имадосте
		hteste	htedoste	znaste	znadoste	imaste	imadoste
3rd p.	(они/оне/ она)	хтеше	хтедоше	знаше	знадоше	имаше	имадоше
		hteše	htedoše	znaše	znadoše	imaše	imadoše

Хтедоше лопови да нас опљачкају док смо спавали.	*Htedoše* lopovi da nas opljačkaju dok smo spavali.	The thieves *wanted* to rob us while we were sleeping.
Одмах знадох о чему се ради.	*Odmah znadoh* o čemu se radi.	*I knew* immediately what it was about.
Рекоше нам да се пазимо.	*Rekoše* nam da se pazimo.	*They told* us to take care.

6.7.2 The negative aorist

The negative particle -не/ne is placed before the verb in the aorist.

Ја *не одох* у Лондон ове године.	Ja *ne odoh* u London ove godine.	*I have not gone* to London this year.
Ти *не рече* кад се враћаш.	Ti *ne reče* kad se vraćaš.	*You have not said* when you will be back.
Не могосмо да им помогнемо.	*Ne mogosmo* da im pomognem.	*We were not able to* help them.

6.7.3 The interrogative aorist

The interrogative aorist expressed in an affirmative meaning can be formed in two ways:

1. With the use of conjunction да/da followed by the interrogative enclitic ли/li and the verb in the aorist tense:

Да ли хтедосте да останете на вечеру?	*Da li htedoste* da ostanete na večeru?	*Did you want* to stay for dinner?

2. With the interrogative enclitic ли/li preceded by the verb in the aorist tense:

Хтедосте ли да останете на вечеру?	*Htedoste li* da ostanete na večeru?	*Did you want* to stay for dinner?
Пођосте ли у биоскоп синоћ?	*Pođoste li* u bioskop sinoć?	*Did you go* to the cinema last night?

6.7.4 The negative interrogative aorist

The negative interrogative can also be formed in two ways:

1. With the use of **зар/zar** followed by the the negative particle and the verb in the aorist tense:

   | Зар не хтедосте да останете на вечеру? | Zar ne htedoste da ostanete na večeru? | Did you not want to stay for dinner? |

2. With the use of the interrogative enclitic **ли/li** preceded by the negative particle and the verb in the aorist tense:

   | Не хтедосте ли да останете на вечеру? | Ne htedoste li da ostanete na večeru? | Did you not want to stay for dinner? |

6.8 Future II

6.8.1 Uses of future II

Also referred to as the future exact, this tense is mainly used to express an action which may take place before or simultaneously with another action in the future:

| Деца ће те волети ако им *будеш* доносио колаче. | Deca će te voleti ako im *budeš* donosio kolače. | The children will love you *if* you *keep bringing* them cakes. |

This tense is usually introduced by one of the following conjunctions expressing time or condition: **кад/kad** (when), **ако/ako** (if), **док/dok** (until), **пошто/pošto** (after), **чим/čim** (as soon as), **да/da** (to be).

| Јави се чим будеш стигао. | Javi se čim budeš stigao. | Call *as soon as you* arrive. |

The present tense of a perfective verb only can replace the future II when these conjunctions are used:

| Јави се чим стигнеш. | Javi se čim стигнеш. | Call *as soon as you* arrive. |
| Деца ће те волети ако им *донесеш* колаче. | Deca će te voleti ako im *doneseš* kolače. | The children will love you if you *bring* them cakes. |

The future II can also be used to express an action which has taken place in the past, expressing the historical present of a verb used in the passive. The verb in this instance has a passive participle ending and there are no conjunctions introducing the tense:

| Крајем те године, он *буде постављен* за председника државе. | Krajem te godine, on *bude postavljen* za predsednika države. | At the end of that year, he *was appointed* as president of the country. |

6.8.2 Formation of the future II

This tense is formed using the present perfect of **бити/biti** (see Section 6.16 Present perfect of **бити/biti**) as an auxiliary, and the main verb with a past participle ending:

Future II of **писати/pisati** (to write)

sg.	1st p.	будем писао	budem pisao
	2nd p.	будеш писао	budeš pisao
	3rd p.m	буде писао	bude pisao
	f	буде писала	bude pisala
	n	буде писало	bude pisalo
pl.	1st p.	будемо писали	budemo pisali
	2nd p.	будете писали	budete pisali
	3rd p.m	буду писали	budu pisali
	f	буду писале	budu pisale
	n	буду писала	budu pisala

6.9 The conditional

6.9.1 Uses of the conditional

The conditional is used when expressing an action which is dependent upon another action taking place. That which is expressed in the main clause depends – is conditional – on that which is expressed in the subordinate (if) clause.

6.9.2 Formation of the conditional

Conditional sentences consist of two clauses:

1. A main clause, containing a main verb with either:

    - the auxiliary short form of the future tense of **хтети/hteti** (will) (see Section 6.6 Future tense):

        Ја ћу певати.   **Ja ću pevati.**   I *will sing*.

    or

    - the auxiliary short form of the aorist tense of **бити/biti** (would) (see Section 6.7 Aorist tense):

        Ја бих певала.   **Ja bih pevala.**   I *would sing*.

2. A subordinate clause containing a main verb and beginning with:

    - **ако/ako** (if)
    - **кад(а)/kad(a)** (were/should)

    and

    - the present perfect form of **бити/biti** (see Section 6.16 Present perfect of **бити/biti**):

        Ако будеш дошао   **Ako budeš došao**   *If you come*

    or

    - the aorist tense form of **бити/biti**:

        Кад би дошао   **Kad bi došao**   *Should you come*

    or

    - **да/da** (have had), followed by a verb in the past, present or future, with or without an auxiliary:

        Ја бих певала   **Ja bih pevala**   I *would have*
        да си дошао.   **da si došao.**   *sung had you come*.

The sentence can begin either with the main clause, in which case the clauses are not separated by a comma, or the subordinate clause, which would be followed by a comma:

Ја ћу певати ако будеш дошао.	**Ja ću pevati ako budeš došao.**	I will sing *if you come*.
Ако будеш дошао, ја ћу певати.	**Ako budeš došao, ja ću pevati.**	*If you come*, I will sing.
Ја бих певала кад би дошао.	**Ja bih pevala kad bi došao.**	I would sing *should you come*.
Кад би дошао, ја бих певала.	**Kad bi došao, ja bih pevala.**	*Should you come*, I would sing.

There are three types of conditionals in Serbian.

Type 1 – the realisable conditional

Type 1 conditional sentences refer to an action or situation in the future which, dependent on the fulfilment of the condition, is realisable. This type of conditional sentence has four forms, in all of which the verb in the main clause is in the future tense. In the first two forms, the subordinate clause begins with **ако/ako** (if), in the third with **уколиико/ukoliko**, and in the fourth form, the particle **ли/li** as a second position enclitic is introduced.

1 In the first form, the verb in the subordinate clause is in the present tense:

Ако дођеш,	*Ako dođeš,*	*If you come,* you will
добићеш поклон.	dobićeš poklon.	get a present.

2 In the second form, the verb in the subordinate clause has the present perfect form of **бити/biti** (see Section 6.8 Future II) as an auxiliary to the verb with a past participle ending (see Section 6.5 Past tense):

Ако будеш дошао,	*Ako budeš došao,*	*If you come,* you'll
добићеш поклон.	dobićeš poklon.	get a present.

3 In the third form, the subordinate clause begins with **уколико/ukoliko**, and the verb in it is in the present or future II:

Уколико стигнеш	*Ukoliko stigneš*	*If you arrive* on
на време, добићеш	na vreme,	time, you will get a
поклон.	dobićeš poklon.	present.

Уколико будеш	*Ukoliko budeš*	
стигао на време,	stigao na vreme,	
добићеш поклон.	dobićeš poklon.	

4 In the fourth form, the particle **ли/li** follows the the verb in the present or future II in the subordinate clause, thus replacing **ако/ako**:

Стигнеш ли на	*Stigneš li na*	*If you arrive* on
време, добићеш	vreme, dobićeš	time, you will get a
поклон.	poklon.	present.

Будеш ли стигао	*Budeš li stigao*	
на време, добићеш	na vreme,	
поклон.	dobićeš poklon.	

Type 2 – the potentially realisable conditional

In Type 2 conditional sentences, although realisable, the action or final outcome is weakened, where **када/kada** (were/should) as well as **ако/ako** (if) are used, implying 'by any chance'. In this type of conditional, the speaker is expressing a desire for something to happen, and not necessarily a belief that it will happen. The subordinate clause begins with **када/kada** or **ако/ako** and the verb in both the subordinate and the main clause has a past participle ending, as well as the auxiliary form of the verb **бити/biti** in the aorist tense:

Када би дошао, добио би поклон.	*Kada bi došao, dobio bi poklon.*	Were (should) you to come, you would get a present.
Ако би се потукли, нико не би победио.	*Ako bi se potukli, niko ne bi pobedio.*	Were they to have a fight, neither would win.
Кад би знао колико га воли, био би пресрећан.	*Kad bi znao koliko ga voli, bio bi presrećan.*	Were he to know how much she loved him, he'd be very happy.
Ако бисте дошли, ишли бисмо у биоскоп.	*Ako biste došli, išli bismo u bioskop.*	If you were to come, we would go to the cinema.

Type 3 – the unrealisable conditional

This conditional is used when speaking about past events, speculating on how the action or situation would have turned out had the condition been fulfilled, thus implying that it had not been fulfilled. It can be used to express reproach or regret. In this type of conditional, the subordinate clause begins with **да/da** (have had). The verb in the subordinate clause is generally in the past tense, while the verb in the main clause has a past participle ending and the auxiliary form of the verb **бити/biti**:

Да си знао, добио би поклон.	*Da si znao, dobio bi poklon.*	Had you known, you would have got a present.
Да сте дошли, отишли бисмо у биоскоп.	*Da ste došli, otišli bismo u bioskop.*	Had you come, we would have gone to the movies.

The aorist of the verb **бити/biti** acts as an auxiliary verb in constructing some forms of the conditional:

6 Verbs

Aorist of **бити/biti** (to be)			
sg.	1st p.	**(ја) бих**	**(ja) bih**	I would
	2nd p.	**(ти) би**	**(ti) bi**	you would
	3rd p.	**(он/а/о) би**	**(on/a/o) bi**	he/she/it would
pl.	1st p.	**(ми) бисмо**	**(mi) bismo**	we would
	2nd p.	**(ви) бисте**	**(vi) biste**	you would
	3rd p.	**(они) бише***	**(oni) biše***	they would

* Third person plural in the conditional is **-би/bi**.

On its own, it is equivalent to the English 'would' and can also be used with other verbs and conjunctions to indicate the following:

1. A readiness or willingness to do something:

Да ли *бисте* **ми** *помогли*?	*Da li* biste mi pomogli?	*Would you help* me, please?
Свако *би* **хтео парче.**	*Svako* bi hteo *parče.*	Everyone *would want* a piece.

2. To express habitual action:

Жене *би* **остајале код куће.**	*Žene* bi ostajale *kod kuće.*	The women *would stay* at home.
Деца *би се играла* **у дворишту.**	*Deca* bi se igrala *u dvorištu.*	The children *would play* in the yard.

3. In polite expressions (**желети/želeti** (to desire), **хтети/hteti** (to want), **волети/voleti** (to like)):

Желео бих чашу воде, молим вас.	*Želeo bih* čašu vode, molim vas.	I *would like* a glass of water, please.
Хтели бисмо да резервишемо собу.	*Hteli bismo da* rezervišemo sobu.	We *would like to* book a room.

4. In expressions of should and ought (**требати/trebati**):

Требало би да кренемо.	*Trebalo bi da* krenemo.	We *should (ought to) go* (set off).

   Not **требали би да кренемо**/trebali bi da krenemo.

| Требало би да се упишете. | Trebalo bi da se upišete. | You should (ought to) sign in. |

Not требал*и* би да се упишете/treba*li* bi da se upišete.

5 As a reason for an action (with conjunction да/da) – 'in order to/for':

| Она ће све урадити *да би* њен син *био* срећан. | Ona će sve uraditi *da bi* njen sin *bio* srećan. | She will do anything *in order for* her son *to be* happy. |
| Отишао је *да би* је *заборавио*. | Otišao je *da bi* je *zaboravio*. | He left *in order to forget* her. |

6 To indicate 'could' (моћи/moći):

| *Могла би* јој рећи. | *Mogla bi* joj reći. | You *could* tell her. |
| *Могли бисте* да се окупате. | *Mogli biste* da se okupate. | You (pl.) *could* take a bath. |

When forming a question, the aorist of бити/biti can be preceded by да ли/da li:

| *Да ли бисте* дошли? | *Da li biste* došli? | *Would you* come? |

Or it can be followed by the interrogative enclitic ли/li:

| *Бисте ли* дошли? | *Biste li* došli? | *Would you* come? |

It can also be preceded by the emphatic зар/zar in first position when asking a question:

| *Зар бисте* дошли? | *Zar biste* došli? | *Would you really* come? |

Or by the negative particle не/ne:

| *Не бисте ли* дошли? | *Ne biste li* došli? | *Would you not* come? |

6.10 Imperative

The imperative is a form of the verb used to give orders, to make suggestions, to give advice or to invite.

6.10.1 Use of the imperative

The imperative form is used in four different situations:

1 When the speaker gives a command to the listener. In this instance, 'you' (sg.) or 'you' (pl.) is implied:

Донеси ми чашу воде, молим те.	*Donesi* mi čašu vode, molim te.	Please *(you)* bring me a glass of water.

This form can be negated with **не/ne** placed before the verb, which is usually an imperfective:

Не доноси ми чашу воде, молим те.	*Ne donosi* mi čašu vode, molim te.	Please *(you)* do not bring me a glass of water.

2 When the speaker gives a command to him or herself plus one or more listeners, the English equivalent of 'let us . . .' is implied:

Прошетајмо пса.	*Prošetajmo* psa.	*Let's* walk the dog.
Хајдемо по чашу воде.	*Hajdemo* po čašu vode.	*Let's* get a glass of water.

This type of imperative cannot be negated.

3 **Нека/neka** (let) is used when a command or permission is being given to a third person:

Нека ми донесе чашу воде.	*Neka* mi donese čašu vode.	*Let* him bring me a glass of water.
Нека га послушају!	*Neka* ga poslušaju!	*Let* them listen to him!

This type can be negated, usually with an imperfective verb:

Нека ми не доноси чашу воде.	*Neka* mi ne donosi čašu vode.	*Let* him not bring me a glass of water.

4 When a command or advice is given 'not to do something'.

Немој да плачеш!	*Nemoj* da plačeš!	*Don't* cry! (you, sg.)
Немојте да га будите!	*Nemojte* da ga budite!	*Don't* wake him up! (you, pl.)

6.10.2 Formation of the imperative

1 In the 2nd person singular and plural, the imperative is formed by dropping the final vowel (**-у/u** or **-е/e**) of the 3rd person plural of the present tense and adding the imperative ending.

The imperative ending can be one of two types, depending on the 3rd person plural present tense ending.

(a) If the final vowel is preceded by the consonant **-ј/j**:

Они певај**у.**   **Oni pevaj**u.   They are singing.

the following applies:

    i   The final vowel is dropped for the 2nd person imperative singular:

        Певај!   **Pevaj!**   Sing! (you)

    ii   For the 2nd person imperative plural -те/te is added to the 2nd person singular:

        Певајте!   **Pevajte!**   Sing! (you, pl.)

(b)   If the 3rd person plural ending is **-е/e** or **-у/u**:

    Они рад**е**.   **Oni rade.**   They are working.

the following applies:

    i   The final vowel is dropped for the 2nd person imperative singular and replaced by **-и/i**:

        Ради!   **Radi!**   Work! (you)

    ii   For the 2nd person plural -те/te is added to the 2nd person singular:

        Радите!   **Radite!**   Work! (you, pl.)

2   When the 1st person plural is implied, the imperative ending **-мо/mo** is added to the 2nd person singular imperative form:

    2nd sg.   **Ради!**   **Radi!**   Work! (you)

    1st pl.   **Радимо!**   **Radimo!**   Let's work!

3   When a command is being given to a third person, the conjunction **нека/neka** is used along with the 3rd person (singular or plural) form of the present tense:

    3rd p.sg.   **Он ради.**   **On radi.**   He is working.

    Pres.
    imperative

        ***Нека* ради!**   ***Neka* radi!**   *Let* him work.

4   When expressing a negative imperative using the **немој/nemoj** (do not) form, the following applies:

    i   The form **немој/nemoj** (do not) is used for the 2nd person singular:

        ***Немој* да излазиш касно!**   ***Nemoj* da izlaziš kasno!**   *Don't* go out late!

    ii   The form **немојте/nemojte** is used for the 2nd person plural:

Немојте да излазите касно!	*Nemojte da izlazite kasno!*	Don't go out late!

iii The form **немојмо/nemojmo** is used for the 1st person plural:

Немојмо да излазимо касно!	*Nemojmo da izlazimo kasno!*	Don't let us go out late!

6.11 Reflexive verbs

Reflexive verbs are used with the reflexive pronoun **се/se** (see Section 8.2 Reflexive pronouns), the short form of the pronoun **себе/sebe**. This pronoun is an enclitic and must follow the enclitic word order whenever and wherever it is used (see Section 13.1 Order and importance of enclitics).

Verbs containing the reflexive pronoun **се/se** can be divided into four groups:

1. Transitive verbs (verbs that take the accusative case and cannot stand on their own but must have a direct object):

Мајко је купала *дете*.	**Majka je kupala *dete*.**	Mother *bathed* the child.

   can be followed by **се/se** instead of the direct object:

Мајка *се* купала.	**Majka *se* kupala.**	Mother had a bath (*bathed* herself).
Мајка је *купала себе*.	**Majka je *kupala sebe*.**	Mother *bathed* herself.

   With this use, although the doer is the subject of the sentence, through the use of the reflexive pronoun **се/se** (or its long form **себе/sebe** which is used only in this group), he/she also becomes the object of the action.

2. When two or more subjects have a reciprocal relationship expressed in English with 'each other' or 'one another', the two can be expressed as the subject while the reflexive pronoun **се/se** denotes a relationship of reciprocity:

Милорад и Љубица *се љубе*.	**Milorad i Ljubica *se ljube*.**	Milorad and Ljubica are *kissing* (each other).
Волети *се* значи поштовати *се*.	**Voleti *se* znači poštovati *se*.**	To *love one another* means to *respect each other*.

3   The short form of the reflexive pronoun **ce/se** is also used to form a passive, impersonal voice from an active verb when the subject of the sentence is in the 3rd person singular or plural, or is not known (see Section 6.12 Impersonal verbs):

Impersonal verbs

| **Зна се да иде у 5 сати.** | **Zna se da ide u 5 sati.** | (It) is known that he/she is going at 5 o'clock. |

This passive form is also used when indicating that something is done regularly (in which case an imperfective verb is used):

| **Заливање баште** *се обавља* **сваког јутра.** | **Zalivanje bašte** *se obavlja* **svakog jutra.** | Watering of the garden *is done* every morning. |

4   Some verbs are reflexive although their meaning indicates neither passivity nor reflexivity:

бојати се	**bojati se**	to be afraid, scared
плашити се	**plašiti se**	to be afraid, scared
борити се	**boriti se**	to struggle, fight
радовати се	**radovati se**	to be happy, look forward to something
догодити се	**dogoditi se**	to happen, occur
десити се	**desiti se**	to happen, occur
надати се	**nadatl se**	to hope
смејати се	**smejati se**	to laugh
чудити се	**čuditi se**	to wonder
коцкати се	**kockati se**	to gamble

6.12   Impersonal verbs

When a statement is being made in which the subject is not present or known, the verb is said to be impersonal. In English this is reflected with the use of 'One says...', 'One thinks...', 'People feel...', 'It is said...', 'It is thought...', 'It is believed...', etc.

In Serbian, this impersonal meaning is expressed by either:

1   Using the 3rd person neuter singular of a verb to which the reflexive pronoun **ce/se** is added (if the verb does not already carry it). The pronoun 'it' (neuter singular) is implied:

Говори се да ме више не волиш.	*Govori se* da me više ne voliš.	*It is said* (people say) that you don't love me any more.
Верује се да се убица крије у селу.	*Veruje se* da se ubica krije u selu.	*It is believed* that the killer is hiding (himself) in the village.
Улази се у зграду кроз главна врата.	*Ulazi se* u zgradu kroz glavna vrata.	*One enters* the building through the main door.

A verb in the past tense, followed by the reflexive **се/se**, is also used to indicate an impersonal meaning:

Плесало се и пило се на забави.	*Plesalo se i pilo se* na zabavi.	*There was dancing* and *drinking* at the party.

2   The impersonal meaning is also conveyed with the verb **бити/biti** (to be) in any tense in the 3rd person singular and an adverb (with the neuter singular pronoun 'it' implied). This is added to the logical subject in the dative case (see Section 7.3.3 Dative case). The reflexive **се/se** does not occur in this form:

Жао ми је што га нисте видели.	*Žao mi je* što ga niste videli.	*I'm sorry* that you did not see him. (it is sorry to me)
Било ми је жао што га нисте видели.	*Bilo mi je žao* što ga niste videli.	*I was sorry* that you hadn't seen him.
Биће ми жао што га нећете видети.	*Biće mi žao* što ga nećete videti.	*I will be sorry* that you won't see him.
Драго ми је да сте дошли.	*Drago mi je* da ste došli.	*I'm glad* that you came. (it is gladdening to me)

6.13   Auxiliary verbs

The auxiliary verbs used for forming various tenses are the short forms of the verbs **бити/biti** (to be) and **хтети/hteti** (to want). All auxiliary verbs are enclitics (see Chapter 13 Enclitics) and must follow the enclitic word order. They indicate person and number, while the main verb they accompany will, depending on the tense, generally only express number.

1   The past tense (see Section 6.5 Past tense) is formed using the short form of **бити/biti** as an auxiliary to the main verb which has a past participle ending:

Ja *сам* гледала тај филм.	Ja *sam* gledala taj film.	I *saw* that film.	Formation of the interrogative

2. The future tense (see Section 6.6 Future tense) is formed using the short form of **хтети/hteti** as an auxiliary to the main verb, which is given in the infinitive:

Ja *ћу* гледати тај филм.	Ja *ću gledati* taj film.	I *will* see that film.

or, by using it with the present tense of the main verb and the conjunction да/da:

Ja *ћу да* гледам тај филм.	Ja *ću da gledam* taj film.	I *will* see that film.

3. The future II (see Section 6.8 Future II) is formed using the present perfective aspect form of **бити/biti** as an auxiliary to the main verb which has a past participle ending:

Једног дана, када *будем живео* на југу Француске	Jednog dana, kada *budem živeo* na jugu Francuske	One day (in the future), when *I'm living* in the South of France

4. Certain forms of the conditional (see Section 6.9 The conditional) are formed using the aorist (see Section 6.7 Aorist tense) of **бити/biti** as an auxiliary to the main verb which has a past participle ending:

Кад *бих гледала* тај филм, рекла бих ти.	Kad *bih gledala* taj film, rekla bih ti.	If *I were to see* that film, I would tell you.

In forming the negative of any of these tenses, the negative marker will be applied to the auxiliary verb and not to the main verb:

нисам гледала	*nisam* gledala	I did not see
нећу гледати	*neću* gledati	I will not see
не будем гледала	*ne budem* gledala	I will not see
не бих гледала	*ne bih* gledala	I would not see

6.14 Formation of the interrogative

There are several ways in which a question may be asked. Question forms to which a 'yes/no' reply is expected are given under (a), (c), (d) and (e), while question forms using question-words are given under (b).

(a) In everyday conversation, raised intonation at the end of the sentence may be sufficient:

Из Београда сте? **Iz Beograda ste?** You're from Belgrade?

(b) An interrogative word may be placed at the beginning of a sentence, followed by the verb:

Где идеш?	**Gde ideš?**	Where are you going?
Шта куваш?	**Šta kuvaš?**	What are you cooking?
Зашто журите?	**Zašto žurite?**	Why are you hurrying?
Ко долази?	**Ko dolazi?**	Who is coming?

(c) When an interrogative word is not used, then the interrogative particle **ли/li** must be used. In the present tense, it will take second position in the sentence and will be preceded by the verb:

Идеш *ли*?	**Ideš** *li*?	Are are you going?
Куваш *ли*?	**Kuvaš** *li*?	Are you cooking?
Журите *ли*?	**Žurite** *li*?	Are you hurrying?

(d) The particle **ли/li** may also be preceded by the conjunction **да/da**, followed (perhaps much later) by the verb:

Да ли стварно тамо идеш?	*Da li* stvarno tamo ideš?	Are you really going there?
Да ли журите?	*Da li* žurite?	Are you hurrying?
Да ли је ово банка?	*Da li* je ovo banka?	Is this the bank?

(e) In the present tense, the particle **ли/li** may be preceded by the verbal **je/je** (3rd person singular of the verb **бити/biti** (to be)), followed by the verb:

Je ли идеш?	*Je li* ideš?	Are you going?
Je ли журите?	*Je li* žurite?	Are you hurrying?
Je ли је ово банка?	*Je li* je ovo banka?	Is this the bank?

Note: With this use, the verbal **je/je** is not an enclitic.

(f) Negative questions are formed by introducing the conjunction **зар/zar** followed by the negative form of the verb:

Зар не идеш?	*Zar ne* ideš?	Are you *not* going?
Зар не журите?	*Zar ne* žurite?	Are you *not* hurrying?
Зар није ово банка?	*Zar nije* ovo banka?	Is this *not* the bank?

When used at the end of a sentence, **зар не/zar ne** invites confirmation or negation of what is stated:

Идеш, *зар не*?	Ideš, *zar ne*?	You are going, *aren't you*?
Журите, *зар не*?	Žurite, *zar ne*?	You are hurrying, *aren't you*?
Ово је банка, *зар не*?	Ovo je banka, *zar ne*?	This is the bank, *isn't it*?

Formation of the negative

(g) As does the conjunction да/da followed by the present tense. This form is used more as a suggestion or an offer:

Да идем?	*Da* idem?	Shall I go?
Да пожурим?	*Da* požurim?	Shall I hurry up?
Да дођем?	*Da* dođem?	Shall I come?

(h) Зар/zar is also used as an emphatic or to express surprise, often expressed in English by 'really':

Зар идеш?	*Zar* ideš?	Are you *really* going?
Зар журите?	*Zar* žurite?	Are you *really* hurrying?
Зар је ово банка?	*Zar* je ovo banka?	Is this *really* the bank?

(i) The particle ли/li is also used following modal verbs (see Section 16.18 Modal verbs) and itself is followed by the conjunction да/da:

Могу ли да идем?	*Mogu li da* idem?	Can I go?
Треба ли да им кувам?	*Treba li da* im kuvam?	Ought I to cook for them?
Смем ли да дођем?	*Smem li da* dođem?	May I come?

For interrogatives in the various tenses, see under each separate tense.

6.15 Formation of the negative

Negation is expressed by using the negative particle не/ne, which can be used independently or as a prefix.

Independently, the negative particle не/ne can be used in two ways:

1 To mean 'no', in which case it is generally accented:

Идете ли у биоскоп вечерас?	Idete li u bioskop večeras?	Are you going to the cinema tonight?
Не, не идемо.	*Ne*, ne idemo.	*No*, we are not.

2   To mean negation:

- with all verbs, excluding **бити/biti** (to be), when inserted before the verb in the present tense and the aorist. Although written separately, the two words are pronounced as one:

Не знам колико је сати.	***Ne znam koliko je sati.***	*I don't know* the time.
Не жели да разговара.	***Ne želi da razgovara.***	*(He/she) doesn't wish* to talk.
Не пољубисмо се до јуче.	***Ne poljubismo se do juče.***	*We hadn't kissed* until yesterday.

- with the verb **бити/biti** (to be) in the aorist when used as an auxiliary to mean the equivalent of the English 'would' or in forming the conditional:

Не бих знала колико је сати.	***Ne bih znala koliko je sati.***	*I wouldn't know* the time.

Не/ne can also be used as a word prefix, when it is generally accented:

1   It can be prefixed to nouns, adjectives or adverbs:

неспоразум	**nesporazum**	misunderstanding
немогућност	**nemogućnost**	impossibility
нељубазан	**neljubazan**	impolite
незаборован	**nezaboravan**	unforgetful

2   And only with the verbs **бити/biti**, **хтети/hteti** (to want) and **имати/imati** (to have):

- with **бити/biti** (to be) in the present tense and when used as an auxiliary in forming the past tense, where it becomes **ни/ni** and is prefixed to the short form of **бити/biti**. The accent falls on the prefixed negative and the form is no longer an enclitic:

Нисам знала колико је сати.	***Nisam znala koliko je sati.***	*I didn't know* the time.
Није желео да разговара.	***Nije želeo da razgovara.***	*(He/she) didn't wish* to talk.

- with **хтети/hteti** (to want) in the present tense and when used as an auxiliary in forming the future tense. **Не/ne** is prefixed to the short form of the verb which is no longer an enclitic, as the **не/ne** carries the stress:

Нећу знати колико је сати.	*Neću znati koliko je sati.*	*I won't know* the time.	Formation of the negative
Неће да разговара.	*Neće da razgovara.*	*(He/she) does not want* to talk.	

- when the verb **имати**/imati (to have) is negated, **не**/ne is prefixed to the verb and replaces the initial -**и**/i. The accent falls on the prefixed negative.

Немам кључ.	*Nemam* ključ.	*I don't have* the key.
Немају кола.	*Nemaju* kola.	*They don't have* a car.

Negation of **имати**/imati occurs only in the present tense. In all other tenses, the auxiliary verb is negated while the original form of **имати**/imati remains and acts as a main verb in accordance with the tense formation:

Нисам имала кључ.	*Nisam imala* ključ.	*I didn't have* the key.
Неће имати кола.	*Neće imati* kola.	*They won't have* a car.

As **имати**/imati can mean 'the existence of' something, **немати**/nemati can also mean 'the non-existence of' something. It can only have this meaning when used in the present tense:

У пекари *нема* млека.	U pekari *nema* mleka.	*There is no* milk in the bakery.

When the past or future of this meaning is expressed, the verb **бити**/biti replaces **имати**/imati, or its negation, and the negation is formed by prefixing the auxiliary verb of the required tense:

Неће бити млека у пекари.	*Neće biti* mleka u pekari.	*There will be no* milk in the bakery.
Није било млека у пекари.	*Nije bilo* mleka u pekari.	*There was no* milk in the bakery.

The present tense **нема**/nema (there is not), the future tense **неће бити**/neće biti (there will not be) and past tense **није било**/nije bilo (there was no) call for the genitive case.

Intensified negation

The negative particle **ни**/ni is often used to emphasise and intensify the meaning of the word immediately following it:

Није нас *ни* сачекао.	*Nije* nas *ni* sačekao.	*He didn't even wait* for us.

Нећемо их ни погледати.	*Nećemo ih ni pogledati.*	We won't even look at them.
Нисам му ни реч рекао.	*Nisam mu ni reč rekao.*	I didn't say a single word to him.

where the following would be equally correct, but not as intensified:

Није нас сачекао.	*Nije nas sačekao.*	He didn't wait for us.
Нећемо их погледати.	*Nećemo ih pogledati.*	We won't look at them.
Нисам му реч рекао.	*Nisam mu reč rekao.*	I didn't say a word to him.

Although **ни/ni** need not ordinarily be included in negating a sentence, if one or more negative pronouns/adverbs are in a sentence, the verb has to be negated with **не/ne** (with **ни/ni-** if there is an auxiliary **сам/sam, си/si, је/je, смо/smo, сте/ste, су/su**). If there is a **ни/ni** of intensified negation, the verb of the sentence also has to be negated.

Нико нас не чека.	*Niko nas ne čeka.*	No-one is waiting for us.
Никоме ништа не говорим.	*Nikome ništa ne govorim.*	I don't say anything to anyone.
Нико их неће погледати.	*Niko ih neće pogledati.*	No-one will look at them.
Нико нас није ни позвао.	*Niko nas nije ni pozvao.*	No-one even called us.

This is often referred to as the 'double negative rule'.

The true double negative

Unlike the preceding 'double negative rule', the true double negative involves the use of two negatives which equate to an affirmative:

Нећу да не спавам.	*Neću da ne spavam.*	I don't want to not sleep.
Не жели да не зна.	*Ne želi da ne zna.*	He/she doesn't want to not know.
Нема особе која није купила тај производ.	*Nema osobe koja nije kupila taj proizvod.*	There isn't a person who hasn't bought that product.

6.16 Present perfective aspect of бити/biti

The verb бити/biti (to be) has two present tense forms. One has been already covered in the present tense (Section 6.4), and the other is the present of the perfective aspect of this verb:

Present of the perfective aspect of **бити/biti** (to be)		
	Singular	Plural
1st p.	будем/budem	будемо/budemo
2nd p.	будеш/budeš	будете/budete
3rd p.	буде/bude	буду/budu

This form of бити/biti is used in constructing the future II (see Section 6.8 Future II) in a subordinate clause, when an action is conceived as being completed at a precise time in the future. The conjunctions кад/kad (when) and ако/ako (if) when referring to an action taking place in the future would always be followed by this form of бити/biti rather than the short form of хтети/hteti used as an auxiliary in forming the regular future (see Section 6.6 Future tense):

Ако буде падала киша, остаћемо код куће.	*Ako bude padala kiša, ostaćemo kod kuće.*	If it rains, we'll stay at home.
Кад будеш завршио домаћи, купићу ти сладолед.	*Kad budeš završio domaći, kupiću ti sladoled.*	When you finish your homework, I'll buy you an ice-cream.

This form is also found with да/da + present tense:

Треба да будемо задовољни с оним што имамо.	**Treba da budemo zadovoljni s onim što imamo.**	We should be happy with what we've got.

6.17 *Ићи/ići* and its derivatives

The verb ићи/ići (to go) has an irregular present tense and an irregular past tense.

In the present tense, -ћи/ći is replaced by -д/d to which the present tense endings are added:

6 Verbs

The present tense of **ићи/ići** (to go)

	Singular	Plural
1st p.	идем idem	идемо idemo
2nd p.	идеш ideš	идете idete
3rd p.	иде ide	иду idu

Наша деца воле да *иду* у школу.	Naša deca vole da *idu* u školu.	Our children like *going* to school.
Не *идем* на посао у понедељак.	Ne *idem* na posao u ponedeljak.	I'm not *going* to work on Monday.

In the past tense, the -ћи/ći is replaced by -ш/š to which the past participle endings -о/o, -ла/la, -ло/lo, -ли/li, -ле/le, -ла/la are added:

The past tense of **ићи/ići** (to go)

	Singular			Plural		
	Masculine	Feminine	Neuter	Masculine	Feminine	Neuter
1st p.	ишао	ишла	ишло	ишли	ишле	ишла
2nd p.	išao	išla	išlo	išli	išle	išla

Ишли смо заједно у школу.	*Išli* smo zajedno u školu.	We *went* to school together.
Зашто си *ишао* тамо?	Zašto si *išao* tamo?	Why did *you go* there?

Verbs derived from **ићи/ići**, many of which have prefixes added to the basic form, with or without the initial и/i, behave in a similar manner in the present tense. With these verbs the **-ћи/ći** ending is generally replaced by **-ђ/đ** rather than **-д/d**, to be followed by the present tense endings. The past tense endings remain the same as for **ићи/ići**:

Infinitive			Present tense	Past tense
			1st p.	Masculine
доћи	doći	to come, to go up to	дођем dođem	дошао došao
отићи	otići	to leave, to go from	одем/отидем odem/otidem	отишао otišao
поћи	poći	to set off, to go off	пођем pođem	пошао pošao
проћи	proći	to pass by, to pass through	прођем prođem	прошао prošao
прићи	prići	to come towards	пpиђем priđem	пришао prišao
наћи	naći	to find	нађем nađem	нашао našao
наићи	naići	to come upon	наиђем naiđem	наишао naišao
обићи	obići	to go around, to tour	обиђем obiđem	обишао obišao
заћи	zaći	to go behind	зађем zađem	зашао zašao
ући	ući	to come into, to go into, to enter	уђем uđem	ушао ušao
изаћи	izaći	to come out of, to go out of, to exit	изађем izađem	изашао izašao

6.18 Modal verbs

Modal verbs (can, may, should, need to, ought to, have to, be able to), express an attitude, judgement, interpretation or feeling, and are usually linked to another verb with the conjunction **да/da** (that/to).

6 Verbs

1. Many modal verbs in Serbian are formed from the verb **требати/trebati** (to need).

Present tense of **требати/trebati** (to need)				
sg.	1st p.	требам	trebam	I need
	2nd p.	требаш	trebaš	you need
	3rd p.	треба	treba	he/she/it needs
pl.	1st p.	требамо	trebamo	we need
	2nd p.	требате	trebate	you need
	3rd p.	требају	trebaju	they need

(a) **Треба да/treba da** + the present tense is used to express the equivalent of 'to need to/to have to/should':

Треба да идемо.   *Treba da idemo.*   We *need to go.*

(b) **Requires да/trebaće da** + the present tense is used to express the equivalent of 'will need to/will have to/should':

Требаће да идемо.   *Trebaće da idemo.*   We *will need to go.*

(c) **Требало је да/trebalo je da** + the past tense is used to express the equivalent of 'needed to/should have':

Требало је да смо отишли.   *Trebalo je da smo otišli.*   We *should have* gone.

(d) **Требало би да/trebalo bi da** + present tense is used to express 'ought to':

Требало би да разговарамо с њом.   *Trebalo bi da razgovaramo s njom.*   We *ought to* talk to her.

The verb following да/da corresponds to the subject in the present tense.

(e) **Требало би да/trebalo bi da** + past tense is used to express 'ought to have':

Требало би да смо разговарали с њом.   *Trebalo bi da smo razgovarali s njom.*   We *ought to have* talked to her.

The verb following да/da corresponds to the subject in the past tense.

All the forms of **требати/trebati** – **треба да/treba da**, **требаће да/trebaće da**, **требало је да/trebalo je da** and **требало би да/trebalo bi da** – remain in the 3rd person singular (3rd person singular *neuter* is used with the past tense formation), while the verb following **да/da** agrees with the subject.

Modal verbs

In addition to its use as a modal verb, **требати/trebati** is used when expressing a need for something. The logical subject of the verb **требати/trebati** is in the dative case and represents the person who *needs* something, while the object, or person, *needed* is in the nominative case and is the grammatical subject of the sentence:

| Њој *треба* кључ. | Njoj *treba* ključ. | She *needs* the key. (The key is needed by/necessary to her.) |
| *Требају* нам нова кола. | *Trebaju* nam nova kola. | We *need* a new car. (A new car is needed by/necessary to us.) |

Although this verb has a regular conjugation, it is often used in the 3rd person singular. And since the subject of the sentence is not the person by whom the object is needed, but the object itself (in the above sentences the subjects are 'the key' and 'the car'), the verb agrees in gender and number with it in all the tenses.

The past tense is formed using **треба/treba** + the past participle (needed):

| *Требали су* јој кључеви за кола. | *Trebali su* joj ključevi za kola. | She *needed* keys for the car. |
| *Требала су* нам нова кола. | *Trebala su* nam nova kola. | We *needed* a new car. |

The future tense is formed using **треба/treba** + **ће/će** (will need):

| *Требаће* јој кључеви за кола. | *Trebaće* joj ključevi za kola. | She *will need* keys for the car. |
| *Требаћете* ми. | *Trebaćete* mi. | I *will need* you (pl.). |

The adjective **потребан/potreban** (necessary) can replace the above. It is used with the auxiliary verb **бити/biti** (to be):

| *Потребан* јој је кључ за кола. | *Potreban* joj je ključ za kola. | She *needs* a key for the car. |
| *Потребна су* нам нова кола. | *Potrebna su nam* nova kola. | We *need* a new car. |

In the past tense, this adjective is used with the auxiliary verb **бити/biti** along with the past tense form of that verb, which will agree in gender and number with the subject:

| Потребан јој је био кључ за кола. | Potreban joj je bio ključ za kola. | She *needed* a key for the car. |
| Потребна су нам била нова кола. | Potrebna su nam bila nova kola. | We *needed* a new car. |

2 **Моћи/moći** (to be able to, can), when used as a modal verb, is followed either by the conjunction да/da and the main verb, or the infinitive of the main verb.

Present tense of **моћи/moći** (to be able to, can)			
sg.	1st p.	могу	mogu	I can
	2nd p.	можеш	možeš	you can
	3rd p.	може	može	he/she/it can
pl.	1st p.	можемо	možemo	we can
	2nd p.	можете	možete	you can
	3rd p.	могу	mogu	they can

| Могу да купе карте преко интернета. | Mogu da kupe karte preko interneta. | They *can buy* the tickets over the internet. |
| Могу купити карте преко интернета. | Mogu kupiti karte preko interneta. | |

It is used in the past tense:

| Могли су да купе карте преко интернета. | Mogli su da kupe karte preko interneta. | They *could have bought* the tickets over the internet. |

And the future tense:

| Моћи ће да купе карте преко интернета. | Moći će da kupe karte preko interneta. | They *will be able to buy* the tickets over the internet. |

Chapter 7
Nouns

Nouns are the names of people, animals, things, places, events, ideas, etc.

Nouns are classified by gender – every noun will be of *masculine*, *feminine* or *neuter* gender (see Section 7.2 Gender of nouns). Nouns are also either singular or plural, a distinction referred to as *number*. A noun has a function in a sentence: it can be the subject or the direct or indirect object of a sentence; it can also show possession or stand after a preposition, and so on. This function is generally identified in English through word order. In Serbian, the function of a noun in a sentence is established by its ending. The ending will indicate what case the noun is in, and therefore what function it has in the sentence (see Section 7.3 Cases of nouns).

The ending a noun will have through the cases will depend on the ending it has in its original form (see Section 7.4 Declension of nouns). In order to apply and recognise the endings of a noun through the cases correctly, and thus ascertain the function of that noun in a sentence, it is important to know the original form of a noun. This is the form in which a noun is given in the dictionary and it corresponds to the nominative case.

Nouns are classified by their gender and the ending they have in the nominative case. Each separate class will decline differently through the cases. There are three basic declensions. For each declension, the basic root of the noun, as it appears in the genitive case, minus the genitive ending, will have endings added to it as it changes through all the cases.

Although the concept of classes and declensions may initially be confusing and difficult to grasp, the student will be able to assign the correct ending to a noun once he or she can recognise the class of nouns to which it belongs.

7.1 Types of nouns

Nouns are classified by type in accordance with what they signify. Nouns belonging to a particular type will often end in a suffix typical of that type:

7 Nouns

1. Proper nouns are names. They include names of people, countries, cities, etc.:

   Елизабета   **Elizabeta**   Elisabeth

   Тексас   **Teksas**   Texas

   The following are some groups of suffixes which proper nouns often have:

   Names of countries:

-ија	Србија	-ija	Srbija	Serbia
-ска	Ирска	-ska	Irska	Ireland
-шка	Норвешка	-ška	Norveška	Norway
-чка	Немачка	-čka	Nemačka	Germany

   Names of male inhabitants:

-ац	Ирац	-ac	Irac	Irish (male)
-анин	Норвежанин	-anin	Norvežanin	a man from Norway
-чанин	Ирачанин	-čanin	Iračanin	an Iraqi man
-лија	Бечлија	-lija	Bečlija	a man from Vienna (Беч/Beč)

   Names of female inhabitants:

-киња	Српкиња	-kinja	Srpkinja	a woman from Serbia
-ка	Норвежанка	-ka	Norvežanka	a woman from Norway
-ица	Немица	-ica	Nemica	a woman from Germany

   Male names often have:

   -ко   Данко   -ko   Danko   Danko (name)

   Female names often have:

   -ица   Милица   -ica   Milica   Milica (name)

Surnames have:

-чић	Љубичић	-čić	Ljubičić	Ljubičić (surname)
-евић	Павићевић	-ević	Pavićević	Pavićević (surname)
-овић	Стевановић	-ović	Stevanović	Stevanović (surname)

2 Common nouns represent entities sharing common traits:

лист	list	leaf
прстен	prsten	ring

Many common nouns end in one of the following groups of suffixes:

-а	жена	-a	žena	woman
-ац	мушкарац	-ac	muškarac	man
-ација	регистрација	-acija	registracija	registration
-ач	отварач	-ač	otvarač	opener
-ача	ломача	-ača	lomača	stake
-ај	лежај	-aj	ležaj	bed, couch
-ак	сељак	-ak	seljak	peasant
-аљка	певаљка	-ljka	pevaljka	singer (pub singer)
-ан	наркоман	-an	narkoman	drug addict
-ана	теретана	-ana	teretana	gym (weight room)
-ар	поштар	-ar	poštar	postman
-ара	стражара	-ara	stražara	guardroom/ house
-аш	робијаш	-aš	robijaš	prisoner
-ба	селидба	-ba	selidba	a move
-че	младунче	-če	mladunče	the young of an animal
-џија	силеџија	-džija	siledžija	bully, rapist
-етина	краветина	-etina	kravetina	cow (derogatory)

Types of nouns

-ица	секретарица	-ica	sekretarica	secretary
-иште	игралиште	-ište	igralište	playground
-иво	пециво	-ivo	pecivo	baked bread, roll, bun
-јак	просјак	-jak	prosjak	beggar
-ка	сељанка	-ka	seljanka	a village woman/peasant
-киња	слушкиња	-kinja	sluškinja	servant (female)
-ко	дебељко	-ko	debeljko	fatso (male)
-лац	посетилац	-lac	posetilac	visitor
-лица	луталица	-lica	lutalica	wanderer
-ло	помагало	-lo	pomagalo	aid
-ница	чекаоница	-nica	čekaonica	waiting room
-ник	службеник	-nik	službenik	official
-оња	носоња	-onja	nosonja	big nose
-ов	лажов	-ov	lažov	liar
-овина	дедовина	-ovina	dedovina	grandfather's inheritance
-тељ	пријатељ	-telj	prijatelj	friend
-тор	мајстор	-tor	majstor	expert, skilled person
-уша	плавуша	-uša	plavuša	a blonde (female)

3   Mass nouns refer to quantity when used in the singular, and to different types of a particular item when used in the plural:

шећер	šećer	sugar	шећери	sēcēri	sugars
кафа	kafa	coffee	кафе	kafe	coffees

Many mass nouns end in one of the following groups of suffixes:

-ада	оранжада	-ada	oranžada	orangeade
-ача	лозовача	-ača	lozovača	grape brandy
-аш	гулаш	-aš	gulaš	meat stew

-ће	воће	-će	voće	fruit
-етина	пилетина	-etina	piletina	poultry
-ица	комовица	-ica	komovica	wine brandy
-ина	говедина	-ina	govedina	beef
-овина	сомовина	-ovina	somovina	salmon

Types of nouns

4   Collective nouns consist of separate entities belonging to a collective entity generally acting as a singular whole:

група	grupa	group
нација	nacija	nation

Many collective nouns end in one of the following groups of suffixes:

-ад*	прасад	-ad*	prasad	piglets
-еж**	младеж	-ež**	mladež	youth
-ија**	старудија	-ija**	starudija	old objects
-ја*	браћа	-ja*	braća	brothers
-је***	дрвеће	-je***	drveće	trees

* Nouns with these suffixes are declined as singular feminine nouns with a plural verb.
** Nouns with these suffixes are declined as singular feminine nouns with a singular verb.
*** Nouns with this suffix: биље/bilje (plants), лишће/lišće (leaves), грање/granje (branches), etc., although plural in meaning, are treated and declined as a singular neuter noun.

5   Abstract nouns refer to intangible concepts and are also a subtype of common nouns:

вера	vera	faith
пријатељство	prijateljstvo	friendship
заробљеништво	zarobljeništvo	captivity

Many abstract nouns end in one of the following groups of suffixes:

-а	мука	-a	muka	nausea
-ација	ситуација	-acija	situacija	situation

7 Nouns

-ај	догађај	-aj	događaj	event
-ак	одлазак	-ak	odlazak	departure
-арија	глупарија	-arija	gluparija	stupidity
-ба	злоупотреба	-ba	zloupotreba	abuse
-еж	трулеж	-ež	trulež	rottenness
-ење	упозорење	-enje	upozorenje	caution
-ић	Божић	-ić	Božić	Christmas
-ија	историја	-ija	istorija	history
-ика	граматика	-ika	gramatika	grammar
-ило	беснило	-ilo	besnilo	rabies
-ина	поштарина	-ina	poštarina	postage
-иште	становиште	-ište	stanovište	point of view
-изам	тероризам	-izam	terorizam	terrorism
-ја	градња	-ja	gradnja	construction
-је	празноверје	-je	praznoverje	superstition
-јење	опкољење	-jenje	opkoljenje	surrounding, blockade
-лук	мамурлук	-luk	mamurluk	hangover
-ња	љутња	-nja	ljutnja	anger
-њава	пуцњава	-njava	pucnjava	shooting
-оћа	самоћа	-oća	samoća	loneliness
-ост	младост	-ost	mladost	youth
-ота	срамота	-ota	sramota	shame
-овина	пустоловина	-ovina	pustolovina	adventure
-ство	лукавство	-stvo	lukavstvo	cunningness
-штина	немаштина	-ština	nemaština	poverty

Nouns formed from verbs belong to this group of nouns. As the name implies, the roots of these nouns originate from verbs. They are neuter singular:

певање	pevanje	singing
пливање	plivanje	swimming

7 Nouns

-ај	догађај	-aj	događaj	event
-ак	одлазак	-ak	odlazak	departure
-арија	глупарија	-arija	gluparija	stupidity
-ба	злоупотреба	-ba	zloupotreba	abuse
-еж	трулеж	-ež	trulež	rottenness
-ење	упозорење	-enje	upozorenje	caution
-ић	Божић	-ić	Božić	Christmas
-ија	историја	-ija	istorija	history
-ика	граматика	-ika	gramatika	grammar
-ило	беснило	-ilo	besnilo	rabies
-ина	поштарина	-ina	poštarina	postage
-иште	становиште	-ište	stanovište	point of view
-изам	тероризам	-izam	terorizam	terrorism
-ја	градња	-ja	gradnja	construction
-је	празноверје	-je	praznoverje	superstition
-јење	опкољење	-jenje	opkoljenje	surrounding, blockade
-лук	мамурлук	-luk	mamurluk	hangover
-ња	љутња	-nja	ljutnja	anger
-њава	пуцњава	-njava	pucnjava	shooting
-оћа	самоћа	-oća	samoća	loneliness
-ост	младост	-ost	mladost	youth
-ота	срамота	-ota	sramota	shame
-овина	пустоловина	-ovina	pustolovina	adventure
-ство	лукавство	-stvo	lukavstvo	cunningness
-штина	немаштина	-ština	nemaština	poverty

Nouns formed from verbs belong to this group of nouns. As the name implies, the roots of these nouns originate from verbs. They are neuter singular:

певање	pevanje	singing
пливање	plivanje	swimming

-ће	воће	-će	voće	fruit
-етина	пилетина	-etina	piletina	poultry
-ица	комовица	-ica	komovica	wine brandy
-ина	говедина	-ina	govedina	beef
-овина	сомовина	-ovina	somovina	salmon

Types of nouns

4 Collective nouns consist of separate entities belonging to a collective entity generally acting as a singular whole:

група	grupa	group
нација	nacija	nation

Many collective nouns end in one of the following groups of suffixes:

-ад*	прасад	-ad*	prasad	piglets
-еж**	младеж	-ež**	mladež	youth
-ија**	старудија	-ija**	starudija	old objects
-ја*	браћа	-ja*	braća	brothers
-је***	дрвеће	-je***	drveće	trees

* Nouns with these suffixes are declined as singular feminine nouns with a plural verb.
** Nouns with these suffixes are declined as singular feminine nouns with a singular verb.
*** Nouns with this suffix: биље/bilje (plants), лишће/lišće (leaves), грање/granje (branches), etc., although plural in meaning, are treated and declined as a singular neuter noun.

5 Abstract nouns refer to intangible concepts and are also a subtype of common nouns:

вера	vera	faith
пријатељство	prijateljstvo	friendship
заробљеништво	zarobljeništvo	captivity

Many abstract nouns end in one of the following groups of suffixes:

-а	мука	-a	muka	nausea
-ација	ситуација	-acija	situacija	situation

The main suffix for these nouns is **-ње/nje**, which is added to the infinitive stem of the verb (see Section 6.1 Infinitives – classification):

-ње	гледање	-nje	gledanje	watching
	чекање		čekanje	waiting
	спавање		spavanje	sleeping
	устајање		ustajanje	getting up
	седење		sedenje	sitting
	ходање		hodanje	walking
	трчање		trčanje	running

7.2 Gender of nouns

Nouns in Serbian have gender. Every noun is either of masculine, feminine or neuter gender. The ending of a noun indicates its gender. In the singular, masculine nouns usually end in a consonant; feminine nouns usually end in **-a**, while neuter nouns end in **-e** or **-o**:

Singular

камион	**kamion**	lorry (m)
кућа	**kuća**	house (f)
село	**selo**	village (n)

There are exceptions to these:

- some masculine nouns end in **-a** and **-o** (see Sections 7.4.1 and 7.4.2);
- some feminine nouns end in a consonant or **-o** (see Section 7.4.3);

Singular

деда	**deda**	grandfather (m)
радост	**radost**	joy (f)
со	**so**	salt (f)

In the plural, most masculine nouns ending in a consonant end in **-и/i**, feminine nouns ending in -a end in -e, while neuter nouns end in -a:

Plural

камиони	**kamioni**	lorries (m)

| куће | kuće | houses (f) |
| села | sela | villages (n) |

Exceptions to these are:

- masculine nouns ending in **-a** have an **-e** ending in the plural;
- feminine nouns ending in a consonant or **-o** have an **-и/i** ending in the plural:

деда – деде	deda – dede	grandfather – grandfathers (m)
радост – радости	radost – radosti	joy – joys (f)
со(л) – соли	so(l) – soli	salt – salts (f)

7.3 Cases of nouns

Regardless of the role (subject, object, etc.) a noun, noun phrase or pronoun plays in a sentence, in English its form generally remains the same. Most changes that occur to endings of nouns are related to the formation of the plural: 'tree – trees, house – houses', etc. (Pronouns, on the other hand, do have a change in form where 'I' is used to express the *subject* of a sentence, and 'me' expresses the *object*.) As the noun essentially remains the same, its function or role in a sentence is generally indicated by word order and/or a preposition.

Serbian, however, is an inflected language. This means that for every role that a noun, noun phrase or pronoun plays in a sentence, a different form of the noun is used. These changes in form are achieved through the use of different endings added to the stem of the noun and any words qualifying it. The various functions are categorised into seven 'cases'. Each case consists of a set of endings for each type of noun, pronoun or adjective. These endings serve as markers as they tell us how a noun (or adjective) is to be construed in relationship to other words depending on the role it plays in the sentence.

This change of noun form through the cases is referred to as a *declension*. It is said that a noun *declines*, 'falls away' from the previous form. With this thought in mind, Roman grammarians named the various cases of a declension after the Latin word *casus*, which means 'fallen' from *cadere* 'to fall'. The idea was that the nominative case (the first case, in which was given the *name* of the noun, thus making it the subject of a sentence) would be at the top and the other cases would be falling away, 'declining', from it.

The seven cases in Serbian are:

> **Cases of nouns**

- Nominative: the nominative case is used to indicate the subject of a sentence:

    | *Мајка* долази. | *Majka* dolazi. | Mother is coming. |

- Genitive: 'possession' is expressed by the genitive – the English ''s' and 'of'; many prepositions also take this case:

    | Идемо у центар *града*. | Idemo u centar *grada*. | We are going to the centre *of town*. |

- Dative: the dative case may express purpose, direction or possession, or personal interest in an event. It is also the only way to express the person 'indirectly' interested in an action:

    | Мајка је дала *сину* поклон. | Majka je dala *sinu* poklon. | Mother gave (to) her *son* a present. |

- Accusative: the only way to express the direct object of a transitive verb is the accusative case:

    | Мајка пева *песму*. | Majka peva *pesmu*. | Mother is singing *a song*. |

- Vocative: the vocative case form is used to indicate words of naming the addressee in direct address:

    | *Мајко*, дођи! | *Majko*, dođi! | *Mother*, come! |

- Instrumental: the instrumental case is used to indicate the company, instrument or vehicle with which or by which an action is taking place:

    | Идемо *са мајком* у град. | Idemo *sa majkom* u grad. | We're going *with mother* to town. |

- Locative: the locative or prepositional case indicates location – it is also the only case which can only be used with a preposition:

    | Били смо јуче у *граду*. | Bili smo juče u *gradu*. | We were *in town* yesterday. |

Although each case is associated with a particular usage or meaning, there are more ways than one to express any given meaning. Equally, no one case offers only one meaning, as one can always put things 'in other words'. However, the cases and their particular usages do offer us the possibility to construct a sentence in which the words are in a particular relationship with each other, thus providing a particular meaning.

7 Nouns

The following are endings for cases of all three genders of nouns:

Singular					
	Masculine		Neuter	Feminine	
	Animate	Inanimate			
Nom.	дечак	аутобус	село	жена	ноћ
	dečak	autobus	selo	žena	noć
Gen.	дечака	аутобуса	села	жене	ноћи
	dečaka	autobusa	sela	žene	noći
Dat.	дечаку	аутобусу	селу	жени	ноћи
	dečaku	autobusu	selu	ženi	noći
Acc.	дечака	аутобус	село	жену	ноћ
	dečaka	autobus	selo	ženu	noć
Voc.	дечаче	аутобусе	село	жено	ноћи
	dečače	autobuse	selo	ženo	noći
Inst.	дечаком	аутобусом	селом	женом	ноћи/ноћу
	dečakom	autobusom	selom	ženom	noći/noću
Loc.	дечаку	аутобусу	селу	жени	ноћи
	dečaku	autobusu	selu	ženi	noći

Plural					
	Masculine		Neuter	Feminine	
	Animate	Inanimate			
Nom.	дечаци	аутобуси	села	жене	ноћи
	dečaci	autobusi	sela	žene	noći
Gen.	дечака	аутобуса	села	жена	ноћи
	dečaka	autobusa	sela	žena	noći
Dat.	дечацима	аутобусима	селима	женама	ноћима
	dečacima	autobusima	selima	ženama	noćima
Acc.	дечаке	аутобусе	села	жене	ноћи
	dečake	autobuse	sela	žene	noći

Voc.	дечаци	аутобуси	села	жене	ноћи	Cases of nouns
	dečaci	autobusi	sela	žene	noći	
Inst.	дечацима	аутобусима	селима	женама	ноћима	
	dečacima	autobusima	selima	ženama	noćima	
Loc.	дечацима	аутобусима	селима	женама	ноћима	
	dečacima	autobusima	selima	ženama	noćima	

Titles of books, plays, films, etc. are declined unless they are preceded by nouns which define them. These nouns themselves are declined: **филм**/film (film), **књига**/knjiga (book), **хотел**/hotel (hotel), etc.

Читам „Харија Потера".	**Čitam „Harija Potera".**	I'm reading 'Harry Potter'.
Читам књигу „Хари Потер".	**Čitam knjigu „Hari Poter".**	I'm reading the book 'Harry Potter'.

An illustration of how cases function:

Петар/Petar... (Peter...)	nominative
је *без сувозача*/je *bez suvozača*. (is *without* a *co-driver*.)	genitive
је писао *сувозачу*/je pisao *suvozaču*. (wrote to his *co-driver*.)	dative
је видео *сувозача*/je video *suvozača*. (saw the *co-driver*.)	accusative
је викнуо "*Сувозаче*"/je viknuo "*Suvozače!*". (shouted Hey, *co-driver!*)	vocative
је видео жену *са сувозачем*/je video ženu *sa suvozačem*. (saw a woman *with* his *co-driver*.)	instrumental
је причао *о сувозачу*/je pričao *o suvozaču*. (spoke *about* the *co-driver*.)	locative

7.3.1 | *Nominative case*

The basic form of a noun, pronoun or adjective, as it is given in the dictionary, will be in the nominative case. This form of the noun is independent of all other words in the sentence which, directly or indirectly, will be dependent on it.

7 Nouns

The nominative case is the case for the subject of a sentence. The subject is the person or thing about which the predicate makes a statement, and the name, 'nominative', in Latin, means 'pertaining to the person or thing designated'.

7.3.1.1 Uses of the nominative case

- When a noun or pronoun is the subject of a verb:

    | Човек ради. | Čovek radi. | The man is working. |
    | Она је јуче дошла. | Ona je juče došla. | She came yesterday. |
    | Јован је наш пријатељ. | Jovan je naš prijatelj. | Jovan is our friend. |

    In Serbian the subject does not always need to be expressed as this information can be expressed by the verb:

    | Воле сладолед. | Vole sladoled. | (They) love ice-cream. |

- When a noun or group of words are in apposition to the subject, i.e. they are re-stating something which has already been expressed by the subject:

    | Наш друг, *Петар*, ради. | Naš drug, *Petar*, radi. | Our friend, *Peter*, is working. |
    | Милош, *голман тима*, никада не касни. | Miloš, *golman tima*, nikada ne kasni. | Miloš, *the team's goalkeeper*, is never late. |

- With a noun, adjective or pronoun used as a predicate with the verb 'to be':

    | Петар је *возач*. | Petar je *vozač*. | Peter is a *driver*. |
    | Филм је *добар*. | Film je *dobar*. | The film is *good*. |

- When a word is used in exclamation:

    Ватра! Vatra! Fire!   **Лопов! Lopov!** Thief!

- The nominative case is used in reply to the following questions:

    Ко? Ko? Who?   and   **Шта? Šta?** What?

    | Ко је дошао на вечеру? | Ko je došao na večeru? | Who came for dinner? |
    | Шта се десило? | Šta se desilo? | What happened? |

    These two interrogatives have no plural form; **ко?/ko?** is masculine and **шта?/šta?** neuter in gender.

The following interrogatives agree both in number and in gender with the noun:

	Which?			What kind?		
	(m)	(n)	(f)	(m)	(n)	(f)
sg.	који	које	која	какав	какво	каква
	koji	koje	koja	kakav	kakvo	kakva
pl.	који	која	које	какви	каква	какве
	koji	koja	koje	kakvi	kakva	kakve

	How big?			Whose?		
	(m)	(n)	(f)	(m)	(n)	(f)
sg.	колики	колико	колика	чији	чије	чија
	koliki	koliko	kolika	čiji	čije	čija
pl.	колико	колика	колике	чији	чија	чије
	koliko	kolika	kolike	čiji	čija	čije

It is important to remember that words in the nominative case are never preceded by a preposition.

7.3.2 Genitive case

There are many uses of the genitive case. It is a convenient way of indicating relationships between nouns and one of its main uses is to attach a noun to a noun, while expressing a relationship of possession. Of all the cases, sentences containing the genitive case are the most complex. In addition to expressing possession, the greatest number of prepositions take this case, as do many adverbs.

7.3.2.1 Uses of the genitive

- To express possession, the equivalent of ''s' in English, and origin. It denotes a sense of belonging to – of – from. The genitive case indicates who possesses an object.

| Ово су кола професора. | Ovo su kola profesora. | This is the car *of the professor* (the professor's car). |
| Да ли је то кућа *дечака*? | Da li je to kuća *dečaka*? | Is that the house of the boy (the boy's house)? |

This case must be used when there is a modifier on the possessor:

| Ово су кола професора Митића. | Ovo su kola Profesora Mitića. | This is *Professor Mitić's* car. |
| Да ли је то кућа малог дечака? | Da li je to kuća malog dečaka? | Is that the house of *the little boy*? |

Otherwise, the ordinary possessive adjective or pronoun can be used:

| Ово су професорова (or Митићева) кола. | Ovo su profesorova (or Mitićeva) kola. | This is *the professor's* (or *Mitić's*) car. |
| Да ли је то дечакова кућа? | Da li je to dečakova kuća? | Is that *the boy's* house? |

The genitive must also be used with words that have no possessive adjectival form:

| Зграбио је дршку *тигања*. | Zgrabio je dršku *tiganja*. | He grabbed the handle *of the frying pan*. (not: the frying pan's handle) |

When a woman's name and surname are used to indicate possession, the first name takes the genitive while the surname remains unchanged:

| Ово је муж *Ане* Маринковић. | Ovo je muž *Ane* Marinković. | This is the husband of *Ana* Marinković. |

The preposition **код/kod** is also followed by the genitive to indicate a person's house/flat/office/room:

| Ми смо *код* маме. | Mi smi *kod* mame. | We are *at (my) mum's*. |

- Like the temporal accusative, the temporal genitive is used in expressions of time and has an adverbial function. It is generally used in response to the question 'When?':

| Она пере косу свaког дана. | Ona pere kosu svakog dana. | She washes her hair *every day*. |
| Идуће недеље идемо на море. | Iduće nedelje idemo na more. | We're going to the coast *next week*. |

- Numerals from five onward in all three genders are followed by the noun and adjective in the genitive plural (numerals from two to four in the feminine gender take the nominative plural, while nouns and adjectives following numerals from two to four in the masculine and neuter genders have an -a ending, which also appears on participles in verb forms):

Cases of nouns

Два човека су дошла.	*Dva* čoveka su došla.	*Two* men came.
Три села су српска.	*Tri* sela su srpska.	*Three* villages are Serbian.
Пет жена је певало.	*Pet* žena je pevalo.	*Five* women sang (were singing).
Двадесетосам мушкараца је седело за столом.	*Dvadesetosam* muškaraca je sedelo za stolom.	*Twenty-eight* men were sitting at the table.

Note: Numbers above and including five take the neuter singular verb, while numbers from two to four take the plural verb (see Chapter 14 Numerals).

- To express a partitive quality (when something is *part of* something else): the genitive is used for the larger whole of which something is a part. An example is **део куће/deo kuće** (part of the house). **Кућа/kuća** (the house) is the whole of which **део/deo** is a part.
- Quantifiers denoting partitive quantity: **нешто/nešto** (some), **превише/previše** (too much), **мало/malo** (a little), **премало/premalo** (too little), **довољно/dovoljno** (an adequate amount of), etc. are followed by the genitive singular:

Дајте нам *мало* воде.	Dajte nam *malo* vode.	Give us *a little* water.

or the genitive plural:

Имамо *нешто* питања.	Imamo *nešto* pitanja.	We have *some* questions.

- Nouns denoting partitive quantity: **векна/vekna** (a loaf of), **кило/kilo** (a kilo of), **метар/metar** (a metre of), **кап/kap** (a drop of), etc. take the genitive singular while **група/grupa** (a group of), **колона/kolona** (a column of), **низ/niz** (a series of), **пар/par** (a couple of) take the genitive plural (see Chapter 15 Quantifiers):

Молим вас, *литар* бензина.	Molim vas, *litar* benzina.	*A litre* of petrol please.
Група студената је прошла поред њих.	*Grupa* studenata je prošla pored njih.	*A group* of students passed them.
Појео је *парче* торте.	Pojeo je *parče* torte.	He ate *a piece* of cake.

- Nouns denoting objects of uncountable quantity (where in English 'some' would be used) go in the genitive singular:

Купили смо шећера.	Kupili smo šećera.	We bought (some) *sugar*.
Јело му се чоколаде.	Jelo mu se čokolade.	He felt like eating (some) *chocolate*.

- Quantifiers expressing a countable quantity (including the English 'a number of'): **неколико**/nekoliko (several), **много**/mnogo (many), **пуно**/puno (a lot of), **доста**/dosta (enough), **довољно**/dovoljno (an adequate number of) take the genitive plural:

Купили смо неколико саксија.	Kupili smo nekoliko saksija.	We bought *a number of (several) flower pots*.
Више студената је чекало.	Više studenata je čekalo.	*A number of students waited*.

- Number nouns: **двојица**/dvojica (a group of two), **тројица**/trojica (a group of three), **четворица**/četvorica (a group of four), etc. take the genitive plural:

Двојица момака чекају своје девојке.	Dvojica momaka čekaju svoje devojke.	(a group of) *Two young men are waiting for their girlfriends.*
Десеторица кондуктера је у аутобусу.	Desetorica konduktera je u autobusu.	(a group of) *Ten conductors are in the bus.*

  As with numerals, this group of nouns takes the singular verb following five and upward, and the plural verb from two to four.

- With the verbs **бити**/biti (in the past tense) and **имати**/imati when used in impersonal constructions – 'there is/there was/there exists/there existed' – and the negative **није било**/nije bilo and **немати**/nemati 'there is not/there was not':

  (a) With a plural countable noun, the genitive plural is used:

У нашем је граду било лепих кућа.	U našem je gradu nije bilo lepih kuća.	*There were beautiful houses in our town.*
У нашем граду има лепих кућа.	U našem gradu ima lepih kuća.	*There are beautiful houses in our town.*
У нашем граду нема лепих кућа.	U našem gradu nema lepih kuća.	*There are no beautiful houses in our town.*

(b) With uncountable nouns, the genitive singular is used:

Било је воде у чесми.	*Bilo je воде u česmi.*	There was water in the tap.
Није било воде у чесми.	*Nije bilo vode u česmi.*	There was no water in the tap.

(c) When the noun is in the singular the nominative case is used:

Овде је некада била фонтана.	*Ovde je nekada bila фонтана.*	There was once a fountain here.
Овде није никада била фонтана.	*Ovde nije nikada bila fontana.*	There was never a fountain here.
Има ли добар хотел овде?	*Ima li dobar hotel ovde?*	Is there a good hotel here?

> Cases of nouns

- The genitive can also be used with the modal verbs **требати/trebati** (to need) and **хтети/hteti** (to want):

Треба нам новца.	*Treba nam novca.*	We need money.
Хоћу торте.	*Hoću torte.*	I want (some) cake.

- The genitive is used with the following adjectives:

вредан	vredan	worthy of
гладан	gladan	hungry for
достојан	dostojan	deserving/worthy of
жедан	žedan	thirsty for
жељан	željan	desirous of
пун	pun	full of
свестан	svestan	conscious of
сит	sit	satiated with

- The genitive is used with the following verbs:

(a) Verbs with **-на/na** prefix:

најести се	najesti se	to eat to satiety
напити се	napiti se	to drink to drunkenness/satiety
наслушати се	naslušati se	to listen until satiated
набрати	nabrati	to pick a quantity of fruit
начекати се	načekati se	to wait for a long time

etc.

(b) Reflexive verbs of which the object is in the genitive:

зажелети се	zaželeti se	to be desirous of
сећати се	sećati se	to remember
сетити се	setiti se	to remember
дохватити се	dohvatiti se	to reach for
држати се	držati se	to hold onto
латити се	latiti se	to undertake
примити се	primiti se	to take onto oneself
тицати се	ticati se	to affect
прихватити се	prihvatiti se	to take on, take responsibility for

(c) The verb доћи/doći (to come) – when implying cost or price:

Живота ће нас доћи овај одмор.	*Života će nas doći ovaj odmor.*	This holiday will cost us our *lives*.
Немој да те то дође главе.	*Nemoj da te to dođe glave.*	Don't let that cost you your head (life).

(d) With negative transitive verbs:

Немамо хлеба.	**Nemamo hleba.**	We don't have bread.

- The genitive is also used with the adverb **жао/žao** (to feel pity/sorry for):

Жао ми је жене.	*Žao mi je žene.*	*I feel sorry* for the *woman*. (it's because of the woman that I feel sorry)

and following words and particles expressing surprise:

гле	gle	look at ...
ево	evo	here (is) ...
ено	eno	over there (is) ...
ето	eto	there (is) ...

- The genitive is used with the following nouns:

крај	**kraj**	the end of
почетак	**početak**	the beginning of
средина	**sredina**	the middle of

- The genitive is used with the following prepositions:

од	od	from (animate)
из	iz	from (inanimate)
са	sa	from (inanimate) off

Cases of nouns

вратити се:	vratiti se:	to return:
од родитеља	*od* roditelja	*from* one's parents (an.)
из позоришта	*iz* pozorišta	*from* the theatre (inan.)
из Србије	*iz* Srbije	*from* Serbia
са Косова	*sa* Kosova	*from* Kosovo
са аеродрома	*sa* aerodroma	*from* the airport
Узела је књигу *са стола*	Uzela je knjigu *sa stola.*	She took the *book from the table.* (off the table)
Он је *са села.*	On je *sa sela.*	He is *from the village* (the country).

до	do	up to, until
испред	ispred	in front of
иза	iza	behind
између	između	between
изнад	iznad	above
испод	ispod	under
код	kod	at/with someone/ someone's place
близу	blizu	near
поред	pored	beside, next to
крај	kraj	next to
дуж	duž	along
испред	ispred	in front of
насред	nasred	in the middle of
ван	van	outside
око	oko	around
након	nakon	after, following
после	posle	after, following, afterwards
пре	pre	before

уочи	uoći	on the eve of
усред	usred	in the middle of
због	zbog	because
ради	radi	for the purpose/sake of
без	bez	without
осим	osim	except, excluding
сем	sem	except, excluding
место	mesto	in the place of
уместо	umesto	instead of

The genitive is used in answer to the following questions:

Кога? Koga Whom? **Чега? Čega** What?

(These have no plural form.)

Кога се сећаш? Koga se sećaš? Whom do you remember?
Чега се сећаш? Čega se sećaš? What do you remember?

	Masculine	Neuter	Feminine	
sg.	ко(је)г/ko(je)g	ко(је)г/ko(je)g	које/koje	Which?
pl.		којих/kojih		
sg.	каквог/kakvog	каквог/kakvog	какве/kakve	What kind/type of?
pl.		каквих/kakvih		
sg.	коликог/kolikog	коликог/kolikog	колике/kolike	What size?
pl.		коликих/kolikih		
sg.	чијег/čijeg	чијег/čijeg	чије/čije	Whose?
pl.		чијих/čijih		

7.3.2.2 Formation of the genitive

The following are the endings for nouns in the genitive:

	Masculine Class I		Neuter Class I	Feminine Class II		Feminine Class III
	aeroplane	policeman	conductor	village	morning	house	country	night
Nom. sg.	авион avion	полицајац policajac	диригент dirigent	село selo	јутро jutro	кућа kuća	земља zemlja	ноћ noć
Nom. pl.	авиони avioni	полицајци policajci	диригенти dirigenti	села sela	јутра jutra	куће kuće	земље zemlje	ноћи noći
Gen. sg.	авиона aviona	полицајца policajca	диригента dirigenta	села sela	јутра jutra	куће kuće	земље zemlje	ноћи noći
Gen. pl.	авионā aviona	полицајāцā policajaca	диригенāтā dirigenata	селā sela	јутāрā jutara	кућā kuća	земāљā zemalja	ноћи noći
	-a	-a	-a	-a	-a	-e, -a	-e, -a	-и
		Note: the fleeting a reappears in the genitive plural	Note: an -a is inserted between the final consonants in gen. pl. where the nom. sg. ends in a consonant group ending with final consonant т.		Note: the fleeting a appears only in the gen. pl. with consonant groups other than ст, шт, шћ, зд.	Note: nom. sg. and the gen. pl.	Note: with some consonant groups before the ending, the fleeting a appears in the gen. pl.	Note: nom. and gen. pl. ending is -и.

7.3.3 Dative case

The dative case is the case of the indirect object, denoting a person (or object) to or for whom something (the direct object) is intended or directed. In 'I gave the pen to him', 'to him' would be in the dative case. This common usage gives the case its name: it is the case that pertains to giving; when something is given or intended or in the interest of someone, it is said to be 'for' that person.

The dative case can be used with or without a preposition, and is common after verbs that indicate particular types of activities.

7.3.3.1 Uses of the dative

Without a preposition

The dative is used with a variety of verbs:

- Verbs of giving and receiving, providing something for/to someone:

Imperfective	Perfective	Imperfective	Perfective	
давати	дати	davati	dati	to give
поклањати	поклонити	poklanjati	pokloniti	to present, donate
уручивати	уручити	uručivati	uručiti	to hand over
намењивати	наменити	namenjivati	nameniti	to intend, earmark
слати	послати	slati	poslati	to send
враћати	вратити	vraćati	vratiti	to return
желети	пожелети	želeti	poželeti	to wish
помагати	помоћи	pomagati	pomoći	to help
пружати	пружити	pružati	pružiti	to offer
куповати	купити	kupovati	kupiti	to buy
служити	послужити	služiti	poslužiti	to serve

Помогао је жртвама.	*Pomogao je žrtvama.*	He *helped* the *victims*.
Пожелели су деци срећан пут.	*Poželeli su deci* srećan put.	They *wished* the *children* a good journey.

- Verbs of telling, advising, complaining, talking to, lying, intending and others:

Imperfective	Perfective	Imperfective	Perfective	
казати		kazati		to say
говорити	рећи	govoriti	reći	to say, tell
јављати	јавити	javljati	javiti	to report, call
писати	написати	pisati	napisati	to write
поручивати	поручити	poručivati	poručiti	to convey
упућивати	упутити	upućivati	uputiti	to address, direct
захваљивати се	захвалити се	zahvaljivati se	zahvaliti se	to thank
објашњавати	објаснити	objašnjavati	objasniti	to explain
жалити	пожалити	žaliti	požaliti	to complain
веровати	поверовати	verovati	poverovati	to believe

Одмах смо *рекли Марку*.	**Odmah smo** *rekli* **Marku.**	We *told Marko* straight away.
Адвокат *ми је саветовао* да сачекам.	**Advokat** *mi je savetovao* **da sačekam.**	The solicitor *advised me* to wait.

- Verbs of motion with -при/pri prefix, denoting an action of approaching or bringing something closer:

Imperfective	Perfective	Imperfective	Perfective	
прилазити	прићи	prilaziti	prići	to approach
приносити	принети	prinositi	prineti	to bring closer to
притицати	притећи	priticati	priteći	to flow, run up to

Чувар је пажљиво *пришао животињи*.	**Čuvar je pažljivo** *prišao* **životinji.**	The keeper carefully *approached the animal*.
Полицајац је *притекао жени* у помоћ.	**Policajac je** *pritekao ženi* **u pomoč.**	The policeman *ran to the woman* to help.

Cases of nouns

- Verbs used in creating idiomatic expressions, including those with impersonal constructions, and verbs used to express a liking for something:

Imperfective	Perfective	Imperfective	Perfective	
дешавати се	десити се	dešavati se	desiti se	to happen*
догађати се	догодити се	događati se	dogoditi se	to happen, occur*
свиђати се	свидети се	sviđati se	svideti se	to like, find attractive
гадити се	згадити се	gaditi se	zgaditi se	to feel sickened, revolted
дивити се	задивити се	diviti se	zadiviti se	to admire
чинити се	учинити се	činiti se	učiniti se	to seem*
изгледати		izgledati		to seem, appear*
допадати се	допасти се	dopadati se	dopasti se	to find attractive
надати се	понадати се	nadati se	ponadati se	to hope
радовати се	обрадовати се	radovati se	obradovati se	to look forward to
сметати	засметати	smetati	zasmetati	to mind, find bothersome

* These verbs are used in the 3rd person, singular or plural, with the impersonal subject 'it', to express a reaction or interest in a thing or quality. Some may be specifically expressions of judgement, **Чини ми се да је добар човек**/**Čini mi se da je dobar čovek** (He seems to me to be a good man; that is, 'in my judgement, from my perspective, he appears to be a good man'):

Свиђа ми се ова хаљина.	**Sviđa mi se ova haljina.**	This dress is *likeable (attractive) to me.*
Десило нам се нешто необично.	**Desilo nam se nešto neobično.**	Something unusual *happened to us.*
Чини ми се да ће падати киша.	**Čini mi se da će padati kiša.**	*It seems to me* that rain will fall.
Изгледа ми да ће падати снег.	**Izgleda mi da će padati sneg.**	*It seems to me* that snow will fall.

- Verbs to which **ce/se** and a dative, usually a pronoun, are added to express a desire to do something:

Игра им се фудбал.	**Igra im se fudbal.**	They feel like playing football. (it feels like *playing to them*)
Не спава јој се сада.	**Ne spava joj se sada.**	She doesn't feel like sleeping now. (it doesn't feel like *sleeping to her*)
Пије му се сок.	**Pije mu se sok.**	He feels like drinking juice. (it feels like *drinking to him*)

- Adverbs followed by personal pronouns and the appropriate short form – auxiliary to the verb **бити/biti** (to be), used to create impersonal constructions, expressing a state of being, feeling or reaction to an external influence whereby someone's reaction or interest in a thing or quality may be specifically that of perspective. For example, **драго јој је/drago joj je** ('it is pleasing to her', implying that, 'for her, in her eyes, it is pleasing'):

Мило (драго) ми је.	**Milo (drago) mi je.**	I feel glad (pleased). (it is *pleasing to me*)
Било нам је хладно на планини.	**Bilo nam je hladno na planini.**	We felt cold in the mountains. (it was *cold to us*)
Досадно ми је.	**Dosadno mi je.**	I feel bored. (it is *boring to me*)
Интересантна му је твоја прича.	**Interesantna mu je tvoja priča.**	He feels interested in your story. (your story is *interesting to him*)
Како ти је?	**Kako ti je?**	How do you feel? (How is it to you?)

- The dative is often used to denote *possession*, especially with personal pronouns. However, it is different from the genitive in that it typically implies a personal connection, enjoyment, etc. that goes beyond the legal possession:

Где ти је муж?	**Gde ti je muž?**	Where is *your* husband?
Ово нам је наставник.	**Ovo nam je nastavnik.**	This is *our* teacher.
Не знам где су ми кључеви.	**Ne znam gde su mi ključevi.**	I don't know where *my* keys are.

Cases of nouns

With a preposition

There are only a few prepositions which take the dative case:

према	prema	towards, according to, facing, opposite
к/ка	k/ka	towards, according to, facing, opposite (with verbs of motion)
насупрот	nasuprot	opposite (increasingly used with genitive)
Авион лети према Лондону.	Avion leti prema Londonu.	The plane is flying towards London.
Они возе ка Лондону.	Oni voze ka Londonu.	They are driving towards London.
Дођи к мени.	Dođi k meni.	Come to me.

The dative is used in response to the following questions:

Коме	Kome	To whom?
Чему	Čemu	To what?

(These have no plural.)

Коме си дао новац?	*Kome si dao* novac?	*To whom* did you give the money?
Према коме је био љубазан?	*Prema kome* je bio ljubazan?	*To whom* was he polite?
Коме је данас рођендан?	*Kome* je danas rođendan?	*To whom* is it a birthday today? (Whose birthday is it today?)
Чему се надаш?	*Čemu* se nadaš?	What are you hoping *for*?

	Masculine	Neuter	Feminine	
sg.	ко(је)м/ko(je)m	ко(је)м/ko(je)m	којој/kojoj	Which?
pl.		којим/kojim		
sg.	каквом/kakvom	каквом/kakvom	каквој/kakvoj	What kind/What type of?
pl.		каквим/kakvim		
sg.	коликом/kolikom	коликом/kolikom	коликој/kolikoj	How big?
pl.		коликим/kolikim		

sg.	чијем/čijem	чијем/čijem	чије/čije	Whose?
pl.		чијим/čijim		

Cases of nouns

Којем студенту си дао књигу?	Kojem studentu si dao knjigu?	To which student did you give the book?
Којем пријатељу је данас рођендан?	Kojem prijatelju je danas rođendan?	Which friend has a birthday today?
Каквом човеку треба помоћ?	Kakvom čoveku treba pomoć?	What kind of man needs help?
Коликом аутомобилу треба велика гаража?	Kolikom automobilu treba velika garaža?	How big (what size of) a car needs a big garage?
Чијем детету си купио џемпер?	Čijem detetu si kupio džemper?	For whose child did you buy a jumper?

Examples of the dative in everyday speech:

1 With expressions of gratitude:

Хвала ти/Вам.	Hvala ti/Vam.	Thank you.
Захваљујем ти/Вам се.	Zahvaljujem ti/Vam se.	I thank you.

2 On meeting someone:

Здраво, ја сам Злата.	Zdravo, ja sam Zlata.	Hello, I'm Zlata.
Драго ми је, ја сам Маја.	Drago mi je, ja sam Maja.	I'm glad to meet you, (it is pleasing to me to meet you) I'm Maja.
Драго ми је.	Drago mi je.	I'm glad to meet you. (It is pleasing to me to meet you.)

3 With expressions of sympathy or condolences:

(Баш) ми је жао.	(Baš) mi je žao.	I'm (really) sorry. (It is sorry to me.)

4 With expressions of good luck etc.:

Срећан ти пут.	Srećan ti put.	Have a good journey. (The journey to you be good.)
Јави ми се.	Javi mi se.	Call me.
Пиши ми.	Piši mi.	Write to me.
Желим вам срећну нову годину.	Želim vam srećnu novu godinu.	I wish you a Happy New Year.

7.3.3.2 Formation of the dative

As in the locative case, consonant alteration occurs, with many exceptions, before the **-и/i** of the feminine singular, and, with hardly any exceptions, before the **-има/ima** of the masculine and neuter plural:

-к/k changes to -ц/c

-г/g -з/z

x/h -с/s

The dative singular of nouns is formed as follows:

Singular:

	Masculine		Neuter	Feminine	
	Consonant ending	-a ending	-o/-e	Consonant ending	-a ending
Dat.	орману	тати	селу/мору	ноћи/мисли	жени
	ormanu	tati	selu/moru	noći/mislii	ženi

Note: Masculine nouns ending in a consonant and neuter nouns have a **-y/u** ending in the dative.
All feminine nouns and masculine nouns ending in -a change to **-и/i**.

The dative plural of nouns is formed as follows:

Plural:

	Masculine		Neuter	Feminine	
	Consonant ending	-a ending	-o/-e	Consonant ending	-a ending
Dat.	-има	-ама	-има	-има	-ама
	-ima	-ama	-ima	-ima	-ama

Note: The dative plural endings for masculine nouns, neuter nouns and feminine nouns ending in a consonant have the same ending **-има/-ima**, while feminine and masculine nouns ending in -a have the ending **-ама/-ama**.

For dative endings of adjectives and pronouns, see appropriate sections.

7.3.4 | Accusative case

The accusative is the case for the direct object – it is the case that indicates the end or ultimate goal of an action or movement. In the example: 'I'm going to hit the ball', 'the ball' is the end or the ultimate goal of my hitting and so becomes the direct object of the action and goes into the accusative case. This is the origin of the direct object.

Specifying the end of movement means that the accusative is attached especially to verbs of motion and to prepositions when they refer to motion. It can be used with or without prepositions. When there is no preposition in the accusative, a transitive verb must be used.

7.3.4.1 | Uses of the accusative case

- The primary use of the accusative case is for the noun (or pronoun) which functions as the direct object of a sentence or clause.

Мирослава воли *сладолед*.	Miroslava voli *sladoled*.	Miroslava loves *ice-cream*. (m inanimate)*
Она такође воли *Јована*.	Ona takođe voli *Jovana*.	She also loves *Jovan*. (m animate)*
Маријан гледа *телевизију*.	Marijan gleda *televiziju*.	Marijan is watching *TV*.
Он такође гледа *Невенку*.	On takođe gleda *Nevenku*.	He is also watching *Nevenka*.

  * Masculine nouns in the accusative singular are divided into animate and inanimate and as such have different endings. (See Section 7.3.4.1 Formation of the accusative case.)

- The direct object is arrived at through questions using the interrogatives 'who?' **ко/ko?** and 'what?' **шта/šta?** with the transitive verb.

  In the accusative, 'Who?' **ко/ko?** changes to **кога/koga** (whom), (as it does in the genitive). The interrogative 'what?' **шта/šta** remains as it is in the nominative case while the interrogative **куда/kuda** (where to?) is used with **ићи/-ići** verbs and their derivatives.

Кога воли Мирослава?	*Koga* voli Miroslava?	*Whom* does Miroslava love?
Шта гледа Маријан?	*Šta* gleda Marijan?	*What* is Marijan watching?
Кога гледа Маријан?	*Koga* gleda Marijan?	*Whom* is he watching?

Cases of nouns

Куда иде Милан?   *Kuda* **ide Milan?**   Where is Milan going?

Милан иде у град.   **Milan ide** *u grad.*   Milan is going *to town.*

- The accusative case is also used after certain prepositions:

    (a) When the verb of the sentence or clause expresses or implies motion. These prepositions are also used with other cases when verbs of motion are not used:

у	**u**	into, in
на	**na**	into, on, at, onto, of
за	**za**	for, about, at
по	**po**	for, to pick up, to collect, one by one

*У*лазим *у* зграду.	**Ulazim** *u* **zgradu.**	I'm *entering the building.*
Идемо *на* одмор.	**Idemo** *na* **odmor.**	We are going *on holiday.*
Идем *по* децу.	**Idem** *po* **decu.**	I'm going *to pick up the children.*
Киша пада *кап по кап.*	**Kiša pada** *kap po kap.*	Rain is falling, *drop by drop.*
Рано је *за ручак.*	**Rano je** *za ručak.*	It's early *for lunch.*

    (b) And several other prepositions:

кроз	**kroz**	through, during the course of
низ	**niz**	down (as in downhill, or in a downward direction)
уз	**uz**	up (as in uphill, or in an upward direction), together with, near
пред	**pred**	just before, in front of
о	**o**	against (e.g. to lean against something)
међу	**među**	among
над	**nad**	directly above
под	**pod**	directly below

Она гледа *кроз* прозор.	**Ona gleda** *kroz* **prozor.**	She is looking *through* the window.

Војници ходају низ брдо.	Vojnici hodaju *niz* brdo.	The soldiers are walking *down* the hill.	Cases of nouns
Шетамо уз обалу.	Šetamo *uz* obalu.	We are walking *along* the shore.	
Шта пијете уз јело?	Šta pijete *uz* jelo?	What do you drink (*along*) *with* your meal?	
Путници су стигли пред хотел.	Putnici su stigli *pred* hotel.	The travellers arrived *in front of* the hotel.	

- In many expressions of time:

цео дан	ceo dan	all day
свако јутро	svako jutro	every morning
по читаву ноћ	po čitavu noć	all night long
сваки дан	svaki dan	every day

- To express greetings or wishes:

добро јутро	dobro jutro	good morning
добар дан	dobar dan	good day
лаку ноћ	laku noć	good evening
срећан пут	srećan put	happy journey

The following are some of the verbs that take the accusative case:

анализирати	analizirati	to analyse
бацити	baciti	to throw
возити	voziti	to drive
волети	voleti	to like/love
гледати	gledati	to watch
донети	doneti	to bring
желети	želeti	to desire
затворити	zatvoriti	to close
играти	igrati	to play
имати	imati	to have
љубити	ljubiti	to kiss

мрзети	mrzeti	to hate
отворити	otvoriti	to open
палити	paliti	to light
писати	pisati	to write
пушити	pušiti	to smoke
свирати	svirati	to play (instrument)
сипати	sipati	to pour
слушати	slušati	to listen
студирати	studirati	to study
тражити	tražiti	to seek
узети	uzeti	to take
чекати	čekati	to wait
читати	čitati	to read

7.3.4.1 Formation of the accusative case

The accusative singular of nouns is formed as follows:

Singular						
	Masculine			Neuter	Feminine	
	Animate	Inanimate	-a ending	-o/-e	consonant ending	-a ending
	soldier	wardrobe	dad	village/sea	night	young woman
Nom.	војник	орман	тата	село/море	ноћ	девојка
	vojnik	orman	tata	selo/more	noć	devojka
Acc.	војника	орман	тату	село/море	ноћ	девојку
	vojnika	orman	tatu	selo/more	noć	devojku

- Masculine inanimate nouns (non-living), neuter nouns and feminine nouns ending in a consonant have endings in the accusative identical to those in the nominative singular:

	Nominative		Accusative		
m inanimate	камион	kamion	камион	kamion	truck
n	пиво	pivo	пиво	pivo	beer
f	ноћ	noć	ноћ	noć	night

- Masculine animate nouns (humans/animals) ending in a consonant end in an -a (as in the genitive singular):

	Nominative		Accusative		
m animate	мушкарац	muškarac	мушкарца*	muškarca	man
	коњ	konj	коња	konja	horse

* The fleeting a in the masculine accusative (see Section 4.1.5 Fleeting a).

- Feminine nouns ending in -a and masculine nouns ending in -a change to -y:

	Nominative		Accusative		
m	тата	tata	тату	tatu	dad
f	мама	mama	маму	mamu	mum

Plural:

	Masculine			Neuter	Feminine	
	Animate	Inanimate	-a ending	-o/-e	Consonant ending	-a ending
	soldiers	wardrobes	dads	villages/seas	nights	young women
Nom.	војници	ормани	тате	села/мора	ноћи	девојке
	vojnici	ormani	tate	sela/mora	noći	devojke
Acc.	војнике	ормане	тате	села/мора	ноћи	девојке
	vojnike	ormane	tate	sela/mora	noći	devojke

- The accusative plural endings for feminine and neuter nouns are the same as the nominative plural, while for masculine nouns the plural ending **-и/i** in the nominative changes to **-е/e** in the accusative.

The accusative is formed with the following endings added to adjectives and pronouns:

Acc.	Singular Masculine		Neuter	Feminine	Plural Masculine	Neuter	Feminine
	Animate	Inanimate	-o	-a	-u/i	-a	-e
Endings	-ог/-ег	-и	-o/-e	-у	-e	-a	-e
	-og/-eg	-i		-u			
Definite adj.	згодно*г* zgodno*g*	згодн*и* zgodn*i*	згодн*о* zgodn*o*	згодн*у* zgodn*u*	згодн*е* zgodn*e*	згодн*а* zgodn*a*	згодн*е* zgodn*e*
Demonstrative pronoun	ов*ог* ov*og*	ов*ај* ov*aj*	ов*о* ov*o*	ов*у* ov*u*	ов*е* ov*e*	ов*а* ov*a*	ов*е* ov*e*
	т*ог* t*og*	т*ај* t*aj*	т*о* t*o*	т*у* t*u*	т*е* t*e*	т*а* t*a*	т*е* t*e*
Possessive pronoun	мој*ег* moj*eg* мо*г* mo*g*	мој moj	мој*е* moj*e*	мој*у* moj*u*	мој*е* moj*e*	мој*а* moj*a*	мој*е* moj*e*
Interrogative pronoun	кој*ег* koj*eg* ко*г* ko*g*	кој*и* koj*i*	кој*е* koj*e*	кој*у* koj*u*	кој*е* koj*e*	кој*а* koj*a*	кој*е* koj*e*
	чиј*ег* čij*eg*	чиј*и* čij*i*	чиј*е* čij*e*	чиј*у* čij*u*	чиј*е* čij*e*	чиј*а* čij*a*	чиј*е* čij*e*

- Definite adjectives and possessive, demonstrative and interrogative pronouns modifying masculine animate nouns have the ending **-ог/og** or **-ег/eg**:

Видео сам тв*ог* (тво*јег*) Јован*а*.	Video sam tv*og* (tvo*jeg*) Jovan*a*.	I saw your Jovan.
Ово дете има млад*ог* (млађ*ег*) тат*у*.	Ovo dete ima mlad*og* (mlađ*eg*) tat*u*.	This child has a young (younger) father.

Cases of nouns

- Definite adjectives and possessive, demonstrative and interrogative pronouns when modifying inanimate masculine or neuter nouns have the same endings as in the nominative singular:

Чoвeк вози стар*и* аутомобил.	Čovek vozi star*i* automobil.	The man is driving an old car.
Кoj*и* аутобус чекате?	Koj*i* autobus čekate?	Which bus are you waiting for?

- Feminine definite adjectives and possessive, demonstrative and interrogative pronouns have the ending **-у/u** in the accusative singular:

Момак је упознао леп*у* девојк*у*.	Momak je upoznao lep*u* devojk*u*.	The young man met a pretty girl.
Чиј*у* си слик*у* купио?	Čij*u* si slik*u* kupio?	Whose painting did you buy?

- Depending on whether the final consonant is soft or hard, neuter definite adjectives and demonstrative pronouns and possessive and interrogative pronouns have the endings **-o** or **-e** in the accusative singular:

Идемо у моj*е* леп*о* сел*о*.	Idemo u moj*e* lep*o* sel*o*.	We are going to my pretty village.
За одмор идемо на наш*е* плав*о* мор*е*.	Za odmor idemo na naš*e* plav*o* mor*e*.	We are going to our blue sea for the holidays.
Где је њихов*о* сел*о*?	Gde je njihov*o* sel*o*?	Where is their village?

- Endings for masculine and feminine genders in the accusative plural are **-e** and **-a** for neuter gender:

Ми волимо своj*е* синов*е*.	Mi volimo svoj*e* sinov*e*.	We love our sons.
Ова деца имају млад*е* тат*е*.	Ova deca imaju mlad*e* tat*e*.	These children have young fathers.
К*у*да иду наш*е* леп*е* девоjк*е*.	K*u*da idu naš*e* lep*e* devojk*e*.	Where to are our pretty girls going.
Идемо у наш*а* леп*а* сел*а*.	Idemo u naš*a* lep*a* sel*a*.	We are going to our pretty villages.

7.3.5 Vocative case

7.3.5.1 Uses of the vocative case

The vocative case is used when addressing someone directly, in person or in writing, and it usually applies to living beings – people and animals. The noun in the vocative stands independently of the other words in a sentence and is usually separated from them by a comma:

| Мама, имамо ли хлеба? | Mama, imamo li hleba? | Mum, do we have some bread? |
| Иване, јави се кући. | Ivane, javi se kući. | Ivan, call home. |

When someone is addressed in writing, his or her name, title or rank is in the vocative, followed by a comma:

| Драги пријатељу, Поштовани господине Младеновићу, | Dragi prijatelju, Poštovani gospodine Mladenoviću, | Dear *friend*, Respected Mr Mladenović, |

The vocative case is also used when calling out to someone:

| Драгане! | Dragane! | (Hey) Dragan! |

This is often preceded by an exclamation: 'Hey, Oi', etc.

7.3.5.2 Formation of the vocative case

Masculine and neuter nouns remain the same in the vocative case as in the nominative. Plural nouns also use the nominative for the vocative case.

The vocative case differs from the nominative case in the following instances:

1   Masculine singular ending is -e after hard consonants:

| Драги син*е*, | Dragi sin*e*, | Dear son, |

and -у/u after soft consonants:

| Драги пријатељ*у*, Поштовани господин*е* Младеновић*у*, | Dragi prijatelj*u*, Poštovani gospodin*e* Mladeniović*u*, | Dear friend, Respected Mr Mladenović, |

The following consonant changes occur before the -e ending:

-к/k to -ч/č   -ц/c to -ч/č

-г/g to -ж/ž   -х/h to -ш/š

отац – оче	otac – oče	father
Бог – Боже	Bog – Bože	God
човек – човече	čovek – čoveče	man

There are no changes to consonants occurring before the **-у/u** ending.

Some nouns ending in hard consonants may take either ending:

| месар – месару/месаре! | mesar – mesaru/mesare! | Butcher! |
| клошар – клошару/клошаре! | klošar – klošaru/klošare! | Tramp! |

2   Although many feminine and masculine nouns ending in an **-a** (second declension) remain as in the nominative:

мама – мама!	mama – mama!	Mum!
тата – тата!	tata – tata!	Dad!
Марија – Марија!	Marija – Marija!	Maria!
Лила – Лила!	Lila – Lila!	Lila!

some masculine and feminine names and nouns ending in **-a** (second declension) have the **a** replaced by an **o**:

мајка – мајко	majka – majko!	Mother!
Нада – Надо!	Nada – Nado!	Nada!
слуга – слуго!	sluga – slugo!	Judge!

3   Collective nouns with an **-a** ending also change to **-o**:

господа – господо!	gospoda – gospodo!	Gentlemen!
деца – децо!	deca – deco!	Children!
браћа – браћо!	braća – braćo!	Brothers!

4   Feminine nouns of three or more syllables ending in **-ица/ica** take the ending **-ице/ice** in the vocative singular:

| комшиница – комшинице! | komšinica – komšinice! | Neighbour! |
| пријатељица – пријатељице! | prijateljica – prijateljice! | Girl-friend! |

Cases of nouns

5   Feminine nouns ending in a consonant (third declension) have an -и/i added to the nominative singular:

   Радости наша!   Radosti naša!   Our joy!

Definite adjectives in the vocative are the same as in the nominative.

7.3.6 | Instrumental case

The instrumental case can be used with or without a preposition to indicate a person, thing or quality associated with the activity of a verb. The two ideas most often expressed with this case are that of company (with whom an action is being carried out) and that of means, manner, agent or instrument associated with the activity of the verb (by which means is an action being carried out).

   Идемо колима.   Idemo kolima.   We're going *by car.*

7.3.6.1 | Uses of the instrumental case

The instrumental case without prepositions has three usages:

- To indicate the instrument or means by which an action is accomplished: where in English the prepositions 'by', 'with' or 'by means of' would be used:

   | **Дете једе *кашиком*.** | **Dete jede *kašikom*.** | The child is eating *with a spoon.* |
   | **Радници су путовали *возом*.** | **Radnici su putovali *vozom*.** | The workers travelled *by train.* |

- To indicate a place in which an action was carried out:

   | **Синоћ смо шетали *градом*.** | **Sinoć smo šetali *gradom*.** | Last night we strolled *through the town.* |
   | **Деца трче *улицом*.** | **Deca trče *ulicom*.** | The children are running *along the street.* |

- When expressing a time-related activity, it can indicate that an action takes place regularly at a certain time, as well as indicating a period of time during which something happens:

   | ***Суботом* идемо у куповину.** | ***Subotom* idemo u kupovinu.** | *On Saturdays* we go shopping. |
   | ***Данима* су га чекали.** | ***Danima* su ga čekali.** | They waited for him *for days.* |

It can also indicate that an action will take or has taken place at a designated point in time:

| Неки су заспали током представе. | Neki su zaspali tokom predstave. | Some fell asleep *in the course of* the show. |
| Крајем недеље идемо у Париз. | Krajem nedelje idemo u Pariz. | *At the end of* the week we're going to Paris. |

Prepositions in the instrumental case are used with the following meanings:

- To indicate company:

| са | sa | with |
| Ана иде у куповину *са Златом*. | Ana ide u kupovinu *sa Zlatom*. | Anna is going shopping *with Zlata*. |

In this use, the person accompanying the subject is considered to be an active participant in the action expressed by the verb: both Anna and Zlata are going shopping.

- Descriptively, to indicate a feature or trait:

| са | sa | with |
| Видео је девојку *са смеђим очима*. | Video je devojku *sa smeđim očima*. | He saw a girl *with brown eyes*. |

In contrast to the previous use of **ca/sa**, here the preposition is followed by a description of the subject, and the object (brown eyes) is not an active participant in the action. The preposition **ca/sa** is nonetheless used as it describes the girl to be 'with brown eyes'. This can also be expressed using the genitive case:

| Видео је девојку плаве косе. | Video je devojku plave kose. | He saw a girl *with blonde hair*. |

- To indicate manner:

| са | sa | with |
| Студенти су слушали професора *са пажњом*. | Studenti su slušali profesora *sa pažnjom*. | The students listened to the professor *attentively* (with attention). |

This can also be expressed using an adverb:

| Студенти су *пажљиво* слушали професора. | Studenti su *pažljivo* slušali profesora. | The students listened *carefully* to the professor. |

7 Nouns

The letter **c/s** (with) is often used on its own as a preposition and is interchangeable with **ca/sa**. However, in instances where the word following the preposition begins with any of the following letters: **c/s, ш/š , з/z** or **ж/ž**, the use of the full **ca/sa** preposition is required in order to avoid occurrence of double consonants. The same rule applies to the preposition **к(а)/k(a)** and its own set of consonants in the dative case.

- To indicate place:

за	za	behind

Жене су стајале једна *за другом*.	Žene su stajale jedna *za drugom*.	The women stood one *behind* the other.

This can also be expressed using the genitive case and the preposition **иза/iza** (behind):

Жене су стајале једна *иза* друге.	Žene su stajale jedna *iza* druge.	The women stood one *behind the other*.

међу	među	amongst/between

Међу путницима је било деце.	*Među* putnicima je bilo dece.	There were children *amongst the passengers*.

This can at times also be expressed using the genitive case and the preposition **између/između** (between).

над	nad	above

Авион лети *над градом*.	Avion leti *nad gradom*.	A plane is flying *above the town*.

This can also be expressed using the genitive case and the preposition **изнад/iznad** (above):

Авион лети *изнад града*.	Avion leti *iznad grada*.	A plane is flying *above the town*.

while the preposition **над/nad** (above) can be followed by the accusative with verbs of motion.

под	pod	under

Мачка је *под столом*.	Mačka je *pod stolom*.	The cat is *under the table*.

This can also be expressed using the genitive case and the preposition испод/ispod (underneath), while the preposition под/pod can be used in the accusative with verbs of motion.

| пред | pred | in front of/ahead of/before |

| Срели су се *пред* самопослугом. | Sreli su se *pred* samoposlugom. | They met *in front of the supermarket.* |

This can also be expressed using the genitive case and the preposition испред/ispred (in front of/ahead of), while the preposition пред/pred can be used in the accusative with verbs of motion.

The instrumental case is used in reply to the following questions:

1   **С(а) ким(е)?**   **S(a) kim(e)?**   With whom?
    Чим(е)?   **Čim(e)?**   With/by what (means)?

These two interrogatives have no plural form or gender in Serbian.

2   The following interrogatives agree both in number and in gender with the noun:

		With which?			With what kind?		
		(m)	(n)	(f)	(m)	(n)	(f)
sg.	с(а)	којим	којим	којом	каквим	каквим	каквом
	s(a)	kojim	kojim	kojom	kakvim	kakvim	kakvom
pl.	с(а)	којим			каквим		
	s(a)	kojim			kakvim		

| *Са којом пријатељицом идеш у биоскоп?* | *Sa kojom prijateljicom ideš u bioskop?* | With which friend are you going to the cinema? |

| *Којим пером пишеш?* | *Kojim perom pišeš?* | With which pen are you writing? |

7.3.6.2 Formation of the instrumental case

The instrumental case is formed with the following endings added to definite adjectives and nouns:

7
Nouns

Singular:

	Adjective	Noun		
Masculine	-им	-ом	or	-ем
	-im	-om		-em
		hard consonant ending		soft consonant ending
Neuter	-им	-ом	or	-ем
	-im	-om		-em
Feminine	-ом	-ом	or	-и	or	-jу
	-om	-om		-i		-ju
		nouns ending in -a		nouns ending in a consonant		

Plural:

	Adjective	Noun		
Masculine	-им	-има		
	-im	-ima		
Neuter	-им	-има		
	-im	-ima		
Feminine	-им	-ама	or	-има
	-im	-ama		-ima
		nouns ending in -a		nouns ending in a consonant

7.3.7 Locative case

The locative case is used to indicate the location and space in which an action is carried out. It is the only case which is always used with a preposition because of which it is also called the prepositional case.

7.3.7.1 Uses of the locative case

This case is used with the following prepositions:

- на/na (on, on top of) and -у/u (in, inside of)

Cases of nouns

To indicate location:

| Даљински управљач је *на телевизору*. | Daljinski upravljač je *na televizoru*. | The remote control is *on the TV*. |
| Деца су *у базену*. | Deca su *u bazenu*. | The children are *in the pool*. |

To indicate time:

На почетку се нису добро слагали.	*Na početku* se nisu dobro slagali.	*At the beginning*, they didn't get on very well.
На крају дана сви су били уморни.	*Na kraju* dana svi su bili umorni.	*At the end of the day*, they were all tired.
У марту понекад још пада снег.	*U martu* ponekad još pada sneg.	Snow sometimes still falls *in March*.

To indicate means:

| Ходали су *на прстима* да не би пробудили дете. | Hodali su *na prstima* da ne bi probudili dete. | They walked *on their toes* so as not to wake up the child. |

To provide further information in a sentence when used with nouns, adjectives and verbs:

| Захваљујемо се *на вашем гостопримству*. | Zahvaljujemo se *na vašem gostoprimstvu*. | We thank you *for your hospitality*. |

The meaning of these two prepositions when followed by the locative differ from their meanings when used with verbs of motion and followed by the accusative (movement onto, into, on top of, inside of, etc.)

- **по/po** (on, in, over, across, through, by)

To indicate movement over a whole surface or area or over only parts of a surface or area:

| Данас смо се шетали *по парку*. | Danas smo se šetali *po parku*. | Today we strolled *through the park*. |
| Ко те је ударио *по лицу*? | Ko te je udario *po licu*? | Who hit you *in the face*? |

To indicate time:

| Јавите нам се *по повратку*. | Javite nam se *po povratku*. | Call us *upon your return*. |

To provide further information in a sentence when used with nouns, adjectives and verbs:

| Препознаћу га *по коси*. | Prepoznaću ga *po kosi*. | I will recognise him *by his hair*. |

| Србин је *по* | Srbin je *po* | He is a Serb *by* |
| националности. | nacionalnosti. | *nationality.* |

To indicate one's opinion or preference:

Какав је он	Kakav je on	What kind of a man is
човек *по теби?*	čovek *po tebi?*	he *according to you?*
Изабрала је	Izabrala je	She chose a dress
хаљину *по*	haljinu *po*	*according to her taste.*
свом укусу.	*svom ukusu.*	

This preposition differs from the same one in the accusative where it is used with the meaning of picking up, fetching, collecting, etc.

- **о/o** (from, on, about, concerning, during, at)
Following verbs of communication and thought:

Разговарамо *о*	Razgovaramo	We're talking *about*
нашем новом	*o našem novom*	*our new doctor.*
доктору.	*doktoru.*	

To indicate means:

Мораћете да	Moraćete da	You will have to travel
путујете *о*	putujete *o*	*at your own expense.*
свом трошку.	*svom trošku.*	

To indicate a location, generally a place from which something is hanging:

| Шешир виси | Šešir visi *o* | The hat is hanging |
| *о чивилуку.* | *čiviluku.* | *from a hat rack.* |

- **при/pri** (at, near, to, with, during, in possession of, having, busy with, in spite of)
To indicate the location of one object in relation to another:

| Изградио је | Izgradio je | He built a garage |
| гаражу *при кући.* | garažu *pri kući.* | *attached to the house.* |

To indicate comparison of one object in relation to another:

| Она није ништа | Ona nije ništa | She is nothing *compared* |
| *при теби.* | *pri tebi.* | *to you.* |

To indicate simultaneous activity expressed by the locative deverbative (noun formed from a verb) and the main verb:

При изградњи	*Pri izgradnji*	*During construction*
моста наишли	mosta naišli	of the bridge they
су на велике	su na velike	encountered great
тешкоће.	teškoće.	difficulties.

This preposition only occurs with the locative case.

- **према/prema** (opposite, facing, in accordance with, in comparison with, suitable for):
  To indicate location, where something is opposite that which is expressed by the noun in the locative:

Седео је леђима окренут *према теби*.	Sedeo je leđima okrenut *prema tebi*.	He sat with his back *towards you*.

  To indicate the equivalent of the English 'in accordance with' or 'therefore':

Према томе, све ће бити у реду.	*Prema tome*, sve će biti u redu.	*Therefore*, everything will be alright.

  This preposition occurs with the dative case as well where its meaning denotes direction.

In general, **у/u** (in) refers to closed spaces, spaces which have 'an inside', while **на/na** (on) refers to open spaces and expansive surfaces, both plateaux and water surfaces. The opposites of these two prepositions are **из/iz** (from, out of) and **са/sa** (from, off) respectively, both of which take the genitive case.

Ми смо били *у ресторану*, да ли сте ви били *на станици*?	Mi smo bili *u restoranu*, da li ste vi bili *na stanici*?	We were *in the restaurant*, were you *at the station*.
Он је *из града* а она је *са села*.	On je *iz grada* a ona je *sa sela*.	He is *from the city* while she is *from the country* (village).

The locative case is used in reply to the following questions:

1 | *О коме?* | *O kome?* | About whom? |
   | *О, у, на чему?* | *O, u, na čemu?* | About, in, on what? |

'In' and 'on' rarely relate to living things.
   These two interrogatives have no plural form.

О коме причате?	*O kome* pričate?	Whom are you talking *about*?
Причамо *о теби*.	Pričamo *o tebi*.	We're talking *about you*.
О чему причате?	*O čemu* pričate?	What are you talking *about*?
Причамо *о филму*.	Pričamo *o filmu*.	We're talking about the film.

Cases of nouns

7 Nouns

2 The following interrogatives agree both in number and in gender with the noun:

		About, in, on which?			About, in, on what kind?		
		(m)	(n)	(f)	(m)	(n)	(f)
sg.	о, у, на	којем	којем	којој	каквом	каквом	каквој
		kojem	kojem	kojoj	kakvom	kakvom	kakvoj
pl.	о, u, na	којим			каквим		
		kojim			kakvim		

У којој школи учите српски?
U kojoj školi učite srpski?
In which school are you studying Serbian?

На каквој плажи сте били?
Na kakvoj plaži ste bili?
What kind of beach were you on?

		How big?			Whose?		
		(m)	(n)	(f)	(m)	(n)	(f)
sg.	о, у, на	коликом	коликом	коликој	чијем	чијем	чијој
		kolikom	kolikom	kolikoj	čijem	čijem	čijoj
pl.	о, u, na	коликим			чијим		
		kolikim			čijim		

У коликој кући живите?
U kolikoj kući živite?
In how big a house do you live?

О чијем детету је реч?
O čijem detetu je reč?
Whose child are you talking about?

7.3.7.2 Formation of the locative case

As in the dative case, alterations of certain consonants occur in both the singular and plural endings of the locative when followed by **-n/i**:

-к/k changes to -ц/c
-г/g -з/z
x/h -c/s

The locative singular is formed with the following endings added to nouns:

Cases of nouns

Singular:						
	Masculine		Neuter	Feminine		
	Consonant ending	-a ending	-o/-e	Consonant ending		-a ending
Loc.	орману	тати	селу/мору	ноћи/мисли		жени
	ormanu	tati	selu/moru	noći/mislii		ženi

Note: Masculine nouns ending in a consonant and neuter nouns have a **-у/u** ending. All feminine nouns and masculine nouns ending in **-a** change to **-и/i**.

Plural:						
	Masculine		Neuter	Feminine		
	Consonant ending	-a ending	-o/-e	Consonant ending		-a ending
Loc.	-има	-ама		-има		-ама
	-ima	-ama		-ima		-ama

Note: The locative plural endings for masculine nouns, neuter nouns and feminine nouns ending in a consonant have the same ending **-има/-ima**, while feminine and masculine nouns ending in **-a** have the ending **-ама/-ama**.

The locative is formed with the following endings added to adjectives and pronouns:

	Singular			Plural		
	Masculine	Neuter	Feminine	Masculine	Neuter	Feminine
Endings	**-ом/-ем**	**-ој**		**-им**		
	-om/-em	**-oj**		**-im**		
Definite adjective	**згодном**	**згодној**		**згодним**		
	zgodnom	**zgodnoj**		**zgodnim**		

	Singular			Plural		
	Masculine	Neuter	Feminine	Masculine	Neuter	Feminine
Demonstrative pronoun	о**вом**		о**вој**	о**вим**		
	том		**тој**	**тим**		
	o**vom**		o**voj**	o**vim**		
	tom		**toj**	**tim**		
Possessive pronoun	мо**јем** (мом/е)		мо**јој**	мо**јим**		
	mo**jem** (mom/e)		mo**joj**	mo**jim**		
Interrogative pronoun	ко**јем** (ком/е)		ко**јој**	ко**јим**		
	ko**jem** (kom/e)		ko**joj**	ko**jim**		
	чи**јем**		чи**јој**	чи**јим**		
	či**jem**		či**joj**	či**jim**		

7.4 Declension of nouns

The concept of declension is closely related to cases (see Section 7.3 Cases of nouns). The change in form of the noun through the cases is brought about by the addition of various endings to the stem of the noun. The stem of the noun is obtained by removing the ending from the genitive singular. However, the stem of a noun and its form in the nominative singular, as given in the dictionary, are often the same. Declensions are distinguished by the particular endings that are added to the stem of nouns as they move through the cases.

There are three main declensions.

The first declension
All animate and inanimate masculine nouns and neuter nouns belong to this declension, with the following exceptions:

- masculine nouns ending in -a in the nominative singular belong to the second declension (деда/deda etc.);
- some masculine nouns which are used to express endearment ending in -o and -e (Иво/Ivo, Владо/Vlado, etc.) also belong to the second or third declension.

A distinction exists in this declension between hard and soft nouns.

Because of its -a endings in the genitive singular (see Section 7.3 Cases of nouns), this declension is referred to as the **A** declension.

Declension of nouns

The second declension

The feminine noun мати/mati and all feminine nouns, both hard and soft, ending in -a, as well as masculine nouns ending in -a, belong to this declension. Because of its -e ending in the genitive singular, this declension is referred to as the E declension.

The third declension

All feminine nouns ending in a consonant and the feminine noun кћи/kći belong to this declension. This declension includes nouns ending in -ост/ost and those ending in -ад/ad.

Because of its **-и/i** ending in the genitive singular, this declension is referred to as the **И/I** declension.

7.4.1 Masculine and neuter nouns

Masculine and neuter nouns belong to the first declension. This declension is also referred to as the **A** declension because of the -a ending of nouns in the genitive singular.

In this declension there exists a distinction between the hard and soft consonant endings of the noun.

The soft consonants include: ј/j, љ/lj, њ/nj, ц/c, ћ/ć, ч/č, ш/š, ђ/đ, џ/dž and ж/ž. The hard consonants include: м/m, р/r, б/b, ф/f, в/v, н/n, т/t, д/d, р/p, л/l, к/k, г/g, с/s з/z and х/h.

Nouns in this declension include masculine nouns ending in a consonant, in -o and in -e in the nominative singular:

Masculine (singular)

прозор	prozor	window
преводилац*	prevodilac*	interpreter/translator
војник**	vojnik**	soldier

* Some masculine nouns ending in -лац/lac in the nominative singular have the letter -л/l replaced by the letter -о in all cases except the genitive plural. A fleeting **a** is inserted here as the noun in the nominative singular ends in a double consonant. This insertion takes place in all cases of double consonant endings except ст/st, зд/zd, шт/št and жд/žd. This fleeting **a** is present only in the nominative singular, the vocative singular and the genitive plural. Elsewhere the case endings allow the presence of two consonants.

** Nouns ending in -к/k, -г/g, -х/h in the nominative singular change to ц/c, з/z and -с/s endings respectively in plural forms of the nominative, dative, vocative, instrumental and locative cases, while the vocative singular takes ч/č, ж/ž and ш/š, respectively.

ниво	nivo	level
решо	rešo	hotplate
парк*	park*	park
такси**	taksi**	taxi

(Masculine nouns ending in -a in the nominative singular, and some masculine nouns ending in -o and -e (endings used with expressions of endearment), may belong to the second or third declensions.)

* Most single-syllable nouns acquire the infixes **-ев/ev** or **-ов/ov** before the plural endings in this declension. In general, nouns ending in a soft consonant in the nominative acquire the **-ев/ev** infix while those ending in a hard consonant acquire the **-ов/ov** ending. Some nouns ending in -o in the nominative singular acquire the **-ов/ov** ending in the plural forms.

** Nouns ending in **-и/i** or **-у/u** are generally of foreign origin. Those ending in **-и/i** acquire a **-j/j** infix before the case endings.

All neuter nouns belong to this declension:

Neuter (singular):

село	selo	village
поље	polje	field
доба	doba	era, season

Several different endings may occur in the following cases depending on the noun being declined:

In the vocative singular:

- Nouns whose stem ends in a hard consonant, a short -e or an -o (changed from л/l, see Section 4.1.6 Change of л/l to -o) have an -e ending:

    | *Госте*! (гост) | *Goste!* (gost) | (Hey) guest! |
    | *Ђорђе*! (Ђорђе) | *Đorđe!* (Đorđe) | (Hey) George! |
    | *Воле*! (во) | *Vole!* (vo) | (Hey) ox! |

- Nouns whose stem ends in a soft consonant, and those with a long accented -e and -o, have an -у/u ending:

    | *Учитељу*! (учитељ) | *Učitelju!* (učitelj) | (Hey) teacher! |
    | *Аташеу*! (аташе) | *Atašeu!* (ataše) | (Hey) attache! |
    | *Бироу*! (биро) | *Birou!* (biro) | (Hey) bureau! |

- Nouns whose stem ends in a short -o have an -o ending:

Данко! (Данко)	**Danko!** (Danko)	(Hey) Danko!
Миленко! (Миленко)	**Milenko!** (Milenko)	(Hey) Milenko!
Златко! (Златко)	**Zlatko!** (Zlatko)	(Hey) Zlatko!

- Foreign names and surnames ending in -ац/ac, -ев/ev, -ов/ov and -ин/in and neuter nouns have the same ending as in the nominative:

Џими! (Џими)	**Džimi!** (Džimi)	(Hey) Jimmy!
Бајац! (Бајац)	**Bajac!** (Bajac)	(Hey) Bajac!
Море! (море)	**More!** (more)	(Hey) sea!

- Nouns (not names) ending in -ац/ac change these two sounds to че/če:

Преводиоче! (преводилац)	**Prevodioče!** (prevodilac)	(Hey) translator!
Гледаоче! (гледалац)	**Gledaoče!** (gledalac)	(Hey) viewer!

In the instrumental singular:

- Nouns whose stem ends in a hard consonant, or whose final syllable contains -e, have an -ом/om ending:

гостом	**gostom**	(with) a guest
селом	**selom**	(with/by way of) the village

- Nouns whose stem ends in a soft consonant generally have an -ем/em ending:

учитељем (учитељ)	**učiteljem** (učitelj)	(with) the teacher
Ђорђем (Ђорђе)	**Đorđem** (Đorđe)	(with) George
певачем (певач)	**pevačem** (pevač)	(with) the singer
пољем (поље)	**poljem** (polje)	(with/by way of) the field

- However, some nouns with an e before the soft consonant have an -ом/om ending:

јежом (јеж)	**ježom** (jež)	(with) a hedgehog

Declension of nouns

In the genitive plural:

- Some masculine nouns denoting quantity have the ending **-и/i**:

пари	pari	(how many) pairs
сати	sati	(how many) hours
месеци	meseci	(how many) months

- The masculine nouns **гост/gost** (guest), **нокат/nokat*** (finger/toe nail), **прст/prst** (finger), and sometimes **уста/usta**** (mouth) end in **-ију/iju**:

гостију	gostiju	(how many) guests
ноктију	noktiju	(how many) fingernails
прсцју	prstiju	(how many) fingers

  * The a drops out when the endings are added.
  ** **Уста/usta** (mouth) like **врата/vrata** are *pluralia tantums*, meaning they only have a plural form.

- Most neuter nouns end in **-a**:

села	sela	(how many) villages
неба	neba	(how many) skies
говеда	goveda	(how many) cattle
имена*	imena*	(how many) names

  * Certain neuter nouns ending in -e have the following infixes through the cases:

име	им + ен +	*ime*	*im + en +*	name
племе	плем + ен +	*pleme*	*plem + en +*	tribe
презиме	презим + ен +	*prezime*	*prezim + en +*	surname
семе	сем + ен +	*seme*	*sem + en +*	seed
време	врем + ен +	*vreme*	*vrem + en +*	time
дугме	дугм + ет +	*dugme*	*dugm + et +*	button
небо	неб + ес +	*nebo*	*neb + es +*	skies
чудо	чуд + ес +	*čudo*	*čud + es +*	miracle
подне	подн + ев +	*podne*	*podn + ev +*	noon

The endings for the first declension are as follows:

Declension of nouns

	Singular		Plural	
	Masculine	Neuter	Masculine	Neuter
Nom.	consonant	-о/o	-и/i	-а/a
	-о/o	-е/e		
	-е/e			
Gen.	-а/a	-а/a	-а/a	-а/a
			-и/i	-и/i
			-иjγ/iju	-иjγ/iju
Dat.	-γ/u	-γ/u	-има/ima	-има/ima
Acc.	consonant/-а	-о/o	-е/e	-а/a
	-о/o	-е/e		
	-е/e			
Voc.	-е/у/u	-о/o	-и/i	-а/a
	-о/o	-е/e		
	consonant			
Inst.	-ом/om	-ом/om	-има/ima	-има/ima
	-ем/em	-ем/em		
Loc.	-γ/u	-γ/u	-има/ima	-има/ima

7 Nouns

First declension – **A** declension

Singular

	Masculine				Neuter	
	Hard		Soft		Hard	Soft
	Animate	Inanimate	Animate	Inanimate		
	soldier	window	lover (of something)	log	village	field
Nom.	војник vojnik	прозор prozor	љубитељ ljubitelj	пањ panj	село selo	поље polje
Gen.	војник*а* vojnik*a*	прозор*а* prozor*a*	љубитељ*а* ljubitelj*a*	пањ*а* panj*a*	сел*а* sel*a*	пољ*а* polj*a*
Dat.	војник*у* vojnik*u*	прозор*у* prozor*u*	љубитељ*у* ljubitelj*u*	пањ*у* panj*u*	сел*у* sel*u*	пољ*у* polj*u*
Acc.	војник*а* vojnik*a*	прозор prozor	љубитељ*а* ljubitelj*a*	пањ panj	село selo	поље polje
Voc.	војни*че* vojni*če*	прозор*е* prozor*e*	љубитељ*у* ljubitelj*u*	пањ*у* panj*u*	село selo	поље polje
Inst.	војник*ом* vojnik*om*	прозор*ом* prozor*om*	љубитељ*ем* ljubitelj*em*	пањ*ем* panj*em*	сел*ом* sel*om*	пољ*ем* polj*em*
Loc.	војник*у* vojnik*u*	прозор*у* prozor*u*	љубитељ*у* ljubitelj*u*	пањ*у* panj*u*	сел*у* sel*u*	пољ*у* polj*u*

Declension of nouns

First declension – **A** declension

Singular

	Masculine				Neuter	
	Hard		Soft			
	Animate	Inanimate	Animate	Inanimate		
	eagle	interview	hunter	judges/jury	name	button
Nom.	орао	интервју	ловац	жири	име	дугме
	orao	intervju	lovac	žiri	ime	dugme
Gen.	орла	интервјуа	ловца	жирија	имена	дугмета
	orla	intervjua	lovca	žirija	imena	dugmeta
Dat.	орлу	интервјуу	ловцу	жирију	имену	дугмету
	orlu	intervjuu	lovcu	žiriju	imenu	dugmetu
Acc.	орла	интервју	ловца	жири	име	дугме
	orla	intervju	lovca	žiri	ime	dugme
Voc.	орле	интервјуу	ловче	жирију	име	дугме
	orle	intervjuu	lovče	žiriju	ime	dugme
Inst.	орлом	интервјуом	ловцем	жиријем	именом	дугметом
	orlom	intervjuom	lovcem	žirijem	imenom	dugmetom
Loc.	орлу	интервјуу	ловцу	жирију	имену	дугмету
	orlu	intervjuu	lovcu	žiriju	imenu	dugmetu

7 Nouns

First declension – **A** declension

Plural

	Masculine				Neuter	
	Hard		Soft		Hard	Soft
	Animate	Inanimate	Animate	Inanimate		
	soldiers	windows	lovers (of something)	logs	villages	fields
Nom.	војни*ци*	прозо*ри*	љуби*те*љ*и*	пањ*еви*	сел*а*	пољ*а*
	vojni*ci*	prozo*ri*	ljubitelj*i*	panj*evi*	sel*a*	polj*a*
Gen.	војни*ка*	прозо*ра*	љубите*ља*	пањ*ева*	сел*а*	пољ*а*
	vojni*ka*	prozo*ra*	ljubitelj*a*	panj*eva*	sel*a*	polj*a*
Dat.	војни*цима*	прозо*рима*	љубите*љима*	пањ*евима*	сел*има*	пољ*има*
	vojni*cima*	prozo*rima*	ljubitelj*ima*	panj*evima*	sel*ima*	polj*ima*
Acc.	војни*ке*	прозо*ре*	љубите*ље*	пањ*еве*	сел*а*	пољ*а*
	vojni*ke*	prozo*re*	ljubitelj*e*	panj*eve*	sel*a*	polj*a*
Voc.	војни*ци*	прозо*ри*	љубите*љи*	пањ*еви*	сел*а*	пољ*а*
	vojni*ci*	prozo*ri*	ljubitelj*i*	panj*evi*	sel*a*	polj*a*
Inst.	војни*цима*	прозо*рима*	љубите*љима*	пањ*евима*	сел*има*	пољ*има*
	vojni*cima*	prozo*rima*	ljubitelj*ima*	panj*evima*	sel*ima*	polj*ima*
Loc.	војни*цима*	прозо*рима*	љубите*љима*	пањ*евима*	сел*има*	пољ*има*
	vojni*cima*	prozo*rima*	ljubitelj*ima*	panj*evima*	sel*ima*	polj*ima*

Declension of nouns

First declension – **A** declension

Plural

	Masculine				Neuter	
	Hard		Soft			
	Animate	Inanimate	Animate	Inanimate		
	eagles	interviews	hunters	judges/juries	names	buttons
Nom.	орлов**и**	интервју**и**	ловц**и**	жириј**и**	имен**а**	дугмет**а**
	orlov**i**	intervju**i**	lovc**i**	žirij**i**	imen**a**	dugmet**a**
Gen.	орлов**а**	интервјy**а**	ловац**а**	жириј**а**	имен**а**	дугмет**а**
	orlov**a**	intervju**a**	lovac**a**	žirij**a**	imen**a**	dugmet**a**
Dat.	орлов**има**	интервјy**има**	ловц**има**	жириј**има**	имен**има**	дугмет**има**
	orlov**ima**	intervju**ima**	lovc**ima**	žirij**ima**	imen**ima**	dugmet**ima**
Acc.	орлов**е**	интервју**е**	ловц**е**	жириј**е**	имен**а**	дугмет**а**
	orlov**e**	intervju**e**	lovc**e**	žirij**e**	imen**a**	dugmet**a**
Voc.	орлов**и**	интервју**и**	ловц**и**	жириј**и**	имен**а**	дугмет**а**
	orlov**i**	intervju**i**	lovc**i**	žirij**i**	imen**a**	dugmet**a**
Inst.	орлов**има**	интервјy**има**	ловц**има**	жириј**има**	имен**има**	дугмет**има**
	orlov**ima**	intervju**ima**	lovc**ima**	žirij**ima**	imen**ima**	dugmet**ima**
Loc.	орлов**има**	интервјy**има**	ловц**има**	жириј**има**	имен**има**	дугмет**има**
	orlov**ima**	intervju**ima**	lovc**ima**	žirij**ima**	imen**ima**	dugmet**ima**

7.4.2 Feminine and masculine nouns ending in -a and the noun мати/mati

Feminine and masculine nouns ending in -a belong to the second declension. This declension is also referred to as the E declension because of the -e endings of nouns in the genitive singular. There are no hard or soft consonant distinctions in this declension, nor are there any animate/inanimate endings.

The following types of nouns belong to this declension:

- All common nouns of feminine gender with an -a ending.
- The feminine noun **мати/mati** (mother), which takes the form **матер/mater** through the cases.
- A small number of common nouns of masculine gender with an -a ending. Although declining as feminine nouns, these nouns are referred to as masculine nouns in the singular and feminine nouns in the plural. These nouns generally refer to masculine animates:

старешина	starešina	officer, chief
вођа	vođa	leader
судија	sudija	judge
слуга	sluga	servant
младожења	mladoženja	bridegroom

- Proper feminine and masculine names and surnames ending in -a:

Нада	Nada	Nada (female)
Никола	Nikola	Nikola (male)

- Nouns declining as feminine but applicable to both genders, ending in -a:

луталица	lutalica	wanderer
пијаница	pijanica	drunk
издајица	izdajica	traitor

- Masculine nouns of foreign origin ending in **-ист/ist, -т/t** to which the letter **-a** has been added, because of which they follow the second declension in the singular, while joining the first declension in the plural:

спортиста	sportista	sportsman
економиста	ekonomista	economist
туриста	turista	tourist
демократа	demokrata	democrat

- Nouns expressing endearment in both genders, ending in -a:

дека	deka	grandpa (m)
меда	meda	teddy bear (m)

- Collective nouns, which are plural in meaning but have a singular form, ending in -a:

господа	gospoda	gentry
живина	živina	poultry

Several different endings may occur in the following cases depending on the noun being declined:

In the dative and locative singular:

- The majority of nouns have an -и/i ending:

кући	kući	(to/on) the house
другарици	drugarici	(to/about) the girl-friend
деди	dedi	(to/about) grandfather

- Nouns denoting names of places with adjectival endings have an -ој/oj ending:

Енглеској	Engleskoj	(to/in) England
Мађарској	Mađarskoj	(to/in) Hungary

In the vocative singular:

- The noun мати/mati (mother) has an -и/i ending;
- Most nouns and bisyllabic nouns ending in -ица/ica have an -o ending:

Птицо! (птица)	*Ptico!* (ptica)	(Hey) bird!
Жено! (жена)	*Ženo!* (žena)	(Hey) woman!
Слуго! (слуга)	*Slugo!* (sluga)	(Hey) servant!

- Proper nouns with short accents and names of places ending in -ска/ska, -чка/čka, -шка/ška have the ending -a:

Лила! (Лила)	*Lila!* (Lila)	(Hey) Lila!
Марија! (Марија)	*Marija!* (Marija)	(Hey) Marija!
Мађарска! (Мађарска)	*Mađarska!* (Mađarska)	(Hey) Hungary!

Declension of nouns

- While some names of places ending in -ка/ka have the ending -o:

  Лико! (Лика)   Liko! (Lika)   (Hey) Lika!

- Nouns of more than two syllables ending in -ица/ica have the ending -e:

  луталице! (луталица)   lutalice! (lutalica)   (Hey) wanderer!

  пијанице! (пијаница)   pijanice! (pijanice)   (Hey) drunkard!

  луткице! (луткица)   lutkice! (lutkica)   (Hey) doll! (dim.)

In the genitive plural:

- Most nouns, including those ending in consonants other than -ст/st, -шт/št, -шч/šč, -шћ/šć, -зд/zd and -жд/žd, where a fleeting a has been inserted, have an -a ending:

  кућа (кућа)   kuća (kuća)   (without) houses

  судија (судија)   sudija (sudija)   (without) judges

  пијаница (пијанице)   pijanica (pijanica)   (without) drunkards

  жртава (жртва)   žrtava (žrtva)   (without) victims

  земаља (земља)   zemalja (zemlja)   (without) countries

- Nouns, the stems of which end in a cluster of consonants, but are without the insertion of a fleeting a, have an -и/i ending:

  фунти (фунта)   funti (funta)   (without) pounds

  лопти (лопта)   lopti (lopta)   (without) balls

  молби (молба)   molbi (molba)   (without) applications

  мајки (мајка)   majki (majka)   (without) mothers

  тајни (тајна)   tajni (tajna)   (without) secrets

- The nouns рука/ruka (hand), нога/noga (leg), слуга/sluga (servant) have a -у/u ending:

  руку (рука)   ruku (ruka)   (without) arms

  ногу (нога)   nogu (noga)   (without) legs

The endings for the second declension are as follows:

Declension of nouns

	Singular		Plural	
	Masculine	Feminine	Masculine	Feminine
Nom.	**-а/a**	**-а/a**	**-е/e**	
		-и/i		
Gen.	**-е/e**		**-а/a**	
			-у/u	
			-и/i	
Dat.	**-и/i**	**-и/i**	**-ама**	
		-ој/oj		
Acc.	**-у/u**		**-е/e**	
Voc.	**-а/a**		**-е/e**	
		-е/e		
		-о/o		
		-и/i		
Inst.	**-ом/om**		**-ама**	
Loc.	**-и/i**	**-и/i**	**-ама**	
		-ој/oj		

7 Nouns

Second declension – **E** declension

Singular

	Feminine				Masculine	
	woman	squirrel	hand	mother	tourist	slave
Nom.	жен*а*	верверищ*а*	рук*а*	мат*и*	турист*а*	слуг*а*
	žen*a*	veveric*a*	ruk*a*	mat*i*	turist*a*	slug*a*
Gen.	жен*е*	верверищ*е*	рук*е*	мат*ере*	турист*е*	слуг*е*
	žen*e*	veveric*e*	ruk*e*	mat*ere*	turist*e*	slug*e*
Dat.	жен*и*	верверищ*и*	руц*и*	мат*ери*	турист*и*	слуг*и*
	žen*i*	veveric*i*	ruc*i*	mat*eri*	turist*i*	slug*i*
Acc.	жен*у*	верверищ*у*	рук*у*	мат*ер*	турист*у*	слуг*у*
	žen*u*	veveric*u*	ruk*u*	mat*er*	turist*u*	slug*u*
Voc.	жен*о*	верверищ*е*	рук*о*	мат*и*	турист*о*	слуг*о*
	žen*o*	veveric*e*	ruk*o*	mat*i*	turist*o*	slug*o*
Inst.	жен*ом*	верверищ*ом*	рук*ом*	мат*ером*	турист*ом*	слуг*ом*
	žen*om*	veveric*om*	ruk*om*	mat*erom*	turist*om*	slug*om*
Loc.	жен*и*	верверищ*и*	руц*и*	мат*ери*	турист*и*	слуг*и*
	žen*i*	veveric*i*	ruc*i*	mat*eri*	turist*i*	slug*i*

Declension of nouns

Second declension – **E** declension

Plural

	Feminine				Masculine	
	woman	squirrel	hand	mother	tourist	slave
Nom.	жен*е*	вевериц*е*	рук*е*	мат*ере*	туристи/turisti	слуг*е*
	žen*e*	veveric*e*	ruk*e*	mat*ere*	First declension	slug*e*
Gen.	жен*а*	вевериц*а*	рук*у*	мат*ера*		слуг*у*
	žen*e*	veveric*e*	ruk*e*	mat*era*		slug*e*
Dat.	жен*ама*	вевериц*ама*	рук*ама*	мат*ерама*		слуг*ама*
	žen*ama*	veveric*ama*	ruk*ama*	mat*erama*		slug*ama*
Acc.	жен*е*	вевериц*е*	рук*е*	мат*ере*		слуг*е*
	žen*e*	veveric*e*	ruk*e*	mat*ere*		slug*e*
Voc.	жен*е*	вевериц*е*	рук*е*	мат*ере*		слуг*е*
	žen*e*	veveric*e*	ruk*e*	mat*ere*		slug*e*
Inst.	жен*ама*	вевериц*ама*	рук*ама*	мат*ерама*		слуг*ама*
	žen*ama*	veveric*ama*	ruk*ama*	mat*erama*		slug*ama*
Loc.	жен*ама*	вевериц*ама*	рук*ама*	мат*ерама*		слуг*ама*
	žen*ama*	veveric*ama*	ruk*ama*	mat*erama*		slug*ama*

7.4.3 Feminine nouns ending in a consonant, in -o, -ост/ost or -ад/ad, and the noun кћи/kći

The third declension is also referred to as the **И/I** declension because of the **-и/i** endings of nouns in the genitive singular. There are no hard or soft consonant distinctions in this declension, nor are there any animate/inanimate endings.

The following types of nouns belong to this declension:

- Feminine nouns ending in a consonant in the nominative singular:

    | ствар | stvar | thing |
    | љубав | ljubav | love |

- Feminine nouns ending in -o:

    | мисао | misao | thought |
    | со | so | salt |

- Abstract feminine nouns ending in -ост/ost:

    | милост | milost | mercy |
    | стварност | stvarnost | reality |

- Collective feminine nouns ending in -ад/ad:

    | телад | telad | calves |
    | јагњад | jagnjad | lambs |

- The feminine noun кћи/kći (daughter).

Several different endings may occur in the following cases depending on the noun being declined:

In the nominative and accusative singular:

- All the nouns have a consonant ending except for кћи/kći, мисао/misao and со/so:

    | љубав | ljubav | love |
    | ствар | stvar | thing |

- The noun кћи/kći has two forms in the nominative -кћи/kći and кћер/kćer:

    | кћи | kći | daughter |
    | кћер | kćer | daughter |

- The nouns **мисао/misao** and **со/so** end with the letter -o in the nominative singular which reverts to л/l in its stem and through the cases.

Declension of nouns

In the instrumental singular:

- The majority of nouns have an **-и/i** ending, particularly when used with a preposition:

    | са ствари | sa stvari | (with) a thing |
    | са мисли | sa misli | (with) a thought |

- For nouns used without a preposition and those whose stem ends in ч/č, ж/ž, ш/š, с/s, з/z, р/r, the **-и/i** ending can be replaced by **-jу/ju*** or **-у/u**:

    | речи | reči | (with) a word |
    | речју | rečju | (with) a word |

    * In the instrumental singular, nouns whose stem ends in the consonants -б/b, -в/v, -м/m or -п/p have the ending -љу/lju while those ending in the letters -л/l, -н/n, -т/t, -д/d change to -љу/lju, -њу/nju, -ћу/ću and -ђу/dju respectively.

    | љубави/љубављу | ljubavi/ljubavlju | (with) love |
    | мисли/мишљу* | misli/mišlju* | (with) a thought |
    | соли/сољу | soli/solju | (with) salt |
    | младости/младошћу* | mladosti/mladošću* | (with) youth |

    * The **-с/s** changes to **-ш/š** before the acquired ending.

In the genitive plural:

- Most nouns have an **-и/i** ending:

    | младости (младост) | mladosti (mladost) | (without) youth |
    | радости (радост) | radosti (radost) | (without) joy |
    | жалости (жалост) | žalosti (žalost) | (without) sorrow |
    | соли (соли) | soli (so) | (without) salt |

мисли (мисли)   misli (misao)   (without) thoughts

телади (телад)   teladi (telad)   (without) calves

- The nouns **очи/oči***, **уши/uši***, **кости/kosti**, have a **-ију/iju** ending:

очију (очи)   očiju (oči)   (without) eyes

ушију (уши)   ušiju (uši)   (without) ears

костију (кости)   kostiju (kosti)   (without) bones

* These nouns have their singular form in the neuter gender which declines in the first declension in the singular.

The endings for the third declension are as follows:

	Singular		Plural
		Feminine	
Nom.	consonant		**-и/i**
Gen.	**-и/i**		**-и/i**
			-ију/iju
Dat.	**-и/i**		**-има/ima**
Acc.	consonant		**-и/i**
Voc.		**-и/i**	
Inst.	**-и/i**		**-има/ima**
	-ју/ju		
	-у/u		
	-љу/lju		
Loc.	**-и/i**		**-има/ima**

Declension of nouns

Third declension – И/I declension

Feminine singular

	thing	thought	word	daughter	hen
Nom.	ствар	мисао	реч	кћи/кћер	кокош
	stvar	misao	reč	kći	kokoš
Gen.	ствари	мисли	речи	кћери	кокоши
	stvari	misli	reči	kćeri	kokoši
Dat.	ствари	мисли	речи	кћери	кокоши
	stvari	misli	reči	kćeri	kokoši
Acc.	ствар	мисао	реч	кћи/кћер	кокош
	stvar	misao	reč	kći/kćer	kokoš
Voc.	ствари	мисли	речи	кћери	кокоши
	stvari	misli	reči	kćeri	kokoši
Inst.	ствари	мисли/мишљу	речи/речју	кћери/кћерју	кокоши/кокошју
	stvari	misli/mišlju	reči/rečju	kćeri/kćerju	kokoši/kokošju
Loc.	ствари	мисли	речи	кћери	кокоши
	stvari	misli	reči	kćeri	kokoši

7 Nouns

Third declension – **И/I** declension

Feminine plural

	thing	thought	word	daughter	hen	ears
Nom.	ствари	мисли	речи	кћери	кокоши	уши
	stvari	misli	reči	kćeri	kokoši	uši
Gen.	ствари	мисли	речи	кћери	кокоши/кокошију	ушију
	stvari	misli	reči	kćeri	kokoši/kokošiju	ušiju
Dat.	стварима	мислима	речима	кћерима	кокошима	ушима
	stvarima	mislima	rečima	kćerima	kokošima	ušima
Acc.	ствари	мисли	речи	кћери	кокоши	уши
	stvari	misli	reči	kćeri	kokoši	uši
Voc.	ствари	мисли	речи	кћери	кокоши	уши
	stvari	misli	reči	kćeri	kokoši	uši
Inst.	стварима	мислима	речима	кћерима	кокошима	ушима
	stvarima	mislima	rečima	kćerima	kokošima	ušima
Loc.	стварима	мислима	речима	кћерима	кокошима	ушима
	stvarima	mislima	rečima	kćerima	kokošima	ušima

7.4.4 | Declension of irregular nouns

Nouns with irregular stems and endings have irregular declensions:

1. Infixes in **-ов/ov** and **-ев/ev**:
   Most monosyllabic masculine nouns, with the exception of **дан/dan** (day), **коњ/konj** (horse), **зуб/zub** (tooth), **сат/sati** (meaning 'hour' and not 'clock', which does have the infix **-ов/ov**), and several others, have in the plural declension the following infixes added to their stem preceding the regular plural case ending: **-ов/ov** added to hard consonants:

град – градови/grad – gradovi (town),
врх – врхови/vrh – vrhovi (top), etc.

and **-ев/ev** added to soft consonants:

муж – мужеви/muž – muževi (husband), **пуж – пужеви/puž – puževi** (snail), **краљ – краљеви/kralj – kraljevi** (king), etc.

The declension of these nouns in the singular is regular in the first declension:

	Singular		Plural	
	Hard	Soft	Hard	Soft
Nom.	град	пуж	градови	пужеви
	grad	puž	gradovi	puževi
Gen.	града	пужа	градова	пужева
	grada	puža	gradova	puževa
Dat.	граду	пужу	градовима	пужевима
	gradu	pužu	gradovima	puževima
Acc.	град	пужа	градове	пужеве
	grad	puža	gradove	puževe
Voc.	граде	пужу	градови	пужеви
	grade	pužu	gradovi	puževi
Inst.	градом	пужем	градовима	пужевима
	gradom	pužem	gradovima	puževima
Loc.	граду	пужу	градовима	пужевима
	gradu	pužu	gradovima	puževima

Declension of nouns

2 Infixes in -ен/en and -ет/et:
Some neuter nouns ending in -e have the following infixes added to the stem in the singular in the genitive, dative, instrumental and locative cases, and in all cases in the plural:

-ен/en:

име/ime (name), **време/vreme** (time/weather), **племе/pleme** (tribe), **раме/rame** (shoulder), **семе/seme** (seed), etc.

-ет/et:

дугме/dugme (button), **теле/tele** (calf), **пиле/pile** (chick) and **дрво/drvo** (tree or wood) which has two plurals with different meanings. The one meaning 'tree' has the above infix.

	Singular		Plural	
	name	button	name	button
Nom.	име	дугме	имена	дугмета
	ime	dugme	imena	dugmeta
Gen.	имена	дугмета	имена	дугмета
	imena	dugmeta	imena	dugmeta
Dat.	имену	дугмету	именима	дугметима
	imenu	dugmetu	imenima	dugmetima
Acc.	име	дугме	имена	дугмета
	ime	dugme	imena	dugmeta
Voc.	име	дугме	имена	дугмета
	ime	dugme	imena	dugmeta
Inst.	именом	дугметом	именима	дугметима
	imenom	dugmetom	imenima	dugmetima
Loc.	имену	дугмету	именима	дугметима
	imenu	dugmetu	imenima	dugmetima

The noun **дете/dete** (child) only declines in the singular, when it declines in the same way as **дугме/dugme** (button).

3   Infixes in **-ec/es**:
    Some neuter nouns ending in -o (**небо/nebo** (sky), **чудо/čudo** (miracle, wonder)) have this infix added in the plural form only:

Declension of nouns

	Singular	Plural
	sky	skies
Nom.	**небо**	**небеса**
	nebo	**nebesa**
Gen.	**неба**	**небеса**
	neba	**nebesa**
Dat.	**небу**	**небесима**
	nebu	**nebesima**
Acc.	**небо**	**небеса**
	nebo	**nebesa**
Voc.	**небо**	**небеса**
	nebo	**nebesa**
Inst.	**небом**	**небесима**
	nebom	**nebesima**
Loc.	**небу**	**небесима**
	nebu	**nebesima**

4   Nouns formed from verbs, where the ending **-лац/lac** replaces the infinitive ending:

читалац/čitalac (reader) **преводилац/prevodilac** (interpreter) **руководилац/rukovodilac** (leader), etc.

have an irregular declension where the ending **-лац/lac** appears only in the nominative singular and the genitive plural:

	Singular	Plural
	reader	readers
Nom.	читалац	читаоци
	čit**a**l**a**c	čitaoci
Gen.	читаоца	читалаца
	čitaoca	čit**a**l**a**ca
Dat.	читаоцу	читаоцима
	čitaocu	čitaocima
Acc.	читаоца	читаоце
	čitaoca	čitaoce
Voc.	читаоче	читаоци
	čitaoče	čitaoci
Inst.	читаоцем	читаоцима
	čitaocem	čitaocima
Loc.	читаоцу	читаоцима
	čitaocu	čitaocima

5   Nouns ending in **-ин/in** which refer to a person belonging to a certain place, nationality, religion, etc. drop the **-ин/in** ending in the plural stem. The singular declension is regular:

Declension of nouns

	Singular	Plural
	Serb	Serbs
Nom.	**Србин**	**Срби**
	Srbin	**Srbi**
Gen.	**Србина**	**Србе**
	Srbina	**Srbe**
Dat.	**Србину**	**Србима**
	Srbinu	**Srbima**
Acc.	**Србина**	**Србе**
	Srbina	**Srbe**
Voc.	**Србине**	**Срби**
	Srbine	**Srbi**
Inst.	**Србином**	**Србима**
	Srbinom	**Srbima**
Loc.	**Србину**	**Србима**
	Srbinu	**Srbima**

6   **брат/brat** (brother) is declined regularly in the singular in the first declension. The plural form is **браћа/braća** and it declines as a regular feminine noun in the second declension.

7   **човек/čovek** (man) has a singular only. Preceded by the numbers 2, 3 and 4, it declines as the genitive singular for masculine nouns in the first declension.

In the plural (and after and including the number 5) **човек/čovek** (man) becomes **људи/ljudi** (people), which also belongs to the first declension, with an **-и/i** ending in the genitive plural.

Chapter 8

Pronouns

Pronouns are words used to replace nouns, adjectives and numbers. They have gender and number, as well as declension.

A pronoun can be any of the following:

1. Personal
2. Reflexive
3. Possessive
4. Demonstrative
5. Relative
6. Interrogative
7. Indefinite
8. Negative
9. Universal
10. Compounded

The following behave as nouns:

1. Personal pronouns
2. Reflexive pronouns
3. Demonstrative pronouns
4. Interrogative pronouns – ко/ko (who?) and шта/šta (what?)
5. Indefinite pronouns – неко/neko (someone)
   нешто/nešto (something)
   ико/iko (anyone)
   ишта/išta (anything) etc.
6. Negative pronouns – нико/niko (no-one)
   ништа/ništa (nothing) etc.

The following pronouns replace adjectives and numbers and answer to the questions: what kind? and which?

Pronouns

1. Possessive pronouns
2. Demonstrative pronouns (these can also replace nouns)
3. Interrogative pronouns – **који/koji** (which?)
   какав/kakav (what kind?)
   чији/čiji (whose?)
4. Indefinite pronouns – **неки/neki** (some)
   некакав/nekakav (some kind)
   нечији/nečiji (someone's)
   икоји/ikoji (any one)
   икакав/ikakav (any kind)
   ичији/ičiji (anyone's) etc.
5. Negative pronouns – **никоји/nikoji** (no-one)
   никакав/nikakav (no kind)
   ничији/ničiji (no-one's) etc.

Some pronouns have the same form for all three genders:

1. Personal pronouns – **ја/ja** (I)
   ти/ti (you)
   ми/mi (we)
   ви/vi (you, pl.)
2. Reflexive pronouns – **се/se** (self)
3. Interrogative pronouns – **ко/ko** (who?)
   шта/šta (what?)

The following pronouns have different suffixes denoting the different genders:

1. Personal pronouns – **он/on** (he)
   она/ona (she)
   оно/ono (it)
2. Possessive pronouns – **мој/moj** (my, m)
   моја/moja (my, f)
   моје/moje (my, n)
3. Demonstrative pronouns – **тај/taj** (that, m)
   та/ta (that, f)
   то/to (that, n)
4. Interrogative pronouns – **чији/čiji** (whose, m)
   чија/čija (whose, f)
   чије/čije (whose, n)
5. Indefinite pronouns – **икакав/ikakav** (any kind, m)
   икаква/ikakva (any kind, f)
   икакво/ikakvo (any kind, n)

6 Negative pronouns –   никакав/nikakav (no kind, m)
                         никаква/nikakva (no kind, f)
                         никакво/nikakvo (no kind, n)

8.1 Personal pronouns

Personal pronouns refer to living and non-living things. They consist of the following:

1st person singular: The person speaking.	I	ja ja
2nd person singular: The person spoken to/listening.	you	ти ti
3rd person singular: The person listening but not participating in the conversation, or the person or thing being spoken about.	he/she/it	он/она/оно on/ona/ono
1st person plural: The person speaking and others.	we	ми mi
2nd person plural: The persons spoken to, or a person spoken to with respect or in formal address. When followed by a verb in the past tense, the past participle ending is in the 2nd p.pl. masculine, regardless of the gender of the subject (where ordinarily 2nd p.pl. feminine or neuter would be expected when addressing a female or a neuter gender body): ви сте читали/vi ste čitali and not ви сте читале/vi ste čitale.	you	ви/Ви vi/Vi (capitalised showing respect or in formal address in correspondence)
3rd person plural: The persons listening but not participating in the conversation, or the persons or things spoken about.	they	они (m/mixed gender) oni оне (f) one она (n) ona

Since it is believed that only humans are able to speak, the 1st and 2nd persons generally refer to humans. The 3rd person, being a passive participant in the conversation, or the object of it, can be either a living or a non-living thing.

Personal pronouns do not indicate gender in the 1st and 2nd persons, but only in the 3rd person. In Serbian, the 3rd person singular and plural forms have different endings for the three genders.

The formation of tenses, along with the appropriate auxiliary verbs, indicating person, number and/or gender make it possible for personal pronouns to frequently be omitted as the subject of a sentence.

| Смејале смо се. (ми) | Smejale smo se. (mi) | We (f) laughed. |
| Није га желео али га је ипак купио. (он) | Nije ga želeo ali ga je ipak kupio. (on) | (He) didn't want it but (he) nonetheless bought it. |

The personal pronoun may also be omitted as the subject of a subordinate clause if it is the same as that in the main clause and whenever the subject has already been referred to and is clearly known:

Они ће доћи код Вас у посету ако се (они) врате до подне.	Oni će doći kod Vas u posetu ako se (oni) vrate do podne.	They will come to visit you if (they) return by noon.
– Био сам код жене у болници јуче.	– Bio sam kod žene u bolnici juče.	– I visited (my) wife in the hospital yesterday.
– Нисам знао да је у болници. (она).	– Nisam znao da je u bolnici. (ona)	– I didn't know (she) was in hospital.

Personal pronouns are divided into stressed and unstressed pronouns. Unstressed personal pronouns are enclitics and as such must follow a given word order (see Chapter 13 Enclitics).

8.1.1 Declension of personal pronouns

In addition to indicating gender and number, personal pronouns also decline. Pronouns for 1st person and 2nd person, both singular and plural, as well as the reflexive pronoun **се/se** (self), decline as feminine nouns ending in **-a** (**кућа/kuća**) in the genitive, dative, locative and instrumental cases. They do not have a form in the vocative case:

8 Pronouns

	Singular			Plural	
	1st p.	2nd p.	Reflexive	1st p.	2nd p.
Nom.	ја	ти	–	ми	ви
	ja	ti		mi	vi
Gen.	мене – ме	тебе – те	себе	нас	вас
	mene – me	tebe – te	sebe	nas	vas
Dat.	мени – ми	теби – ти	себи	нама – нам	вама – вам
	meni – mi	tebi – ti	sebi	nama – nam	vama – vam
Acc.	мене – ме	тебе – те	себе – се	нас	вас
	mene – me	tebe – te	sebe – se	nas	vas
Voc.	–				
Inst.	мном, мноме	тобом	собом	нама	вама
	mnom, mnome	tobom	sobom	nama	vama
Loc.	мени	теби	себи	нама	вама
	meni	tebi	sebi	nama	vama

Personal pronouns in the 3rd person belong to the pronominal declension:

	Singular			Plural		
	Masculine	Neuter	Feminine	Masculine	Neuter	Feminine
Nom.	он	оно	она	они	она	оне
	on	ono	ona	oni	ona	one
Gen.	њега – га	ње – је		њих – их		
	njega – ga	nje – je		njih – ih		
Dat.	њему – му	њој – јој		њима – им		
	njemu – mu	njoj – joj		njima – im		
Acc.	њега – га – њ	њу, ју, је		њих – их		
	njega – ga – nj	nju, ju, je		njih – ih		
Voc.	–	–		–		
Inst.	њиме – њим	њоме, њом		њима		
	njime – njim	njome – njom		njima		
Loc.	њему	њој		њима		
	njemu	njoj		njima		

The masculine and neuter forms in the singular are the same except in the nominative, while the plural forms for all three genders are the same in the genitive and accusative, and in the dative, instrumental and locative.

Personal pronouns

8.1.2 Stressed personal pronouns

Stressed personal pronouns are the long pronouns in the genitive, dative and accusative cases. The instrumental case also has a long form. They decline as follows:

	Singular					Plural		
	1st p.	2nd p.	3rd p.			1st p.	2nd p.	3rd p.
	I	you	he	she	it	we	you	they
Gen.	мене	тебе	њега	ње	њега	нас	вас	њих
	mene	tebe	njega	nje	njega	nas	vas	njih
Dat.	мени	теби	њему	њој	њему	нама	вама	њима
	meni	tebi	njemu	njoj	njemu	nama	vama	njima
Acc.	мене	тебе	њега	њу	њега	нас	вас	њих
	mene	tebe	njega	nju	njega	nas	vas	njih
Inst.	мном(е)	тобом	њим(е)	њом(е)	њим(е)	нама	вама	њима
	mnom(e)	tobom	njim(e)	njom(e)	njim(e)	nama	vama	njima

They can take almost any position in the word order, and are used in the following instances:

1 When a personal pronoun begins a sentence, it has to be stressed:

   ***Тебе* су позвали.**   ***Tebe* su pozvali.**   They invited *you*.

   ***Њега* сви воле.**   ***Njega* svi vole.**   Everybody likes *him*.

2 Following conjunctions **а/a** (and, but), **и/i** (and) and **ни/ni** (neither):

   Писали су *и* вама *и* нама.   **Pisali su *i* vama *i* nama.**   They wrote *to you and to us*.

   Њој су купили цвеће *а* њему флашу вина.   **Njoj su kupili cveće *a njemu* flašu vina.**   They bought flowers for her *and* a bottle of wine for him.

3 In the dative and genitive when used with a preposition:

| Да ли је ово поклон *од тебе*? | Da li je ovo poklon *od tebe*? | Is this a present *from you*? |
| Дете је отишло *ка њему*. | Dete je otišlo *ka njemu*. | The child went *towards him*. |

4 When emphasis or contrast are required:

| Не обраћа се *теби*! | Ne obraća se *tebi*! | He's not speaking *to you*! |
| *Њега* ми је доста! | *Njega* mi je dosta! | I've had enough *of him*! |

In the instrumental singular, the 1st person and all three genders in the 3rd person have two forms: **мном**/**mnom** and **мноме**/**mnome**, **њим**/**njim** and **њиме**/**njime**, and **њом**/**njom** and **њоме**/**njome**. Although the first form is short, it is not an enclitic and is usually used with a preposition, while the longer form is usually used without a preposition:

Хајде *са мном* у биоскоп.	Hajde *sa mnom* u bioskop.	Come *with me* to the cinema.
Моји се родитељи поносе *мноме*.	Moji se roditelji ponose *mnome*.	My parents are proud *of me*.
Били смо у биоскопу *са њом*.	Bili smo u bioskopu *sa njom*.	We were in the cinema *with her*.
Мој се брат оженио *њоме*.	Moj se brat oženio *njome*.	My brother married *her*.

8.1.3 | Unstressed personal pronouns

Unstressed personal pronouns are the short form of pronouns given in the genitive, dative and accusative cases. They are also called pronominal enclitics and are as follows:

	Singular					Plural		
	1st p.	2nd p.	3rd p.			1st p.	2nd p.	3rd p.
	I	you	he	she	it	we	you	they
Gen.	ме	те	га	је	га	нас	вас	их
	me	te	ga	je	ga	nas	vas	ih
Dat.	ми	ти	му	јој	му	нам	вам	им
	mi	ti	mu	joj	mu	nam	vam	im
Acc.	ме	те	га – њ	ју – је	га – њ	нас	вас	их
	me	te	ga – nj	ju – je	ga – nj	nas	vas	ih

Feminine pronouns in the accusative have two short forms: **ју/ju** and **је/je**. When the pronominal enclitic is followed by the verbal enclitic **је/je** ('is', auxiliary to past tense), or the word preceding the enclitic ends with -**је/je**, the short form **ју/ju** is used. Otherwise **је/je** is used:

Она *је* купила књигу.	Ona *je* kupila knjigu.	She *bought* the book.
Она *ју је* купила.	Ona *ju je* kupila.	She *bought* it. (book – f.)

Masculine and neuter pronouns also have two short, enclitic forms in the accusative. The **га/ga** form is generally used. **њ/nj** is used only with prepositions taking that case (with the stress being transferred from the pronoun onto the preposition), where ordinarily the long, stressed form would be used.

Хоћете ли *га* позвати?	Hoćete li *ga* pozvati?	Will you call *him*?
Овај позив је *за њ* (*за њега*).	Ovaj poziv je *za nj* (*za njega*).	This invitation is *for him*.

Unstressed personal pronouns cannot begin a sentence. They cannot ordinarily follow a preposition or the conjunctions **и/i** (and) and **а/a** (and, but). They are enclitics and must follow the enclitic word order. (See Chapter 13 Enclitics.)

8.1.4 Order of unstressed personal pronouns

The following order of the short form of personal pronouns, enclitics, must be followed when two or more pronominal enclitics appear together:

1   The dative case:

ми	ти	му	јој	му	нам	вам	им
mi	ti	mu	joj	mu	nam	vam	im

2   The genitive case:

ме	те	га – њ	је	га	нас	вас	их
me	te	ga – nj	je	ga	nas	vas	ih

3   The accusative case:

ме	те	га – њ	ју – је	га – њ	нас	вас	их
me	te	ga – nj	ju – je	ga – nj	nas	vas	ih

Ана је купила књигу брату.	Ana je kupila knjigu bratu.	Anna bought *a book for her brother*.
Купилу *му ју* је. (dat./acc.)	Kupila *mu ju* je. (dat./acc.)	She bought *it for him*.
Младен је дао новац сестри.	Mladen je dao novac sestri.	Mladen gave *the money to his sister*.
Дао *јој га* је. (dat./acc.)	Dao *joj ga* je. (dat./acc.)	He gave *it to her*.
Сећаш ли *се* куће?	Sećaš li *se* kuće?	Do you remember *the house*?
Сећаш ли *је* се! (gen.)	Sećaš li *je* se? (gen.)	Do you remember *it*?

Enclitics in the genitive are generally used with verbs that take that case.

8.2 Reflexive pronouns

Reflexive pronouns are intrinsically related to reflexive verbs. When the subject of an action is also the object of that action, it is said that the action is reflected back onto the subject, thus making the subject the bearer, i.e. the object, of its own action. This reflection is expressed through the use of the reflexive pronoun **себе/sebe** (oneself) or its short, enclitic form **се/se** (see Chapter 13 Enclitics). True reflexiveness is expressed with the use of the enclitic form **се/se** in the accusative case, while the long form **себе/sebe** is used as an emphatic.

Себе увек мораш да поштујеш.	*Sebe* uvek moraš da poštuješ.	You must always respect *yourself*.
Смири *се*.	Smiri *se*.	(*You*) calm (*yourself*) down.

Another reflexive pronoun with an emphatic function is the pronoun **сам/sam** (oneself) which is used with the long or the short form of **себе/sebe**:

Обећао је *самом себи* да неће пити.	Obećao je *samom sebi* da neće piti.	He promised to *himself* that he won't drink. (dat.)

The reflexive pronoun **себе/sebe** has no person, gender or number marker, while the reflexive pronoun **сам/sam** has gender and number.

Reflecting the traits of the subject, reflexive pronouns can be used in the following manner:

Reflexive pronouns

- As the direct object – in the accusative, both forms are used without a preposition. The reflexive pronoun has to be traced back to the subject, which in this instance is also the object, reflected by the pronoun:

Мајка *се* вратила.	Majka *se* vratila.	Mother has returned (*herself*).
Човек треба *самог себе* да воли.	Čovek treba *samog sebe* da voli.	One needs to love *oneself*.

- The reflexive pronoun **себе/sebe** can also be used in a context of reciprocity when the subject and object have a reciprocal relationship with each other, expressed through the verb (the English equivalent of 'each other' or 'one another'). In this case the two can be expressed as the subject while the reflexive pronoun **се/se** denotes the relationship of reciprocity and reflexivity:

(Џон воли Анку.)	(Džon voli Anku.)	(John loves Anka.)
Џон и Анка *се* воле.	Džon i Anka *se* vole.	John and Anka love *each other*.
Они *се* воле.	Oni *se* vole.	They love *each other*.

- As the indirect object – excluding the accusative case, in the long form:

Човек треба да се *собом* поноси.	Čovek treba da se *sobom* ponosi.	One should be proud of *oneself*. (inst.)

- Following prepositions – all cases, in the long form:

Он даје све *од себе*.	On daje sve *od sebe*.	He is giving all *of himself*.
Изађи на крај *са собом*.	Izađi na kraj *sa sobom*.	Sort *yourself* out.
Ја имам довољно *за себе*.	Ja imam dovoljno *za sebe*.	I have enough *for myself*.

The reflexive pronouns **себе/sebe** and **сам/sam** decline as follows:

Reflexive pronouns								
себе/sebe		**сам/sam**						
Long form	Enclitic	Singular			Plural			
		Masculine	Neuter	Feminine	Masculine	Neuter	Feminine
Nom.	–		сам	само	сама	сами	сама	саме
			sam	samo	sama	sami	sama	same
Gen.	себе		самог		саме	самих		
	sebe		samog		same	samih		
Dat.	себи		самом		самој	самима		
	sebi		samom		samoj	samima		
Acc.	себе	се	самог	само	саму	саме	сама	саме
	sebi	se	samog	samo	samu	same	sama	same
Voc.	–							
Instr.	собом		самим		самом	самима		
	sobom		samim		samom	samima		
Loc.	себи		самом		самој	самима		
	sebi		samom		samoj	samima		

The reflexive pronoun **себе/sebe** has no nominative or vocative case and has the same form for both singular and plural. Its enclitic form exists only in the accusative case (and sometimes in the genitive case), taking on the role of the object through reflection.

8.3 Possessive pronouns

Possessive pronouns indicate to whom or to what something belongs:

Чија је ово оловка?   **Čija je ovo olovka?**   Whose pencil is this?

Моја је.   *Moja* je.   It is *mine*.

Моја/moja (mine) refers to the pencil as well as to the person to whom it belongs, while **оловка/olovka** (pencil) is a feminine noun in the nominative singular. The pronoun **моја/moja** is given a feminine ending to reflect this.

In Serbian, possessive pronouns behave and decline as adjectives, and are referred to as adjectives and pronouns (see Section 9.4 Possessive adjectives). They have person and agree in case, number and gender with the noun that they qualify or to which they refer. The 3rd person singular and plural decline like indefinite adjectives (see Section 9.2 Indefinite adjectives), while the 1st and 2nd persons singular and plural decline as definite adjectives (see Section 9.3 Definite adjectives).

Possessive pronouns include the following in the nominative singular:

my	**мој, моје, моја**
	moj, moje, moja
your	**твој, твоје, твоја**
	tvoj, tvoje, tvoja
reflexive possessive pronoun:	**свој, своје, своја**
one's own	**svoj, svoje, svoja**
our	**наш, наше, наша**
	naš, naše, naša
your (pl.)	**ваш, ваше, ваша**
	vaš, vaše, vaša
his	**његов, његово, његова**
	njegov, njegovo, njegova
her	**њен, њено, њена**
	njen, njeno, njena
	њезин, њезино, њезина
	njezin, njezino, njezina
their	**њихов, њихово, њихова**
	njihov, njihovo, njihova

Possessive pronouns

Possessive pronouns: **твој/tvoj, наш/naš, ваш/vaš**, and the reflexive possessive pronoun **свој/svoj**, decline like **мој/moj**. The pronouns **наш/naš** (ours) and **ваш/vaš** (yours) take the soft consonantal endings -ег(а)/eg(a) instead of -ог(а)/og(a), and -ем(у)/em(u) instead of -ом(е)/om(e):

8 Pronouns

Possessive pronoun **мој/moj** (my)

	Singular			Plural		
	Masculine	Neuter	Feminine	Masculine	Neuter	Feminine
Nom.	мој	моје	моја	моји	моја	моје
	moj	moje	moja	moji	moja	moje
Gen.	мојег(а) – мог(а)	мојег(а) – мог(а)	моје		мојих	
	mojeg(a) – mog(a)	mojeg(a) – mog(a)	moje		mojih	
Dat.	мојем(у) – мом(е)	мојем(у) – мом(е)	мојој	мојима – мојим		
	mojem(u) – mom(e)	mojem(u) – mom(e)	mojoj	mojima – mojim		
Acc.	Same as nom./gen.	моје	моја	моје	моја	моје
		moje	moja	moje	moja	moje
Voc.	мој	моје	моја	моји	моја	моје
	moj	moje	moja	moji	moja	moje
Inst.	мојим	мојим	мојом	мојима – мојим		
	mojim	mojim	mojom	mojima – mojim		
Loc.	мојем(у) – мом(е)	мојем(у) – мом(е)	мојој	мојима – мојим		
	mojem(u) – mom(e)	mojem(u) – mom(e)	mojoj	mojima – mojim		

The possessive pronoun **свој/svoj** means 'one's own', and has gender, number and case. It is used when the object it describes belongs to the subject of the sentence or clause:

Ја волим своју жену.	Ja volim svoju ženu.	I love *my (own)* wife.
Ти волиш своју жену.	Ti voliš svoju ženu.	He loves *his (own)* wife.
Он воли *своју* жену.	On voli *svoju* ženu.	He loves *his (own)* wife.
Он воли његову жену.	On voli *njegovu* ženu.	He loves *his* wife.

The last sentence may mean that he loves someone else's wife as his own is not stipulated. Equally, the possessive pronoun cannot stand on its own, without a subject to trace it back to:

Possessive pronouns

| **Био је на вечери** | **Bio je na večeri** | He went to dinner |
| **са својом женом.** | **sa svojom ženom.** | with his wife. |

But not

| **Он и своја жена су** | **On i svoja žena** | He and his own wife |
| **били на вечери.** | **su bili na večeri.** | went to dinner. |

since the 'own' has no subject to belong to.

The possessive pronoun can also be omitted when it is clear from the context who the 'owner' is:

| **Он и жена су били** | **On i žena su bili** | He and (his) wife went |
| **на вечери.** | **na večeri.** | to dinner. |

The possessive pronouns **његов/njegov, њен/njen, њезин/njezin** decline as both indefinite and definite adjectives, with the latter being more frequently used:

Possessive pronoun **његов/njegov** (his)					
Singular			Plural		
Masculine	Neuter	Feminine	Masculine	Neuter	Feminine

	Masculine	Neuter	Feminine	Masculine	Neuter	Feminine
Nom.	његов	његово	његова	његови	његова	његове
	њен – њезин	њено – њезино	њена – њезина	њени – њезини	њена – њезина	њене – њезине
	njegov	njegovo	njegova	njegovi	njegova	njegove
	njen – njezin	njeno – njezino	njena – njezina	njeni – njezini	njena – njezina	njene – njezine
Gen.	његовог	његовог	његове		његових	
	њеног – њезиног	њеног – њезиног	њене – њезине		њених – њезиних	
	njegovog	njegovog	njegove		njegovih	
	njenog – njezinog	njenog – njezinog	njene – njezine		njenih – njezinih	
Dat.	његовом	његовом	његовој		његовим	
	њеном(е) – њезином(е)	њеном – њезином	њеној – њезиној		њеним – њезиним	
	njegovom	njegovom	njegovoj		njegovim	
	njenom(e) – njezinom(e)	njenom – njezinom	njenoj – njezinoj		njenim – njezinim	

Possessive pronoun **његов/njegov** (his)

		Singular			Plural		
		Masculine	Neuter	Feminine	Masculine	Neuter	Feminine
Acc.	Same as nom./gen.	његово	његову	његове	његова	његове
		њено – њезино	њену – њезину	њене – њезине	њена – њезина	њене – њезине
		njegovo	njegovu	njegove	njegova	njegove
		njeno – njezino	njenu – njezinu	njene – njezine	njena – njezina	njene – njezine
Voc.	његов	његово	његова	његови	његова	његове
	њен – њезин	њено – њезино	њена – њезина	њени – њезини	њена – њезина	њене – њезине
	njegov	njegovo	njegova	njegovi	njegova	njegove
	njen – njezin	njeno – njezino	njena – njezina	njeni – njezini	njena – njezina	njene – njezine
Inst.	његовим	његовим	његовом		његовим	
	њеним – њезиним	њеним – њезиним	њеном – њезином		њеним – њезиним	
	njegovim	njegovim	njegovom		njegovim	
	njenim njezinim	njenim njezinim	njenom njezinom		njenom njezinim	
Loc.	његовом	његовом	његовој		његовим	
	њеном(е) – њезином(е)	њеном – њезином	њеној – њезиној		њеним – њезиним	
	njegovom	njegovom	njegovoj		njegovim	
	njenom(e) njezinom(e)	njenom – njezinom	njenoj – njezinoj		njenin – njezinim	

8.4 Demonstrative pronouns

Demonstrative pronouns refer to the distance, size or type of thing or person that is being spoken about. The reference points are:

- The speakers themselves, whereby **овај/ovaj** (this one) refers to the 1st person or speaker, **тај/taj** (this/that one) refers to the 2nd person, listener or participant, and **онај/onaj** (that one) refers to the 3rd person, or the person or thing spoken about:

    Ова је моја соба, та је твоја а она је његова.

    Ova je moja soba, ta je tvoja a ona je njegova.

    This is my room, *that* one is yours and *that* one (over there) is his.

- Or the location of the speakers, whereby 'this' or 'that one', to whom reference has already been made, is demonstrated by *т*ај/*t*aj. 'This one over here', located close by, is demonstrated by *ов*ај/*ov*aj and 'that one over there', not so close by, is demonstrated by *он*ај/*on*aj. Other demonstrative pronouns formed from the stem of these, *толи*ки/*t*oliki (one this or that big), *ово*лики/*ov*oliki (one this big) and *оно*лики/*on*oliki (one that big), have the same distinction.

> Demonstrative pronouns

The demonstrative pronoun **ово/ovo**, when followed by a verb, equates to the English use of 'this (is)':

Ово је наша соба. **Ovo je naša soba.** *This is* our room.

Demonstrative pronouns include the following:

this one, that one	тај, то, та
	taj, to, ta
this one (over here)	овај, ово, ова
	ovaj, ovo, ova
that one (over there)	онај, оно, она
	onaj, ono, ona
such, like that one (over here)	такав, такво, таква
	takav, takvo, takva
such, like this one	овакав, овакво, оваква
	ovakav, ovakvo, ovakva
such, like that one (over there)	онакав, онакво, онаква
	onakav, onakvo, onakva
(one) so big	толики, толико, толика
	toliki, toliko, tolika
(one) this big	оволики, оволико, оволика
	ovoliki, ovoliko, ovolika
(one) that big	онолики, онолико, онолика
	onoliki, onoliko, onolika
the same	исти, исто, иста
	isti, isto, ista

8 Pronouns

The demonstrative pronouns **овај/ovaj** and **онај/onaj** decline like **тај/taj**:

Demonstrative pronoun **тај/taj** (this, that)						
	Singular			Plural		
	Masculine	Neuter	Feminine	Masculine	Neuter	Feminine
Nom.	тај	то	та	ти	та	те
	taj	to	ta	ti	ta	te
Gen.	тога – тог		те		тих	
	toga – tog		te		tih	
Dat.	том(е) – том		тој		тима – тим	
	tom(e) – tom		toj		tima – tim	
Acc.	Same as nom./gen.	то	ту	те	та	те
		to	tu	te	ta	te
Voc.	–					
Inst.	тим		том		тима – тим	
	tim		tom		tima – tim	
Loc.	том(е) – том		тој		тима – тим	
	tom(e) – tom		toj		tima – tim	

The demonstrative pronouns **такав/takav**, **овакав/ovakav** and **онакав/onakav** decline like demonstrative (indefinite) adjectives:

Demonstrative pronoun **такав/takav** (like this/that)						
	Singular			Plural		
	Masculine	Neuter	Feminine	Masculine	Neuter	Feminine
Nom.	такав	такво	таква	такви	таква	такве
	takav	takvo	takva	takvi	takva	takve
Gen.	таквог		такве		таквих	
	takvog		takve		takvih	
Dat.	таквом		таквој		таквим	
	takvom		takvoj		takvim	
Acc.	Same as nom./gen.	такво	такву	такве	таква	такве
		takvo	takvu	takve	takva	takve

Voc.	–		
Inst.	таквим	таквом	таквим
	takvim	takvom	takvim
Loc.	таквом	таквој	таквим
	takvom	takvoj	takvim

8.5 Relative pronouns

Relative pronouns begin a subordinating clause and refer to the noun preceding the clause:

| Ово је кућа, *коју* желимо да купимо. | Ovo je kuća, *koju* želimo da kupimo. | This is the house, *which* we wish to buy. |
| Ово је кућа, *какву* нисте још видели. | Ovo je kuća, *kakvu* niste još videli. | This is a house, the *kind of which* you have not seen before. |

There are seven basic types of relative pronouns in Serbian. These are divided into two categories:

1. **ко**/**ko** (who), has case and is masculine singular, and **шта**/**šta** (what) and (**оно**) **што**/(ono) što (that which), have case and are neuter singular:

Свако *ко* дође код нас похвали нашу башту.	Svako *ko* dođe kod nas pohvali našu baštu.	Everyone *who* comes to our place praises our garden.
Џон је човек *кога* Ана воли.	Džon je čovek *koga* Ana voli.	John is the man *whom* Ana loves.
Оно *чиме* пишеш се зове оловка.	Ono *čime* pišeš se zove olovka.	That *what* (which) you are writing with is called a pencil.

2. **који**/**koji** (which), **чији**/**čiji** (whose), **какав**/**kakav** (the quality/kind/type of), **колики**/**koliki** (the amount/size/extent of) have number, gender and case:

| Траже кафану у *којој* је дозвољено пушење. | Traže kafanu u *kojoj* je dozvoljeno pušenje. | They're looking for a pub *in which* smoking is allowed. |

8 Pronouns

Назови жену *чија* је ово хаљина.	Nazovi ženu *čija* je ovo haljina.	Call the woman *whose* dress this is.
Ово је жена *са чијом* сестром смо били на мору.	Ovo je žena *sa čijom* sestrom smo bili na moru.	This is the woman *with whose* sister we were at the coast.

The relative pronouns **ко/ko** (who) and **шта/šta** (what) decline in the following manner:

Relative pronouns **ко/ko** (who) and **шта/šta** (what)		
	Masculine	Neuter
Nom.	ко – ko	шта – šta
Gen.	кога – koga	чега – čega
Dat.	ком(е) – kom(e)	чему – čemu
Acc.	кога – koga	шта – šta
Voc.		–
Inst.	ким – kim	чим – čim
Loc.	ком(е) – kom(e)	чему – čemu

The relative pronoun **што/što** does not decline.

The relative pronouns **који/koji** (which) and **чији/čiji** (whose) decline like definite adjectives:

Relative pronouns **који/koji** (which) and **чији/čiji** (whose)						
	Singular			Plural		
	Masculine	Neuter	Feminine	Masculine	Neuter	Feminine
Nom.	који / koji	које / koje	која / koja	који / koji	која / koja	које / koje
Gen.	којег(а) – ког(а) / kojeg(a) – kog(a)	којег(а) – ког(а) / kojeg(a) – kog(a)	које / koje	којих / kojih	којих / kojih	којих / kojih
Dat.	ком(е) – ком / kom(e) – kom	ком(е) – ком / kom(e) – kom	којој / kojoj	којима – којим / kojima – kojim	којима – којим / kojima – kojim	којима – којим / kojima – kojim
Acc.	Same as nom./gen.	које / koje	којy / koju	које / koje	која / koja	које / koje

Voc.	–			
Inst.	којим kojim	којом kojom		којим(a) kojim(a)
Loc.	ком(е) – ком kom(e) – kom	којој kojoj		којима – којим kojima – kojim

The relative pronouns **какав/kakav** (the quality/kind/type of) and **колики/koliki** (the amount/size/extent of) decline like indefinite adjectives:

Relative pronoun **какав/kakav** (the quality/kind/type of)

	Singular			Plural		
	Masculine	Neuter	Feminine	Masculine	Neuter	Feminine
Nom.	какав kakav	какво kakvo	каква kakva	какви kakvi	каква kakva	какве kakve
Gen.	каквог kakvog		какве kakve	каквих kakvih		
Dat.	каквом kakvom		каквој kakvoj	каквим kakvim		
Acc.	Same as nom./gen.	какво kakvo	какву kakvu	какве kakve	каква kakva	какве kakve
Voc.	–	–	–	–	–	–
Inst.	каквим kakvim		каквом kakvom	каквим kakvim		
Loc.	каквом kakvom		каквој kakvoj	каквим kakvim		

8.6 Interrogative pronouns

Interrogative pronouns are used when asking questions and they generally begin a sentence. In form, they are closely related to relative pronouns and, excluding the pronoun **што/što** which as an interrogative takes on the meaning of 'Why?' as a short form of the adverb **зашто/zašto**, the list of pronouns is the same:

ко **ko**	who?	Is masculine singular and declines. Applicable to humans. All verbs used with it are in the singular, except the verb **бити/biti** (to be) which can be used in either the singular or the plural.
шта **šta**	what?	Is neuter singular and declines. Applicable to inanimate nouns. Verbs used with it are in the singular.
који **koji**	which?	Has number, gender and case. Applicable to animate and inanimate nouns. Verbs used with it can be in either the singular or the plural.
чији **čiji**	whose?	Same as **који/koji**.
какав **kakav**	what kind/type?	Has number, gender and case. Applicable to animate and inanimate nouns. Refers to the quality of the noun.
колики **koliki**	what size/extent?	Has number, gender and case. Applicable to animate and inanimate nouns. Refers to the quantity of the noun.

Ко су она деца?	*Ko* su ona deca?	*Who* are those children?
Кога сте позвали на вечеру?	*Koga* ste pozvali na večeru?	*Whom* have you invited for dinner?
Шта су вам купили за рођендан?	*Šta* su vam kupili za rođendan?	*What* have they bought you for your birthday?
Коју кошуљу да купим?	*Koju* kopulju da kupim?	*Which* shirt shall I buy?
Чија је ово кућа?	*Čija* je ovo kuća?	*Whose* house is this?
Какви су ови колачи?	*Kakvi* su ovi kolači?	*What kind* of cakes are these?
Колика вам је тераса?	*Kolika* vam je terasa?	*How big* is your terrace?

8.7 Universal pronouns

Used with animate and inanimate nouns, universal pronouns refer to a total sum or an individual part of a total sum.

| Он се са *сваким* дружи. | On se sa *svakim* druži. | He socialises with *everyone*. |

The following are the most common universal pronouns used in Serbian:

свако svako	everybody/ everyone	Is masculine singular and declines. Applicable to animate nouns. All verbs used with it are in the singular.
свашта svašta	all kinds of things	Is neuter singular and declines. Applicable to inanimate nouns. When used as subject in the sentence, verbs used with it can only be in the singular. Also means 'Really! Nonsense'!
сваки svaki	every, everybody	Has gender and case and is normally singular. Neuter form also overlaps in meaning with above pronoun **свако/svako**. Applicable to animate and inanimate nouns. Verbs used with it are in the singular.
свачији svačiji	everybody's	Has number, gender and case. Applicable to animate and inanimate nouns. Refers to possession.
свакакав svakakav	all kinds, types	Has number, gender and case. Applicable to animate and inanimate nouns. Refers critically or dismissively to the quality of the noun.
сви svi	everybody, all	Has case and gender. Applicable to plural nouns. Verbs used with it are in the plural. Refers to the quantity of the noun.
све sve	all, everything	Has case. Refers to inanimate nouns. Verbs used with it are in the singular.

Свако се жали на њу.	*Svako* se žali na nju.	*Everyone* complains about her.
Свашта сте ми испричали.	*Svašta* ste mi ispričali.	You've told me *all kinds of things*.
Свако дете воли да се игра.	*Svako* dete voli da se igra.	*Every* child loves to play.
Он је *свачији* љубимац.	On je *svačiji* ljubimac.	He is *everyone's* pet.

Свакакви се људи овде скупљају.	*Svakakvi* se ljudi ovde skupljaju.	*All kinds* of people gather here.
Сви су дошли на њен рођендан.	*Svi* su došli na njen rođendan.	*Everybody* came to her birthday (party).
Са њеном мајком можеш слободно о *свему* да разговараш.	Sa njenom majkom možeš slobodno o *svemu* da razgovaraš.	You can talk freely with her mother about *everything*.

The universal pronouns **свако/svako** (everybody/everyone) and **сваки/ сваки – сваки, свако, свака/svaki, svako, svaka** (every/everybody) decline like a definite adjective, while **свашта/svašta** (all kinds of things) declines like **шта/šta** (what).

The universal pronoun **свачији/svačiji** (everybody's) declines like the relative pronoun **чији/čiji** (whose) while **свакакав/svakakav** (all kinds/ types) declines like the relative pronoun **какав/kakav** (the quality/kind/ type of).

The pronouns **све/sve** (all) and **сви/svi** (everybody, all) decline in the following manner:

Universal pronouns **све/sve** (all) and **сви/svi** (everybody, all)

	Singular			Plural		
	Masculine	Neuter	Feminine	Masculine	Neuter	Feminine
Nom.		све sve		сви svi	сва sva	све sve
Gen.		свега svega			свих svih	
Dat.		свему svemu			свим/свима svim/svima	
Acc.		Same as nom.			све sve	
Voc.		–			–	
Inst.		свим svim			свим/свима svim/svima	
Loc.		свему svemu			свим/свима svim/svima	

Chapter 9
Adjectives

Unlike pronouns, which replace nouns, adjectives describe or modify nouns. They agree with the noun they describe in number, gender and case and every adjective has a form for all three genders, in the singular and in the plural.

Adjectives can describe a noun attributively – by either preceding or immediately following it:

Нова хаљина је била скупа.	*Nova* haljina je bila skupa.	The *new* dress was expensive.
Хаљина *нова* је била скупа.	Haljina *nova* je bila skupa.	The *new* dress was expensive.

or predicatively – by following the linking (copular) verb – 'to be, to become, to feel, to remain, to seem', etc.:

Нова хаљина је била *скупа*.	Nova haljina je bila *skupa*.	The new dress was *expensive*.
Предавање постаје *досадно*.	Predavanje postaje *dosadno*.	The lecture is becoming *boring*.

The following are the most common types of adjectives:

Type	Answers to the question	Adjective (given in m.sg.)	
Descriptive (indefinite)	какав/kakav (what kind)?	плав/plav	blue
Descriptive (definite)	који/koji (which)?	плави/plavi	blue
Possessive (definite)	чији/čiji (whose)?	сестрин/sestrin српски/srpski	sister's Serbian

9 Adjectives

Type	Answers to the question	Adjective (given in m.sg.)	
Material (indefinite)	чега/čega (of what material is it made – constructed)?	гвозеден/gvozden стаклен/staklen мастан/mastan	(made of) iron (made of) glass greasy
Time related (definite)	када/kada (when)?	летњи/letnji прошли/prošli	summer past
Place related (definite)	где/gde (where)?	доњи/donji последњи/poslednji	lower last

Какав је он човек?	*Kakav* je on čovek?	*What kind of* man is he?
Поштен.	*Pošten.*	Honest.
Који ти се човек допада?	*Koji* ti se čovek dopada?	*Which* man do you like?
Онај *црни* с брковима.	Onaj *crni* s brkovima.	The *dark-haired* one with a moustache.
Где је ваш стан?	*Gde* je vaš stan?	*Where* is your flat?
На *последњем* спрату.	Na *poslednjem* spratu.	On the *top* floor.

Descriptive adjectives have two forms: a definite and an indefinite form. In their use, definite adjectives could be said to be similar to the English definite article 'the', while indefinite adjectives are similar to the English indefinite article 'a/an'.

Стари шешир ме је добро служио.	*Stari* šešir me je dobro služio.	The *old* hat served me well. (def.)

The remaining adjectives have either one or the other form.

Adjectives cannot stand on their own in a sentence unless they follow the verb, in which case the indefinite form is used:

Овај шешир је *стар*.	Ovaj šešir je *star*.	This hat is *old*. (indef.)

Descriptive adjectives, and adverbs formed from them, have a comparative and a superlative form. Both forms agree with the noun in gender, number and case. The comparative form is formed by the addition of a suffix to the main adjective.

The suffix will depend on the adjective and its ending:

Овај шешир је *старији* од тебе.	Ovaj šešir je *stariji* od tebe.	This hat is *older* than you.
Мој пешкир је *мекши* од њеног.	Moj peškir je *mekši* od njenog.	My towel is *softer* than hers.

The superlative form is formed by the addition of one particular prefix: нај/naj, to the comparative form:

Ја сам овде *најстарији*.	Ja sam ovde *najstariji*.	I'm the *oldest* here.
Твој пешкир је стварно *најмекши*.	Tvoj peškir je stvarno *najmekši*.	Your towel really is the *softest*.

9.1 Classification of adjectives

Adjectives are classified into hard and soft, and definite and indefinite:

1   Adjectives are hard or soft depending on the last consonant of their base. The base of an adjective is the part without the feminine and neuter gender endings:

слободна/**слободн**о   **slobodn**a/**slobodn**o   free, vacant

слободн-   **slobodn-**

The following consonants are the base endings of soft adjectives:

Ј	J
Љ	Lj
Њ	Nj
Ц	C
Ћ	Ć
Ч	Č
Ш	Š
Ђ	Đ
Ж	Ž

Hard adjectives are those that end in any of the remaining consonants.

9 Adjectives

2 Descriptive adjectives have two forms, the definite and the indefinite. Both forms have gender, number and case, although they belong to different declensions.

(a) Definite adjectives carry a similar meaning to the English definite article 'the', and are used when describing a known, already mentioned thing or being:

Ово је *млади*	Ovo je *mladi*	This is *the young*
човек о којем сам	čovek o kojem	*man* about whom
ти причала.	sam ti pričala.	I spoke to you.

(b) Indefinite adjectives, similar in meaning to the English indefinite articles 'a' and 'an', are used when describing an unknown, until that particular point in time, unmentioned thing or being:

Паметан човек	*Pametan čovek*	*An intelligent*
размишља о	razmišlja o	*person* thinks
свему.	svemu.	about everything.

The following differences occur between the two forms:

(i) The main difference is in the masculine singular in the nominative case, where indefinite adjectives end in a consonant:

стар камион   **star kamion**   (an) old truck

while definite adjectives end in **-и/i**:

стари камион   **stari kamion**   (the) old truck

(ii) Adjectives describing nouns in the feminine gender differ only in accent, with the definite form having a longer unaccented final vowel than the indefinite form: лепā/lepā, and the indefinite form having a shorter accent: лепа/lepa;

(iii) Indefinite adjectives in the masculine and neuter gender decline as masculine nouns in the first declension (see Section 7.4.1 Masculine and neuter nouns), except in the instrumental case where indefinite adjectives have an **-им/im** rather than **-ом/om** ending. Indefinite adjectives in the feminine singular decline in the same way as definite adjectives, as do all three genders in the plural.

(iv) Definite adjectives follow an adjectival declension, which distinguishes between adjectives in the masculine and neuter singular base ending in hard and soft consonants. Where there is a hard adjectival ending, -o/o is included in the endings through the cases, and where the adjectival ending is soft, -e/e is included. This distinction is relevant only in the genitive, dative and locative cases for both genders, and the nominative case for the neuter gender. The definite form is becoming predominant in use in the modern language.

старог камиона	starog kamiona	(of the) old truck (gen.)
млађег камиона	mlađeg kamiona	(of the) younger truck (gen.)
чисто стакло	čisto staklo	clean glass (nom.)
веће стакло	veće staklo	larger glass (nom.)

(v) Feminine adjectives end in -a in both the definite and the indefinite form in the nominative singular, although the final vowel can be longer in the definite form:

| стара кућа | stara kuća | (an) old house (indefinite) |
| старā кућа | starā kuća | (the) old house (definite) |

(vi) Hard neuter adjectives end in -o, both in the definite and the indefinite form in the nominative singular, while soft neuter adjectives end in -e:

| старо дрво | staro drvo | (an/the) old tree – (indefinite/definite) |
| млађе дрво | mlađe drvo | (a/the) younger tree – (indefinite/definite) |

9.2 Indefinite adjectives

Indefinite adjectives are used when describing someone or something unknown, being mentioned for the first time. They are given in response to the question **какав/kakav?** (what kind/type?). Indefinite adjectives often carry the same reference as the English indefinite articles 'a' and 'an'.

Although the indefinite form is older than the definite form, in the spoken language today the definite form is more commonly used.

The indefinite form is mostly used when following a verb, and in those instances the adjective often stands alone:

| Имате ли слободан сто? | Imate li *slobodan* sto? | Do you have a *free* table? |
| Да, овај сто је слободан. | Da, ovaj sto je *slobodan*. | Yes, this table is *free*. |

9 Adjectives

The form following the numbers два/dva (two), три/tri (three), четири/četiri (four) for masculine and neuter nouns always has the ending -a:

Два лепа вука су легла да спавају.	**Dva lepa** vuka su legla da spavaju.	**Two beautiful** wolves lay down to sleep.
Три вештачка језера су изграђена.	**Tri veštačka** jezera su izgrađena.	**Three artificial** lakes have been built.

The following have only the indefinite form:

1. Adjectives created from nouns to indicate possession by the addition of the following suffixes:

    (a) -ов/ov, if the noun ends in a hard consonant for nouns of masculine and neuter gender;
    (b) -ев/ev, if the noun ends in a soft consonant for nouns of masculine and neuter gender;
    (c) љев/ljev, added to the base of masculine nouns ending in -в/v
    (d) -ин/in for feminine and masculine nouns endings in -a:

братов (брат) шешир	bratov (brat) šešir	brother's (brother) hat
младићев (младић) ауто	mladićev (mladić) auto	young man's (young man) car
Бранков (Бранко) сат	Brankov (Branko) sat	Branko's (Branko) watch
сестрин (сестра) мобител	sestrin (sestra) mobitel	sister's (sister) mobile phone
Лукина (Лука) тетка	Lukina (Luka) tetka	Luka's (Luka (man's name)) aunt

    Created from nouns and proper names, these adjectives take the indefinite form in the nominative and accusative (masculine inanimate) cases. In the remaining cases, including the accusative masculine animate, the definite form endings can also be used.

2. The number један/jedan (one) – often used to mean the equivalent of the English indefinite articles 'a' or 'an':

Успут смо срели **једног** слепог човека.	Usput smo sreli **jednog** slepog čoveka.	We met *a* blind man on the way.

3. When the adjective ends in two consonants, other than -ст/st, -зд/zd, -шт/št, -жд/žd, which can stand together, a fleeting **a** is inserted before the final consonant in the masculine singular:

ведр-а	**vedr-a**	clear feminine
ведар	**ved*a*r**	m indefinite

Declension of indefinite adjectives						
	Singular			Plural		
	Masculine	Neuter	Feminine	Masculine	Neuter	Feminine
Nom.	**добар** dobar	**добро** dobro	Same declension as for definite adjectives			
Gen.	**добр*а*** dobr*a*					
Dat.	**добр*у*** dobr*u*					
Acc.	inanimate (as nom.)	**добро** dobro				
	animate (as gen.)	**dobro**				
Voc.	**добр*и*** dobr*i*	**добро** dobro				
Inst.	**добр*им*** dobr*im*					
Loc.	**добр*у*** dobr*u*					

> Definite adjectives

9.3 Definite adjectives

Definite adjectives are used when describing something or someone already known to us, or possessing a particular or permanent quality. They are given in response to the question **који/koji?** (which?). The definite adjective is comparable in usage to the English definite article 'the', and is generally becoming the preferred form of adjective in use today.

9 Adjectives

The definite adjective differs from indefinite adjectives most apparently in the nominative masculine singular, where it ends in **-и/i**:

| Уморни путник се синоћ вратио кући. | Umorni putnik se sinoć vratio kući. | The tired traveller returned home last night. |

as compared to:

| Уморан, путник се синоћ вратио кући. | Umoran, putnik se sinoć vratio kući. | Tired, the traveller returned home last night. |

It does not differ from the indefinite adjective in the other genders in the nominative case.

The definite adjective is used attributively and stands next to the noun it describes:

| Вруђа супа нас чека. | Vruća supa nas čeka. | Hot soup awaits us. |

In the genitive, dative, accusative and locative cases, masculine and neuter definite adjectives ending in a hard consonant will include an -o in the case ending, and those ending in a soft consonant will include an -e:

| Младог лава су видели у Африци. | Mladog lava su videli u Africi. | They saw the young lion in Africa. |
| Носила је прстен на средњем прсту. | Nosila je prsten na srednjem prstu. | She wore a ring on her middle finger. |

Masculine and neuter definite adjectives have a short and a long form in the genitive, dative and locative cases. Although the short form is in general use today, the long form is used when the noun described by the adjective is omitted:

| Којем шефу сте се јавили? | Kojem šefu ste se javili? | Which boss did you report to? |
| Староме. | Starome. | The old one. |

It is also used when the noun precedes the adjective or for stylistic reasons.

While descriptive adjectives have both the definite and the indefinite form, the following adjectives have only the definite form, apparent when describing masculine singular nouns:

Possessive adjectives ending in -ји/ji, -ски/ski, -шки/ški, -чки/čki, many of them created from names of countries and cities: српски/srpski (Serbian), лондонски/londonski (London's), мађарски/mađarski (Hungarian), трговачки/trgovački (merchant), etc.

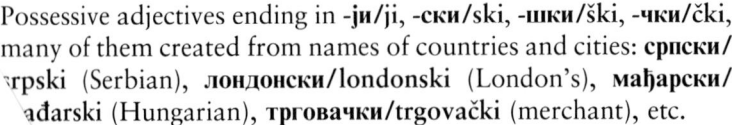

| ведр-а | vedr-a | clear feminine |
| ведар | ved*a*r | m indefinite |

Definite adjectives

Declension of indefinite adjectives

	Singular			Plural		
	Masculine	Neuter	Feminine	Masculine	Neuter	Feminine
Nom.	добар dobar	добро dobro	Same declension as for definite adjectives			
Gen.	добр*а* dobr*a*					
Dat.	добр*у* dobr*u*					
Acc.	inanimate (as nom.) animate (as gen.)	добро dobro				
Voc.	добри dobri	добро dobro				
Inst.	добр*и*м dobr*i*m					
Loc.	добр*у* dobr*u*					

9.3 Definite adjectives

Definite adjectives are used when describing something or someone already known to us, or possessing a particular or permanent quality. They are given in response to the question **који/koji?** (which?). The definite adjective is comparable in usage to the English definite article 'the', and is generally becoming the preferred form of adjective in use today.

9 Adjectives

The definite adjective differs from indefinite adjectives most apparently in the nominative masculine singular, where it ends in -и/i:

Уморни путник се синоћ вратио кући.	**Umorni** putnik se sinoć vratio kući.	*The* tired traveller returned home last night.

as compared to:

Уморан, путник се синоћ вратио кући.	**Umoran**, putnik se sinoć vratio kući.	*Tired*, the traveller returned home last night.

It does not differ from the indefinite adjective in the other genders in the nominative case.

The definite adjective is used attributively and stands next to the noun it describes:

Врућа супа нас чека.	**Vruća** supa nas čeka.	*Hot* soup awaits us.

In the genitive, dative, accusative and locative cases, masculine and neuter definite adjectives ending in a hard consonant will include an -o in the case ending, and those ending in a soft consonant will include an -e:

Младог лава су видели у Африци.	**Mladog** lava su videli u Africi.	They saw *the young* lion in Africa.
Носила је прстен на *средњем* прсту.	Nosila je prsten na *srednjem* prstu.	She wore a ring on her *middle* finger.

Masculine and neuter definite adjectives have a short and a long form in the genitive, dative and locative cases. Although the short form is in general use today, the long form is used when the noun described by the adjective is omitted:

Ко**јем** шефу сте се јавили?	Ko**jem** šefu ste se javili?	Which boss did you report to?
Стар**оме**.	Star**ome**.	The old one.

It is also used when the noun precedes the adjective or for stylistic reasons.

While descriptive adjectives have both the definite and the indefinite form, the following adjectives have only the definite form, apparent when describing masculine singular nouns:

1. Possessive adjectives ending in -ји/ji, -ски/ski, -шки/ški, -чки/čki, many of them created from names of countries and cities: српски/srpski (Serbian), лондонски/londonski (London's), мађарски/mađarski (Hungarian), трговачки/trgovački (merchant), etc.

2 Adjectives of time and place ending in -ни/ni, -њи/nji, -шњи/šnji: десни/desni (right), летњи/letnji (summer), данашњи/današnji (today's), овдашњи/ovdašnji (of this place).
3 Adjectives used as part of a name: **Нови Београд/Novi Beograd** (New Belgrade), **Нова година/Nova godina** (New Year), **црни лук/crni luk** (onions).
4 Ordinal numbers: први/prvi (first), други/drugi (second), etc.
5 Comparatives and superlatives: лепши/lepši (prettier), **спорији/sporiji** (slower), **бољи/bolji** (better), **најбољи/najbolji** (best), **дужи/duži** (longer), **најдужи/njaduži** (longest), **тежи/teži** (heavier), **најтежи/najteži** (heaviest), etc.
6 Adjectives: **мали/mali** (small, little), **исти/isti** (the same), **јарки/jarki** (bright, scorching), **неки/neki** (some), **бојни/bojni** (battle, combat), **велики/veliki** (big), etc.

Definite adjectives

Declension of definite adjectives

	Singular			Plural		
	Masculine	Neuter	Feminine	Masculine	Neuter	Feminine
Nom.	лаки	лако	лака	лаки	лака	лаке
	laki	lako	laka	laki	laka	lake
Gen.	лаког(а)		лаке		лаких	
	lakog(a)		lake		lakih	
Dat.	лаком(е/у)		лакој		лаким	
	lakom(e/u)		lakoj		lakim	
Acc.	inanimate (as nom.)	лако	лаку	лаке	лака	лаке
	animate (as gen.)	lako	laku	lake	laka	lake
Voc.	лаки	лако	лака	лаки	лака	лаке
	laki	lako	laka	laki	laka	lake
Inst.	лаким		лаком		лаким	
	lakim		lakom		lakim	
Loc.	лаком(е/у)		лакој		лаким	
	lakom(e/u)		lakoj		lakim	

9.4 Possessive adjectives

Possessive adjectives are given in response to the interrogative **чији/čiji?** (whose?). These adjectives correspond to the English possessive ending in ''s'. They can be formed from singular nouns denoting persons, from proper names, names of animals, deities, countries, cities, etc.:

о**чев** капут	o**čev** kaput	father's coat
брат**ова** кола	brat**ova** kola	brother's car
мам**ина** маза	mam**ina** maza	mother's pet

Possessive adjectives are created by the addition of the following suffixes:

- **-ов/ov** — added to the base of masculine nouns ending in a hard consonant
- **-ев/ev** — added to the base of masculine nouns ending in a soft consonant
- **-љев/ljev** — added to the base of masculine nouns ending in **-в/v** (**Јаковљев/Jakovljev** but also **синовљев/sinovljev**)
- **-ин/in** — added to the base of nouns ending in **-a** which is dropped prior to the suffix ending
- **-ски/ski** — added to the base of names of countries, cities or areas
- **-чки/čki**
- **-шки/ški**

Adjectives ending in -ов/ov, -ев/ev and -ин/in, when formed from nouns denoting nationality, proper names, surnames, names of deities and nicknames, are capitalised:

Енглескињ**ин**	Engleskinj**in**	the English woman's
Србин**ов**	Srbin**ov**	the Serbian man's
Марк**ов** новчаник	Mark**ov** novčanik	Marko's wallet
Мађар**ев** колач	Mađar**ev** kolač	the Hungarian man's cake
Ан**ина** лутка	An**ina** lutka	Anna's doll

Adjectives with the following endings are formed from names of countries or cities and are not capitalised. These adjectives decline as definite adjectives:

Possessive adjectives

-ски/ski	енглески – Енглеска	engle*ski* – **Engleska**	England's – England
	српски – Србија	sr*pski* – **Srbija**	Serbia's – Serbia
	европски – Европа	evro*pski* – **Evropa**	Europe's – Europe
-чки/čki	словеначки – Словенија	slovena*čki* – **Slovenija**	Slovenia's – Slovenia
-шки/ški	хашки – Хаг	ha*ški* – **Hag**	the Hague's – the Hague

However, the first word in a title or name of a region or administrative unit is capitalised.

Прва армијска област	*Prva armijska* oblast	the First Military District
Северноатлантска алијанса	*Severnoatlantska* alijansa	the North Atlantic Alliance

Possessive adjectives agree with the noun they qualify in gender, number and case:

Где је *братов* штап?	Gde je *bratov* štap?	Where is *my brother's* walking stick?
брат-*ов*	brat-*ov*	
Маринина пријатељица стиже данас.	*Marinina* prijateljica stiže danas.	*Marina's* friend is arriving today.
Марин(а)-*ина*	Marin(a)-*ina*	
Нисам био ни на једном *европском* првенству.	Nisam bio ni na jednom *evropskom* prvenstvu.	I haven't been to any *European* championships.
Да ли идете на *Европско* првенство у фудбалу 2004?	Da li idete na *Evropsko* prvenstvo u fudbalu 2004?	Are you going to the 2004 *European* Football Championship?

The very nouns from which possessive adjectives were formed can replace these adjectives:

Где је штап моје *sestre*? (сестрин штап)	Gde je štap moje *sestre*? (sestrin štap)	Where is the walking stick of my *sister*? (sister's)
Дечак је купио нове патике за *спорт*. (спортске патике)	Dečak je kupio nove patike za *sport*. (sportske patike)	The boy bought a new pair of trainers for *sports*. (sports trainers)

9.5 Adjectival declension

Adjectival declension (definite)						
	Singular			Plural		
	Masculine	Neuter	Feminine	Masculine	Neuter	Feminine
Nom.	-и/i	-о/o	-а/a	-и/i	-а/a	-е/e
Gen.	-ог(а)/og(a)		-е/e	-их/ih		
Dat.	-ом(е/у)/om(e/u)		-ој/oj	-им/im		
Acc.	inanimate -о/o (same as nom.) animate (same as gen.)		-у/u	-е/e	-а/a	-е/e
Voc.	-и/i	-о/o	-а/a	-и/i	-а/a	-е/e
Inst.	-им/im		-ом/om	-им/im		
Loc.	-ом(е/у)/om(e/u)		-ој/oj	-им/im		

Adjectival declension

Comparison of definite and indefinite adjectival declensions for masculine and neuter singular

	Singular	
	Masculine	Neuter
Nom.	млад/mlad	млад-о/mlad-o
	млад-и/mlad-i	млад-о/mlad-o
Gen.	млад-а/mlad-a	
	млад-ог/mlad-og	
Dat.	млад-у/mlad-u	
	млад-ом(е)/mlad-om(e)	
Acc.	млад/mlad and млад-а/mlad-a*	млад-о
	млад-и/mlad-i and млад-ог/mlad-og*	mlad-o
Voc.	млад-и	
	mlad-i	
Inst.	млад-им	
	mlad-im	
Loc.	млад-у/mlad-u	
	млад-ом(е)/mlad-om(e)	

* used with animate nouns

9 Adjectives

9.6 Comparative adjectives

Only descriptive adjectives have comparison. The three stages of comparison are the positive, the comparative and the superlative.

The basic form of the adjective is referred to as the positive adjective. Comparative adjectives are formed by the addition of suffixes to the positive masculine indefinite form:

1. **-иjи/iji** masculine Some monosyllabic and most polysyllabic
   -иjе/ije neuter   adjectives take this ending.
   -иjа/ija feminine

Positive	Comparative	
стар – star	**стар***иjи* **– star***iji*	old/older
смрдљив – smrdljiv	**смрдљив***иjи* **– smrdljiv***iji*	smelly/smellier
хладан* – hladan*	**хладн***иjи* **– hladn***iji*	cold/colder

   * The fleeting **a** is removed before the addition of the comparative suffix.

2. **-jи/ji** masculine Most monosyllabic adjectives take this ending.
   -jе/je neuter   The **-j** merges with the preceding consonant and
   -jа/ja feminine   softens it (see Section 4.1.7 **J** changes).

Positive	Comparative	
млад – mlad	**мла-ђи – mla-đi**	young/younger
брз – brz	**бр-жи – br-ži**	fast/faster

3. **-jи/ji** masculine The endings **-ак**, **-ок**, **-ек** in the masculine, **-тко**,
   -jе/je neuter   **-око**, **-еко** in the neuter and **-тка**, **-ока**, **-ека**
   -jа/ja feminine   in the feminine are replaced by these endings.
                          The **-j** merges with the preceding consonant and
                          softens it (see Section 4.1.7 **J** changes).

Positive	Comparative	
крат*ак* **– krat***ak*	**кра-ћи – kra-ći**	short/shorter
близ*ак* **– bliz***ak*	**бли-жи – bli-ži**	close/closer
дуб*ок* **– dub***ok*	**дуб-љи – dub-lji**	deep/deeper
дал*ек* **– dal***ek*	**да-љи – da-lji**	far/further

4. **-ши/ši** masculine Only three adjectives have this ending:
   -ше/še neuter
   -ша/ša feminine

Comparative adjectives

Positive	Comparative	
лак – lak	лак-ши – lak-ši	easy, light/easier, lighter
леп – lep	леп-ши – lep-ši	beautiful, pretty/more beautiful, prettier
мек – mek	мек-ши – mek-ši	soft/softer

5 Adjectives with irregular comparatives:

Positive	Comparative	
добар – dobar	бољи – bolji	good/better
лош/зао – loš/zao	гори – gori	bad/worse
велик(и) – velik(i)	већи – veći	big/bigger
мали (мален) – mali (malen)	мањи – manji	small/smaller, at least
дебео – debeo	дебљи – deblji	fat/fatter

6 The comparative of adjectives ending in -ски/ski, and adjectives with three or more syllables, is sometimes formed with the adverbs **више/više** (more) or **мање/manje** (less) preceding the positive adjective:

Positive	Comparative	
родитељски – roditeljski	више родитељски – više roditeljski	parent-like/more parent-like
академски – akademski	мање академски – manje akademski	academic/less academic

Note: мање/manje can be put before any adjective.

Comparison can be expressed with the use of the conjunctions **него/nego** or **но/no**, where the beings or objects compared remain in the same case, or with the conjunction **од/od**, in which case the second being or object compared is in the genitive case:

Њихова кућа је *старија* него наша.	Njihova kuća je *starija* nego naša.	Their house is *older* than ours.
Њихова кућа је *старија* од наше.	Njihova kuća je *starija* od naše.	Their house is *older* than ours.

Comparative adjectives may also be formed with the addition of the prefix **пре/pre-** with the meaning of 'too', added to the positive adjective:

Positive	Comparative	
добар	**пре**добар	good/too good
dobar	**pre**dobar	

The adverb **сувише/suviše** (too much) can precede an adjective to give the same meaning:

Positive	Comparative	
добар	*сувише* **добар**	good/too good
dobar	*suviše* **dobar**	

This form of comparative adjective does not have a superlative form.

9.7 Superlative adjectives

Only descriptive adjectives have a comparative and a superlative form. The superlative adjective is formed by the addition of the prefix **нај/naj-** to the comparative adjective:

Positive	Comparative	Superlative	
груб – grub	грубљи – grublji	*нај*грубљи – *naj*grublji	rough/rougher/roughest
здрав – zdrav	здравији – zdraviji	*нај*здравији – *naj*zdraviji	healthy/healthier/healthiest
бистар* – bistar*	бистрији – bistriji	*нај*бистрији – *naj*bistriji	transparent/more transparent/*most transparent*

* The fleeting **a** is removed before the addition of the comparative suffix.

The superlative prefix **нај/naj-** is added to the comparative form of adjectives with an irregular comparative:

Positive	Comparative	Superlative	
добар – dobar	бољи – bolji	*нај*бољи – najbolji	good/better
лош/зао – loš/zao	гори – gori	*нај*гори – najgori	bad/worse
велик(и) – velik(i)	већи – veći	*нај*већи – najveći	big/bigger

Where the comparative form is formed by the addition of the adverb **више/više** (more) (or **мање/manje** (less)) to the positive adjective, the superlative is formed by the addition of the superlative prefix нај/naj- to више/više (or мање/manje):

Positive	Comparative	Superlative	
родитељски – roditeljski	више родитељски – više roditeljski	*нај*више родитељски – *naj*više roditeljski	parent-like/most parent-like
академски – akademski	мање академски – manje akademski	*нај*мање академски – *naj*manje akademski	academic/least academic

As the superlative form involves more than two elements in comparison, it is followed by the preposition од/od which takes the genitive:

| Њихова кућа је *најстарија од* свих кућа у селу. | Njihova kuća je *najstarija od* svih kuća u selu. | Their house is the *oldest* of all the houses in the village. |

9.8 Verbal adjectives

There are four types of participles in the Serbian language, all of which are derived from verbs. Two of these are adjectival forms and are described as adjectival and referred to as verbal adjectives. The other two are adverbial forms, and are described as adverbial and referred to as verbal adverbs (see Section 10.4 Verbal adverbs).

The two verbal adjectives have gender and number. The first of these is indeclinable, while the other is declinable.

9.8.1 The active past participle

This verbal adjective is also referred to as the indeclinable active past participle. It denotes an action which had been carried out or was being carried out some time, often in the past, by the subject, who or which may or may not be known. This participle is often referred to as the -л/-l participle as its endings mostly include this letter:

| *Седео је* Иван на клупи. | *Sedeo je* Ivan na klupi. | Ivan *was sitting* on the bench. |
| Мира га *је видела и дозвала.* | Mira ga *je videla i dozvala.* | Mira *saw* him and *called* out to him. |

9
Adjectives

На мом рођендану гости *су* јели и пили.	**Na mom rođendanu gosti *su* je*li* i pi*li*.**	The guests *ate* and *drank* on my birthday.
Како *сте* путова*ли*?*	**Kako *ste* putova*li*?***	How was your journey (how did *you* travel)?*

* When using the 2nd person plural as an expression of politeness, the masculine plural of this participle is used regardless of the person's gender.

This is the most frequently used of all the participles due to its role in the formation of the past tense and most compound tenses, excluding the future tense:

Марија *је* воле*ла* свог пса.	**Marija *je* vole*la* svog psa.**	Maria *loved* her dog.
Ако *би* доша*о*, отиш*ли бисмо* у град.	**Ako *bi* doša*o*, otiš*li bismo* u grad.**	If you *were to come*, we *would go* to town.

This participle can also take a purely adjectival role to describe a particular quality of the noun:

поседе*ла* коса/posede*la* kosa	hair that has turned grey
изгладне*ло* дете/izgladne*lo* dete	a child that is worn out by hunger
преплану*ло* лице/preplanu*lo* lice	a suntanned face
оболе*ли* људи/obole*li* ljudi	sick/ailing people

When used in this way, it will decline as an adjective. Many such participles have become proper adjectives:

*зре*ла* жена/zre*la* žena*	a mature woman
*зре*о* човек/zre*o* čovek*	a mature man
*зре*ло* воће/zre*lo* voće*	ripe fruit

The active past participle is also used as an expression of good wishes, salutations and curses:

Живе*ли*!/Žive*li*!	Cheers!
Живе*о* краљ!/Žive*o* kralj!	Long live the King!

9.8.2 *Formation of the active past participle*

This participle may be formed from all verbs types, imperfective, perfective, transitive and intransitive. It is formed from the infinitive base with the following endings:

Verbal adjectives

Singular			Plural		
Masculine	Feminine	Neuter	Masculine	Feminine	Neuter
-о/o	-ла/la	-ло/lo	-ли/li	-ле/le	-ла/la

- With infinitives ending in -ти/ti:

To be	He was	She was	It was	They were	They were	They were
бити	био	била	било	били	биле	била
biti	bio	bila	bilo	bili	bile	bila
To want	He wanted	She wanted	It wanted	They wanted	They wanted	They wanted
хтети	хтео	хтела	хтело	хтели	хтеле	хтела
hteti	hteo	htela	htelo	hteli	htele	htela
To give	He gave	She gave	It gave	They gave	They gave	They gave
дати	дао	дала	дало	дали	дале	дала
dati	dao	dala	dalo	dali	dale	dala

- With infinitives ending in -сти/sti, the form of the participle depends on that of the present tense. When the last consonant of the present tense is dental, д/d, т/t, дн/dn or тн/tn, the participle is formed from the infinitive base as in the -ти/ti ending.

Infinitive		Present	Past participle					
			Masculine	Feminine	Neuter	Masculine	Feminine	Neuter
јести	to eat	једем	јео	јела	јело	јели	јеле	јела
jesti		jedem	jeo	jela	jelo	jeli	jele	jela
провести	to spend	проведем	провео	провела	провело	провели	проведе	провела
provesti		provedem	proveo	provela	provelo	proveli	provele	provela

When the last consonant of the present tense base is not dental, the ending for masculine singular has a fleeting **a** inserted before the final -o.

- With infinitives ending in -ћи/ći, the participle endings above apply, in addition to the reappearance of the original г/g or к/k from which the -ћи/ći developed. A fleeting **a** is inserted before the final -o in the masculine singular. The present tense will often contain the original consonant.

9
Adjectives

Infinitive		Present	Participle					
			Masculine	Feminine	Neuter	Masculine	Feminine	Neuter
вући	to pull	вучем	вукао	вукла	вукло	вукли	вукле	вукла
vući		vučem	vukao	vukla	vuklo	vukli	vukle	vukla
моћи	to be	могу	могао	могла	могло	могли	могле	могла
moći	able to	mogu	mogao	mogla	moglo	mogli	mogle	mogla

Exceptions to this are **-ићи/ići** and its derivatives (see Section 6.17 **Ићи/ići** and its derivatives).

9.8.3 The passive participle

Also referred to as the past passive participle and the declinable passive past participle, this verbal adjective is used to form the passive, signifying that an action has been carried out on or to something or someone. It functions as a regular adjective, having gender and number as well as declension. In English it is usually translated by the 'ed' ending to a word.

It is often used when the subject carrying out the action is unknown or of no relevance. In addition to its purely adjectival function, it is also expressed as the second half of a 'to be . . .' sentence:

This participle is often referred to as the **-н-т/n-t** participle as its endings always include either one of these letters:

Фарба*на* коса понекад лепо изгледа.	Farba*na* kosa ponekad lepo izgleda.	Dy*ed* (pain*ted*) hair sometimes looks good.
Зидови наше собе *су* офарба*ни*.	Zidovi naše sobe *su* ofarba*ni*.	The walls of our room *are* pain*ted*.
Волим да видим опра*не* чаше.	Volim da vidim opra*ne* čaše.	I like to see wash*ed* glasses.
Кажу да *је* та кућа прокле*та*.	Kažu da *je* ta kuća prokle*ta*.	The say that house *is* curs*ed*.

9.8.4 Formation of the passive past participle

The passive past participle has both gender and declension and is formed from the infinitive base of transitive verbs only by the addition of the following endings:

Verbal adjectives

Singular			Plural		
Masculine	Feminine	Neuter	Masculine	Feminine	Neuter
-ен/en	-ена/ena	-ено/eno	-ени/eni	-ене/ene	-ена/ena
-н/n	-на/na	-но/no	-ни/ni	-не/ne	-на/na
-т/t	-та/ta	-то/to	-ти/ti	-те/te	-та/ta

- Before the -е/e of the -ен/en endings, velars change into palatals, so the к/k of рек-/rek- changes to ч/č. Dentals (only in the и-ти/i-ti type of verb) change into palatals, so the т/t of платити/platiti and the ц/c of бацити/baciti change into ћ/ć and ч/č respectively. Н/n also changes to њ/nj and л/l to љ/lj: labials add љ/lj; only р/r and consonants that are already palatal fail to undergo further changes.

Infinitive		Participle		
		Masculine	Feminine	Neuter
рећи	to say – said	речен	речена	речено
reći		rečen	rečena	rečeno
платити	to pay – paid	плаћен	плаћена	плаћено
platiti		plaćen	plaćena	plaćeno
бацити	to throw – thrown	бачен	бачена	бачено
baciti		bačen	bačena	bačeno
запленити	to confiscate – confiscated	заплењен	заплењена	заплењено
zapleniti		zaplenjen	zaplenjena	zaplenjeno
хвалити	to praise – praised	хваљен	хваљена	хваљено
hvaliti		hvaljen	hvaljena	hvaljeno

9 Adjectives

- Infinitives in **-ати/ati** take **-н/n, -на/na, -но/no**:

Infinitive		Participle		
		Masculine	Feminine	Neuter
писати	to write – written	**писан**	**писана**	**писано**
pisati		**pisan**	**pisana**	**pisano**
читати	to read – read	**читан**	**читана**	**читано**
čitati		**čitan**	**čitana**	**čitano**

- Infinitives whose root ends in **-р/r** or whose linking vowel is **-у/u** or **-е/e** usually take the **-т/t, -та/ta, -то/to** endings:

Infinitive		Participle		
		Masculine	Feminine	Neuter
прострти	to spread out – spread out	**прострт**	**прострта**	**прострто**
prostrti		**prostrt**	**prostrta**	**prostrto**
напети	to tighten – tight	**напет**	**напета**	**напето**
napeti		**napet**	**napeta**	**napeto**

This participle has given rise to a whole category of nouns created in a similar way to English nouns formed from a verb and the suffix '-ing' or '-ion'.

Infinitive		Participle	Noun	
		Masculine	Neuter	
решити	to resolve, decide	**решен**	**решење**	resolution
rešiti		**rešen**	**rešenje**	
ослободити	to liberate	**ослобођен**	**ослобођење**	liberation
osloboditi		**oslobođen**	**oslobođenje**	

Chapter 10
Adverbs

Adverbs are words used to modify or describe a verb or another adverb. Adverbs do not decline, nor do they mark person or number. They provide the following information about the action described by the verb:

1. Manner – how? When modifying verbs:

   | **Брзо** отвори прозор! | ***Brzo** otvori prozor!* | Open the window *quickly!* |

2. Time – when? When modifying verbs:

   | **Сада** сам стигао кући. | ***Sada** sam stigao kući.* | I have arrived home *now*. |

3. Place – where? When modifying verbs:

   | Можете да видите море **одавде**. | *Možete da vidite more **odavde**.* | You can see the sea *from here*. |

4. Quantity – how much? When modifying verbs (and nouns as a quantifier):

   | Она **много** једе. | *Ona **mnogo** jede.* | She eats *a lot*. |
   | Имамо **много** хлеба. | *Imamo **mnogo** hleba.* | We have *a lot* of bread. |

5. Frequency – how often? When modifying verbs:

   | **Никад** не говоримо за време ручка. | ***Nikad** ne govorimo za vreme ručka.* | We *never* talk during lunch. |

6. Cause – why? When modifying verbs:

   | Био је гладан и **зато** је појео твоје парче. | *Bio je gladan i **zato** je pojeo tvoje parče.* | He was hungry and *that is why* he ate your piece. |

7 Degree – intensifying or toning down. When modifying verbs:

| Стварно мрзим зиму. | *Stvarno* mrzim zimu. | I *really* hate winter. |
| Сваког дана деца *радо* иду у школу аутобусом. | Svakog dana deca *rado* idu u školu autobusom. | Every day the children *gladly* go to school by bus. |

The following adverb and adverbial expressions are used in the above sentence:

the time that the children go to school:	сваког дана/svakog dana every day
the manner in which they go:	радо/rado gladly
and	аутобусом/autobusom by bus

The latter is a noun to which an adverbial function has been given by its use in the instrumental case.

Most adverbs in Serbian have developed from nouns, adjectives, pronouns or verbs. As such, they can be divided into four groups:

(a) Substantival (nominal) adverbs – adverbs formed from nouns;
(b) Adjectival adverbs – adverbs formed from adjectives;
(c) Pronominal adverbs – adverbs formed from pronouns;
(d) Verbal adverbs – adverbs formed from verbs.

10.1 Substantival (nominal) adverbs

There are two types of adverbs formed from nouns.

1 Those with various endings, prefixes and prepositions:

зими	zimi	in winter
изјутра	izjutra	in the morning
кришом	krišom	by stealth, secretly
лети	leti	in summer
напокон	napokon	finally, in the end

> **Substantival adverbs**

напоље	napolje	outside
натраг	natrag	back, backwards
низбрдо	nizbrdo	downhill
ноћу	noću	in the night, by night
оберучке	oberučke	with both hands
одмах	odmah	immediately
по подне	po podne	in the afternoon
поименце	poimence	by name, particularly
прексиноћ	preksinoć	night before last
прексутра	preksutra	the day after tomorrow
прекјуче	prekjuče	the day before yesterday
синоћ	sinoć	last night
сутра	sutra	tomorrow
сутрадан	sutradan	the next day
увек	uvek	always
узастопце	uzastopce	one after another, successively
узбрдо	uzbrdo	uphill
ујутро	ujutro	in the morning

2 And those ending with -с/s:

пролетос	proletos	this spring
летос	letos	this summer
јесенас	jesenas	this autumn
зимус	zimus	this winter
ноћас	noćas	this night/tonight
јутрос	jutros	this morning
вечерас	večeras	this evening

10 Adverbs

10.2 Adjectival adverbs

Adjectival adverbs are formed from either indefinite neuter nominative singular adjectives:

Добро пева.	*Dobro* peva.	(He/she) sings *well*.
Лепо је украсила јелку.	*Lepo* je ukrasila jelku.	She decorated the Christmas tree *beautifully*. (*nicely*)

in which case the stress between the adjective and the adverb may be different:

Ово је *jáко* дете.	Ovo je *jáko* dete.	This is a *strong* child. (adj.)
Jâко си га ударио.	*Jâko* si ga udario.	You hit him *hard*. (*strongly*) (adv.)

or from definite masculine nominative singular adjectives, most of which end in ски/ski, чки/čki and шки/ški:

Спортски се понашао.	*Sportski* se ponašao.	He behaved in *a sports-like manner*.
Дамски се обукла.	*Damski* se obukla.	She dressed in *a lady-like manner*.

in which case there is no difference in stress between the adjective and the adverb.

Adverbs may also have a comparative and superlative degree, which is formed in the same manner as with adjectives:

добро – dobro	боље – bolje	најбоље – najbolje	well/better/best
брзо – brzo	брже – brže	најбрже – najbrže	quickly/more quickly/most quickly

The prefix пре/pre- and preposition по/po indicate respectively an excessive (too) and an intermittent frequency of the action described by the verb:

Прерано сте стигли.	*Prerano* ste stigli.	You arrived *too early*.
Добру ракију треба пити *по мало*.	Dobru rakiju treba piti *po malo*.	Good brandy should be drunk *a little at a time*.

10.3 Pronominal adverbs

Pronominal adverbs are formed from the basic stem of pronouns to which particular endings are added to indicate place, direction, time, manner and extent:

Question	Pronoun	Adverb				
		Place	Direction	Time	Manner	Extent
који? koji? which?	тај taj this/that	ту tu here	отуд(а) otud(a) from that direction	тамо/туда tamo/tuda there/that way	тако tako in that way/like that/so	толико toliko so much/to that extent
				тада tada then, at that time		
	овај ovaj this	овде ovde here	овамо/овуда ovamo/ovuda over here/this way	— —	овако ovako thus/in this way	оволико ovoliko this much
		одавде odavde from here				
	онај onaj that	онде onde there	онамо/онуда onamo/onuda over there/that way	онда onda then	онако onako thus/in that way	онолико onoliko that much
		онанде odande from there/that direction				
ко ko	ко ko	где gde	камо/куда kamo/kuda	када kada	како kako	колико koliko

Question	Pronoun	Adverb				
		Place	Direction	Time	Manner	Extent
			откуд(а) **otkud(a)** from whence/ how come?			
	ико **iko** anyone	**игде** **igde** anywhere	**икамо/икуда** **ikamo/ikuda** anywhere/by any route	**икада** **ikada** ever/any time	**икако** **ikako** in any way	**иколико** **ikoliko** in any amount/ even a little
	неко **neko** someone	**негде** **negde** somewhere	**некамо/некуда** **nekamo/nekuda** somewhere/by some route	**некада** **nekada** sometime	**некако** **nekako** in some way/ somehow	**неколико** **nekoliko** some/several
	нико **niko** no-one	**нигде** **nigde** nowhere	**никамо/никуда** **nikamo/nikuda** nowhere/by no route	**никада** **nikada** never	**никако** **nikako** in no way	**николико** **nikoliko** to no extent/ none at all
	свако **svako** everyone	**свуда/свугде/** **свагде** **svuda/svugde/** **svagde** everywhere	**свакамо/** **свакуда** **svakamo/** **svakuda** everywhere/ every way	**свакада** **svakada** always	**свакако** **svakako** in every way/ of course	**свеколико** **svekoliko** completely/ entirely
						These are rarely used.

10.4 Verbal adverbs

There are four types of participles in the Serbian language, all of which are derived from verbs. Two of these are adjectival forms are known as verbal adjectives (see Section 9.8 Verbal adjectives). The other two are adverbial forms, and are known as adverbial participles or verbal adverbs. These adverbial forms are derived from verbs, they have no number or gender, and are indeclinable. There are two types of verbal adverbs.

10.4.1 The present verbal adverb

Also referred to as the present participle, or the declinable active participle of simultaneous action, this verbal adverb describes an action occurring at the same time as that of the main verb. It relates to present or contemporaneous time and translates into English as 'whilst' or with the verbal suffix '-ing'.

| *Ходајући* по леду, дечак је склизнуо и пао. | *Hodajući* po ledu, dečak je skliznuo i pao. | *Whilst walking* on the ice, the boy slipped and fell. |
| *Читајући* новине, заспала је. | *Čitajući* novine, zaspala je. | *Whilst reading* the newspapers, she fell asleep. |

In addition to denoting the simultaneous aspect of an action, this verbal participle can also describe:

1   The manner in which the action occurs:

   | Отишли су у град *певајући*. | Otišli su u grad *pevajući*. | They went to town (whilst) singing. |

2   The condition under which the action occurs:

   | *Радећи* непрекидно, можемо да успемо. | *Radeći* neprekidno, možemo da uspemo. | (Whilst) working continuously, we can succeed. |

3   The cause or reason why the action occurs:

   | *Плачући* од жалости, жена се срушила. | *Plačući* od žalosti, žena se srušila. | (Whilst) crying with grief, the woman collapsed. |

The rule in Serbian is similar to that in English: the understood subject of the adverb should be the same as the subject of the main verb.

If it is not, this needs to be explained with a new clause or sentence. However, although grammatically incorrect, there are exceptions to this rule. In the following instances, the two verbs share a logical subject:

Заболела га је глава *гледајући* **у екран.**	**Zabolela ga je glava** *gledajući* **u ekran.**	His head started hurting *whilst looking* at the screen.

This adverbial form can be placed either before or after the main verb in the sentence. When it is used after the main verb, no punctuation is required. However, when it occurs before the main verb, a comma separates the two:

Излазећи из воде, гласно је удахнуо.	*Izlazeći* iz vode, glasno je udahnuo.	*(Whilst) coming out* of the water, he inhaled loudly.
Удахнуо је гласно *излазећи* из воде.	Udahnuo je glasno, *izlazeći* iz vode.	He inhaled loudly *(whilst) coming out* of the water.

Adjectives are increasingly formed with this verbal participle. Many expressions formed with these adjectives are set expressions:

текући рачун тећи	tekući račun teći	current account	(from to flow)
гостујућа екипа гостовати	gostujuća ekipa gostovati	visiting (away) team	'from to visit'

When used as adjectives, these verbal adverbs take on all the characteristics of adjectives:

идући ићи	idući ići	coming/next	(from to come/go)
следећи следити	sledeći slediti	following	(from to follow)
могући моћи	mogući moći	possible	(from to be able)

Formation of the present verbal adverb
As simultaneous action refers to a present or contemporaneous action, this participle is formed from the present tense of imperfective verbs only, by the addition of **-ћи/ći** to the 3rd person plural.

Verbal adverbs

Infinitive		Present tense	Participle	
		3rd person plural		
ходати	to walk	ходају	ходајући	whilst
hodati		hodaju	hodajući	walking
певати	to sing	певају	певајући	whilst
pevati		pevaju	pevajući	singing
радити	to work	раде	радећи	whilst
raditi		rade	radeći	working
плакати	to cry	плачу	плачући	whilst
plakati		plaču	plačući	crying
излазити	to exit/	излазе	излазећи	whilst
izlaziti	come out of	izlaze	izlazeći	exiting

10.4.2 The past verbal adverb

Also referred to as the active participle of past action, this verbal adverb describes an action that has occurred *prior* to the action described by the main verb. It translates into English as 'having' followed by the verb, or 'after . . .' followed by a verb ending in '-ing'

Запаливши цигарету, странац ми је вратио упаљач.	*Zapalivši* cigaretu, stranac mi je vration upaljač.	*Having lit* the cigarette, the stranger returned the lighter to me.
Ухвативши лопту, дете је потрчало.	*Uhvativši* loptu, dete je potrčalo.	*Having caught* the ball, the child started running.

When a verbal adverb is formed from an imperfective verb, the exact duration of the action it expresses should be stated:

Радивши 9 сати без престанка, човек је легао да се одмори.	*Radivši* 9 sati bez prestanka, čovek je legao da se odmori.	*Having worked for 9 hours* without a break, the man lay down to rest.

This adverbial form is often replaced by када/kada (when), док/dok (while), пошто/pošto (after, since), чим/čim (as soon as):

Пробудивши се, девојчица је заплакала.	*Probudivši se*, devojčica je zaplakala.	*Having woken up*, the little girl started crying.

10 Adverbs

Када се пробудила, девојчица је заплакала.	*Kada se probudila,* devojčica je zaplakala.	*When she woke up,* the little girl started crying.
Показавши мајци модрицу, дечак је пошао у школу.	*Pokazavši* majci modricu, dečak je pošao u školu.	*Having shown* his mother the bruise, the boy set off to school.
Пошто је показао мајци модрицу, дечак је пошао у школу.	*Pošto je pokazao* majci modricu, dečak je pošao u školu.	*After he showed* his mother the bruise, the boy set off to school.

The verbal adverb can be placed either before or after the main verb in the sentence. When it is used after the main verb, no punctuation is required. When it occurs before the main verb, a comma separates the two.

Оправши руке, Мирко је сео да једе.	*Opravši* ruke, Mirko je seo da jede.	*Having washed* his hands, Mirko sat down to eat.
Мирко је сео да једе *оправши* руке.	Mirko je seo da jede *opravši* ruke.	Mirko sat down to eat *having washed* his hands.

Infrequently, these verbal adverbs may also be used as adjectives. An example of this is the adjective **бивши, бивша, бивше/bivši, bivša, bivše** (former, past) from **бити/biti** (to be).

Formation of the past verbal adverb

This verbal adverb is formed from the infinitive stem of mainly perfective verbs (although it can be formed from both aspects) by the addition of **-вши/vši** (after a vowel) or **-авши/avši** (after a consonant). Sometimes **-в/v** or **-ав/av** may be added respectively.

Infinitive	Infinitive stem	Participle	
запалити	запали	запаливши	to (set) light (to)
zapaliti	zapali	zapalivši	
радити	ради	радивши	to work
raditi	radi	radivši	
пробудити	пробуди	пробудивши	to wake up
probuditi	probudi	probudivši	
опрати	опра	оправши	to wash
oprati	opra	opravši	

Chapter 11
Prepositions

Prepositions indicate the position, direction, time or manner in which one noun or pronoun relates to another noun or pronoun. They cannot be placed independently of a noun or pronoun, but come before it. Prepositions can link the noun or pronoun either to another noun or to a verb or other parts of the sentence.

Prepositions have no gender or number and do not inflect. They have an unchanging form (with the exception of a few prepositions, such as **с/s** and **к/k** which can also take the form **са/sa** and **ка/ka**).

Prepositions reflect a relationship between:

1   Living beings:

  Јелена седи   **Jelena sedi**   Jelena is sitting *in*
  испред Марка.   **ispred Marka.**   *front of* Marko.

2   Non-living things:

  Улица пролази   **Ulica prolazi**   The street passes
  кроз град.   **kroz grad.**   *through* town.

3   Living and non-living things:

  Она седи *поред* **Ona sedi *pored***   She is sitting *by* the
  реке.   **reke.**   river.

Although one preposition generally stands with one noun or pronoun, when linked by a conjunction two prepositions can stand with just one noun or pronoun:

  ***Испред и иза* куће**   ***Ispred i iza* kuće**   There was rubbish *in*
  је стајало смеће.   **je stajalo smeće.**   *front of and behind* the
                                                      house.

Prepositions can be divided into two groups:

1   Simple prepositions;
2   Compound prepositions.

11 Prepositions

Some prepositions are used with only one case, but others appear in more than one case. Only in the nominative and the vocative cases are prepositions not used.

11.1 Simple prepositions

Simple prepositions consist of one word only:

из **iz** from, out of

Several simple prepositions, **с(а)/s(a)** (with, off, from), **к(а)/k(a)** (towards), **под(а)/pod(a)** (under, underneath) have a final **a** in some instances. Although this use may be optional, there are certain situations in which it is required:

с(а)	s(a)	The final **a** is required when the word following the preposition begins with any of the following letters: **с/s, ш/š, з/z, ж/ž**:

Враћамо се са села./Vraćamo se sa sela.
We're returning from the village.

к(а)	k(a)	The final **a** is required when the word following the preposition begins with any of the following letters: **г/g, х/h, к/k**:

Јахачи су кренули ка коњима./Jahaći su krenuli ka konjima.
The riders set off towards the horses.

под(а)	pod(a)	The final **a** is required when the preposition is followed by the short form of a personal pronoun or by the pronoun **мном/mnom**:

Пода мном није било ничега./Poda mnom nije bilo ničega.
There was nothing below me.

Some simple prepositions govern only one case, while some govern more than one case:

Марија је ишла са пријатељицама у биоскоп.	Marija je išla *sa prijateljicama* u bioskop.	Maria went *with her friends* to the cinema.
Радник је пао *са мердевина*.	Radnik je pao *sa merdevina*.	The worker fell *off (of)* the ladder.

11.2 Compound prepositions

Compound prepositions are either formed from two prepositions:

| усред – у сред | usred – u sred | in the middle of, amidst |

or they originate from a prepositional phrase:

| упркос – у пркос | uprkos – u prkos | in spite of |

The two prepositions acquire a somewhat new shade of meaning when combined:

| крај | kraj | next to, beside |
| покрај | pokraj | alongside |

All compound prepositions govern the genitive case (see Section 7.3.2 Genitive case) except for **упркос/uprkos**, which may also take the dative case (see Section 7.3.3 Dative case).

11.3 Accentuation

Prepositions act as proclitics in that they are words which are linked in meaning to the word immediately following them. As such, they do not normally carry stress. There are, however, instances when they are stressed.

When the first syllable of the following word is rising, the preposition will normally carry no stress:

| бра́ку | bráku | marriage |
| у бра́ку | u bráku | in marriage |

However, when a preposition occurs immediately before a word which normally has a falling stress on the first syllable, the stress might fall on to the preposition. In this case, the preposition would either have a short falling (ˋ) or a short rising stress (ˊ):

| сӯ̏нце | sȕnce | sun |
| нȁ сӯнце | nà sūnce | in the sun |

If the preposition is bi- or tri-syllabic, the stress will fall on the last syllable if it is a rising accent, or on the first syllable if it is a falling accent, though neither shift is very frequent nowadays:

| нама | nama | us |
| међу̀ нама | međù nama | between us |

11 Prepositions

11.4 Prepositions through the cases

Prepositions are not straightforward to learn. Their meaning does not always translate easily nor is it necessarily set. It is therefore recommended that attention should be paid to the use of prepositions in any text one comes across and that these examples be taken into consideration when learning prepositions.

The following prepositions govern the genitive:

без	bez	without
близу	blizu	near
ван	van	outside
до	do	up to, as far as, until, before, to, next to
дуж	duž	alongside of
из	iz	behind
иза	iza	behind
изван	izvan	outside of
изнад	iznad	above
између	između	between, among
због	zbog	because of
код	kod	at, with, by
крај	kraj	beside, near
место	mesto	instead of, in place of
наврх	navrh	on the top of
надомак	nadomak	in the vicinity of
након	nakon	following, at the end of
насред	nasred	in the middle of
насупрот	nasuprot	opposite
ниже	niže	below, beneath
од	od	from, of
око	oko	around, about
осим	osim	except

поврх	povrh	over, above
покрај	pokraj	alongside
попут	poput	like
поред	pored	next to, in addition to
после	posle	after
пре	pre	before
преко	preko	across, over
против	protiv	against, opposite, for
ради	radi	for the sake of
с(а)	s(a)	from, off
уочи	uoči	on the eve of
усред	usred	in the middle of

Preposi-tions through the cases

Отишао је на посао без кравате.	*Otišao je na posao bez kravate.*	He went to work *without a tie*.
Дуж друма је стајао човек до човека.	*Duž druma je stajao čovek do čoveka.*	*All along the road* people were standing *next to each other*.
Изнад нас је пролетео авион.	*Iznad nas je proleteo avion.*	A plane flew *above us*.
Пробудила их је галама усред ноћи.	*Probudila ih je galama usred noći.*	The noise woke them up *in the middle of the night*.
После ручка идемо у парк.	*Posle ručka idemo u park.*	*After lunch* we're going to the park.
Имам лек против мамурлука.	*Imam lek protiv mamurluka.*	I have a cure *for hangovers*.
Он то ради ради тебе.	*On to radi radi tebe.*	He is doing that *for your sake*.
Разишли смо се због његове мајке.	*Razišli smo se zbog njegove majke.*	We parted *because of his mother*.
Добићеш поклон уочи Божића.	*Dobićeš poklon uoči Božića.*	You will get your gift *on Christmas Eve*.

11 Prepositions

The following prepositions govern the dative:

к(а)	k(a)	towards, to (direction) (used mainly with verbs of motion)
према	prema	towards, to (direction)
насупрот	nasuprot	opposite (used increasingly with the genitive)
надомак	nadomak	in the vicinity of (used increasingly with the genitive)
упркос	uprkos	in spite of
према	prema	according to, towards, opposite

Он гледа *према граду*.	On gleda *prema gradu*.	He is looking *towards* town.
Окрени се *ка прозору*.	Okreni se *ka prozoru*.	Turn *towards* the window.
Завршили смо посао *упркос лошем времену*.	Završili smo posao *uprkos lošem vremenu*.	We finished the job *in spite of* the bad weather.

The following prepositions govern the accusative:

за	za	for
кроз	kroz	through, over
међу	među	together with, between, among
на	na	on, in, onto, to (with motion)
над	nad	above, over (with motion)
низ	niz	down
о	o	against (to lean against)
по	po	for, to collect, gather, pick up
под	pod	under (with motion)
пред	pred	in front of (with motion)
у	u	in, into (when it expresses motion)
уз	uz	alongside of (upward direction), together, near, up

Уђите *у воз* чим стигне.	Uđite *u voz* čim stigne.	Get *onto the train* as soon as it arrives.
Идемо *на паузу*.	Idemo *na pauzu*.	We're going *on* (our) break.

У 3 сата идем по децу.	U tri sata idem po decu.	At 3 o'clock I'm going to pick up the children.
Пењаћемо се уз планину.	Penjaćemo se uz planinu.	We'll climb *up* the mountain.

The following prepositions govern the instrumental:

за	za	behind, following
међу	među	between, amongst
над	nad	above, over (denotes position)
под	pod	under (denotes position)
пред	pred	in front of, before (denotes position)
с(а)	s(а)	with

Над градом се наоблачило.	*Nad* gradom se naoblačilo.	The clouds gathered *above* the town.
Дуго смо стајали *под* кишобраном.	Dugo smo stajali *pod* kišobranom.	We stood *under* the umbrella for a long time.
Деца су се играла *за* кућом.	Deca su se igrala *za* kućom.	The children played *behind* the house.
Они чекају *пред* болницом.	Oni čekaju *pred* bolnicom.	They're waiting *in front of* the hospital.

The following prepositions govern the locative:

на	na	on, at (location)
о	o	about, concerning,
по	po	in accordance with, through, all over, on top of, around
при	pri	at, near, adjoining, a part of
у	u	in, into (location)

Скини капу *при* уласку у цркву.	Skini kapu *pri* ulasku u crkvu.	Take your hat off *on* entering church.
Управо смо говорили *о* теби.	Upravo smo govorili *o* tebi.	We've just been talking *about* you.
Шетали смо се *по* граду.	Šetali smo se *po* gradu.	We walked *around* town.
Заборавила сам кључеве *на* столу.	Zaboravila sam ključeve *na* stolu.	I forgot my keys *on the* table.
Сладолед је *у* фрижидеру.	Sladoled je *u* frižideru.	The ice-cream is *in the* fridge.

Prepositions through the cases

Chapter 12
Conjunctions

Conjunctions are divided into two main categories: coordinating conjunctions, which connect two independent clauses of equal status, and subordinating conjunctions, which connect a dependent clause to a main clause.

Each of these groups of conjunctions can generally be divided into six sub-groups. In addition to these sub-groups, there are also conjunctions used when asking questions as well as when connecting corresponding clauses.

12.1 Coordinating conjunctions

Coordinating conjunctions connect two independent clauses of equal status and they include the following:

1   The 'and' conjunctions:

и	i	and
а	a	and (requires a difference), while
те	te	and, and so
и . . . и	i . . . i	both . . . and
како . . . тако	kako . . . tako	both . . . and, as . . . so
Марио *и* Нада су муж *и* жена.	Mario *i* Nada su muž *i* žena.	Mario *and* Nada are husband *and* wife.
Марио је из Сплита *а* Нада је из Ниша.	Mario je iz Splita *a* Nada je iz Niša.	Mario is from Split *and* (while) Nada is from Niš.
И он *и* она воле море.	*I* on *i* ona vole more.	*Both* he *and* she love the sea.

240

| *Како* Марио *тако и* Нада воли море. | *Kako* Mario *tako i* Nada voli more. | *Both* Mario *and* Nada love the sea. |

2 The 'but' conjunctions:

а*	a*	but*
али**	ali**	but
него	nego	but (comes after a negative first clause and corrects a wrong impression)
но	no	but
већ	već	see него/nego
па	pa	but, and also, and so
(и)пак	(i)pak	but, nevertheless
па ипак	pa ipak	and yet
док	dok	whereas
само	samo	only
ма	ma	at least
макар	makar	at least

* This form of 'but' is not strong as it does not indicate total opposition.
** This is the most common form of 'but'.

Он је дошао *а* њих нема.	On je došao *a* njih nema.	He came *but* they are not here.
Миленко је добар човек *али* је наиван.	Milenko je dobar čovek *ali* je naivan.	Milenko is a good man *but* he is naïve.
То није моје *него* његово.	To nije moje *nego* njegovo.	It's not mine *but* his.
Она је вредна *док* њена сестра није.	Ona je vredna *dok* njena sestra nije.	She is hardworking *whereas* her sister is not.
Уморан сам *но* ћу те сачекати.	Umoran sam *no* ću te sačekati.	I am tired *but* I'll wait for you.

3 The 'either/or' conjunctions:

или	ili	or
или . . . или	ili . . . ili	either . . . or

12 Conjunctions

било... било	bilo... bilo	either... or
ни	ni	neither
ни... ни	ni... ni	neither... nor
нити... нити	niti... niti	neither... nor

Дођи *или* нам пошаљи новац.	Dođi *ili* nam pošalji novac.	Come *or* send us the money.
Они ће доћи *или* код мене *или* код тебе.	Oni će doći *ili* kod mene *ili* kod tebe.	They will come *either* to your place *or* to mine.
Ни Ана *ни* Марко нису знали колико је сати.	*Ni* Ana *ni* Marko nisu znali koliko je sati.	*Neither* Ana *nor* Marko knew what the time was.
Нити је њему *нити* је њој то било важно.	*Niti* je njemu *niti* je njoj to bilo važno.	*Neither* he *nor* she thought it was important.

4 The да/da conjunction:

да*	da*	that
што*	što*	that, that which, that (for) the fact that (used after verbs and adjectives showing emotion or feeling: **бринути се/brinuti se** (to be worried), **радовати се/radovati se** (to be glad, to rejoice), **мило/milo** (glad), **драго/drago** (glad), **жао/žao** (sorry), etc.)
да	da	in order to
да	da	let's (do something)
да	da	(used to connect present tense verbs)

* These conjunctions are used to introduce a subordinate clause.

| Рекао је *да* ће доћи. | Rekao je *da* će doći. | He said (*that*) he will come. |
| Радујем се *што* вас видим. | Radujem se *što* vas vidim. | I'm glad to (*that I*) see you. |

5 The 'therefore' conjunctions:

дакле	dakle	and so, thus, therefore
зато	zato	therefore, that's why
стога	stoga	therefore

| Уморан је *зато* плаче. | Umoran je *zato* plače. | He is tired, *therefore* he is crying. |
| Рекли сте да одлазите *стога* смо поранили. | Rekli ste da odlazite *stoga* smo poranili. | You said you were leaving, *therefore* we came early. |

6   The 'although' conjunctions:

иако	iako	although, though
мада	mada	although, though
премда	premda	although, though

| *Иако* је било вруће, носили смо џемпере. | *Iako* je bilo vruće, nosili smo džempere. | *Although* it was hot, we wore sweaters. |
| Седео је још два сата *мада* је знао да каснимо. | Sedeo je još dva sata *mada* je znao da kasnimo. | He sat for two more hours, *although* he knew we were late. |

12.2 Subordinating conjunctions

Subordinating conjunctions connect a dependent clause to a main clause and consist of the following sub-groups:

1   Pertaining to time:

чим	čim	as soon as, when
док	dok	while
док не	dok ne	until
када, кад	kada, kad	when, while
откако	otkako	since
пре него што	pre nego što	before
тек	tek	just
тек што	tek što	just, only just, no sooner, hardly

| Дошао сам *чим* сам чуо. | Došao sam *čim* sam čuo. | I came *as soon as* I heard. |
| Седните *док* чекате. | Sednite *dok* čekate. | Take a seat *while* you are waiting. |

12 Conjunctions

Остаћемо *док не* престане киша.	Ostaćemo *dok ne* prestane kiša.	We will stay *until* the rain stops.
Откако је постала богата, никоме се не јавља.	*Otkako* je postala bogata, nikome se ne javlja.	*Since* she became rich, she doesn't speak to anyone.
Тек што смо стигли, морали смо да кренемо.	*Tek što* smo stigli, morali smo da krenemo.	We had *just* arrived and we had to leave.

2 Used for comparisons, the 'than' conjunctions:

него	nego	than
неголи	negoli	than
а камоли	a kamoli	let alone, not to mention

Више волим чоколаду *него* сладолед.	Više volim čokoladu *nego* sladoled.	I like chocolate more *than* ice cream.
Не воли себе *а камоли* друге.	Ne voli sebe *a kamoli* druge.	He doesn't love himself, *let alone* others.

3 The 'because' conjunctions:

јер*	jer*	because
пошто	pošto	since, because, after
тако да	tako da	so (that)
зато што	zato što	because, for that reason

* јер/jer is a milder form of 'because', expressing not the cause but the reason.

Она не може да дође на телефон *јер* је у купатилу.	Ona ne može da dođe na telefon *jer* je u kupatilu.	She cannot come to the phone *because* (she) is in the bathroom.
Деца су гладна *тако да* морамо да пожуримо.	Deca su gladna *tako da* moramo da požurimo.	The children are hungry *so* we must hurry.
Зашто? *Зато што*!	Zašto? *Zato što*!	Why? *Because*!
Закаснио је на воз *зато што* се успавао.	Zakasnio je na voz *zato što* se uspavao.	He was late for the train *because* he overslept.

4. The 'if' conjunctions:

ако	ako	if
кад	kad	if (were to)
да	da	if (had, had been)

| Ићи ћемо у биоскоп *ако* стигнете на време. | Ići ćemo u bioskop *ako* stignete na vreme. | We will go to the cinema *if* you arrive on time. |
| *Да* сте стигли на време, отишли бисмо у биоскоп. | *Da* ste stigli na vreme, otišli bismo u bioskop. | *Had* you arrived on time, we would have gone to the cinema. |

5. The 'how' conjunctions:

како	kako	how, like, as
као	kao	how, like, as
као што	kao što	as
као да	kao da	as if

Гледала је децу *како* се играју.	Gledala je decu *kako* se igraju.	She watched the children *as* they played.
Понашали су се *као да* су знали шта се догодило.	Ponašali su se *kao da* su znali šta se dogodilo.	They acted (behaved) *as if* they knew what had happened.
Као што знате, ми смо позната фирма.	*Kao što* znate, mi smo poznata firma.	*As* you know, we are a well-known firm.

6. The 'in order to' conjunctions:

| да/да би | da/da bi | to, in order to |
| како би | kako bi | so as to |

| Морали су да се сликају *да би* добили пасоше. | Morali su da se slikaju *da bi* dobili pasoše. | They had to have their pictures taken *in order to* get their passports. |

Miscellaneous conjunctions:

нека	neka	let (it be), and (let)
макар	makar	although, though, at least, even though
бар, барем	bar, barem	at least

Subordinating conjunctions

Дуг је пут, *нека* се добро одморе.	Dug je put, *neka* se dobro odmore.	The journey is long, *let* them rest well.
Назови ме *макар* било касно.	Nazovi me *makar* bilo kasno.	Call me *even if* it's late.
Напиши нам *барем* једно писмо.	Napiši nam *barem* jedno pismo.	Write us *at least* one letter.

Conjunctions used when asking questions:

да ли	da li	whether
где	gde	where
одакле	odakle	from where
откуд	otkud	whence, how come
ко	ko	who
што/шта	što/šta	what, why
куда	kuda	whither – where to

Да ли му је помогао брат да купи кућу?	*Da li* mu je pomogao brat da kupi kuću?	*Did* his brother help him to buy the house?
Одакле су Марко и Нада?	*Odakle* su Marko i Nada?	*Where* are Marko and Nada *from*?
Откуд ви овде?	*Otkud* vi ovde?	*How come* you are here?
Куда иду деца на одмор?	*Kuda* idu deca na odmor?	*Whither* are the children going for their holidays?

12.3 Differences in usages of *што*/*što* and *који*/*koji*

Што/**što** (which) is a relative conjunction used in relative clauses to link a dependent clause to the main clause. **Који/koji** (which, who) is a relative pronominal adjective and it also is used to link a dependent clause to the main clause. However, there is difference as to when each should be used.

Relative clauses describe or provide information about something or someone that has usually already been specified in the main clause.

This is Jane *who* drives me to work.

I've just finished reading a novel *which* I enjoyed very much.

In both of these sentences, the words 'who' and 'which' refer to the noun preceding them. In Serbian the relative pronominal adjective **који/ koji** would be used in both cases:

Usages of што/što and који/koji

| Ово је Џејн, *која* ме вози на посао. | Ovo je Džejn, *koja* me vozi na posao. | This is Jane *who* drives me to work. |
| Управо сам прочитао роман, *који* ми је јако пријао. | Upravo sam pročitao roman, *koji* mi je jako prijao. | I've just finished reading a novel *which* I enjoyed very much. |

Since **који/koji** is an adjective, it reflects gender and number and declines as an adjective.

However, instead of the above sentences, consider the following:

Jane drives fast, *which* scares me.

The food finally arrived, *which* made us all happy.

'Which' relates to the verb and not the noun in the previous clause. In these instances, the relative conjunction **што/što** would be used:

| Џејн вози брзо, *што* ме плаши. | Džejn vozi brzo, *što* me plaši. | Jane drives fast, *which* scares me. |
| Храна је коначно стигла, *што* нас је све обрадовало. | Hrana je konačno stigla, *što* nas je sve obradovalo. | The food finally arrived, *which* made us all happy. |

Unlike **који/koji**, **што/što** has no gender, number, nor case. It remains unchanged in all cases.

Што/što as a relative conjunction is also used after the words **нешто/ nešto** (something), **то/to** (that – determiner), **ово/ovo** (this over here), **оно/ono** (that over there), and wherever something is not named:

| Он је ипак постигао *нешто*, *што* не може да се каже и за тебе. | On je ipak postigao *nešto*, *što* ne može da se kaže i za tebe. | He still achieved *something*, *which* can't be said about you. |

Both **који/koji** and **што/što** have other uses, i.e. **који/koji** as an interrogative (see Section 8.6 Interrogative pronouns), and **што/što** as a conjunction used to replace **да/da** (that) after verbs expressing emotion or feelings: **бринути се/brinuti se** (to worry), **радовати се/radovati se** (to be glad, to rejoice), and following constructions in the dative case which express emotion or feelings: **мило/milo** (glad), **драго/drago** (glad), **жао/žao** (sorry), etc.

12 Conjunctions

Она се *брине што* јој се ниси јавио.	Ona se *brine što* joj se nisi javio.	She is *worried that* you haven't called her.
Радујемо се што сте положили испит.	*Radujemo se što* ste položili ispit.	We are *glad that* you passed your exam.

Chapter 13
Enclitics

Although the structure of a sentence in Serbian generally follows the basic Subject, Verb, Object word order, it is by no means rigid or fixed, and the language, in fact, moves quite freely with respect to this structure:

Милан је купио кућу у јуну.	Milan je kupio kuću u junu.	Milan bought a house in June.
Кућу је Милан купио у јуну.	Kuću je Milan kupio u junu.	The house Milan bought in June.
У јуну је Милан кућу купио.	U junu je Milan kuću kupio.	In June Milan (the house) bought.

In contrast to this generally flexible word order, there exists a fixed order with respect to the use of enclitics, both relative to each other and relative to the other elements in the sentence.

As words consisting of one or two syllables, enclitics, though written separately, cannot stand on their own in a sentence. They are dependent on the word preceding them (while proclitics, e.g. prepositions, are dependent on the word following them). Although proclitics may take on the accent of the word following them (see Sections 8.1.3 Unstressed personal pronouns and 11.3 Accentuation), enclitics never carry an accent themselves.

| Деца су изашла *на* сунце. | Deca su izašla *na* sunce. | The children went out *into* the sun. (proclitic) |
| Рекао *ми је* да ће закаснити. | Rekao *mi je* da će zakasniti. | He told *me* he would be late. (enclitic) |

Due to this close dependency on the word preceding them, and their taking second position with regard to it, enclitics are known as second-position clitics. Although this strict word order relevant to enclitics is in such contrast to the otherwise quite free word order of the language, it must be respected and understood in order to both speak and learn the language correctly and with understanding.

13 Enclitics

13.1 Order and importance of enclitics

There are four types of enclitics in Serbian. An enclitic can never begin a sentence (or clause), but takes second position to the word beginning the sentence. Enclitics appear in the following order:

1. Interrogative enclitic – particle ли/li: when present, this enclitic stands in first position in relation to all the other enclitics. The particle ли/li is only used when a question is being asked:

Хоћете *ли* да идете на плажу данас?	Hoćete *li* da idete na plažu danas?	*Will* you go to the beach today?
Је *ли* идете на плажу данас?	Je *li* idete na plažu danas?	*Are* you going to the beach today?
Идете *ли* данас на плажу?	Idete *li* danas na plažu?	*Are* you going to the beach today?

Although the word order in all three sentences is different, the particple ли/li, as an enclitic, is always in the second position. Note that in the second example, the **je/je** is not a verbal enclitic (see Sections 8.1 Personal pronouns and 8.1.4 Order of unstressed personal pronouns), but part of an interrogative form with the verb **бити/biti** (to be) (see Section 6.14 Formation of the interrogative).

2. Verbal enclitics – auxiliary verbs used in forming various tenses:

Past tense:	**сам/sam, си/si, je/je, смо/smo, сте/ste, су/su**
Future tense:	**ћу/ću, ћеш/ćeš, ће/će, ћемо/ćemo, ћете/ćete, ће/će**
Aorist tense:	**бих/bih, би/bi, би/bi, бисмо/bismo, бисте/biste, би/bi**

These take second position in the enclitic word order. Since each sentence or clause will have only one subject, verbal enclitics will appear on their own and will not compete with another verbal enclitic for position. It is important to remember that the verbal enclitic **je/je** is excluded from this position in the word order, as it falls in the last position of the enclitic word order.

Да *ли* бисте желели парче торте?	Da *li* biste želeli parče torte?	*Would* you *like* a piece of cake?
Ја *сам* рекао да ћу да дођем.	Ja *sam* rekao da ću da dođem.	I *said* that I *will* come.

3. Pronominal enclitics: the short or unstressed forms of personal pronouns are called pronominal enclitics (see Sections 8.1.3 Unstressed personal pronouns and 8.1.4 Order of unstressed personal pronouns). In position, they follow the verbal enclitics, in the following order:

> Dative: ми/mi, ти/ti, му/mu, joj/joj, нам/nam, вам/vam, им/im
>
> Genitive and accusative: ме/me, те/te, га/ga, je/je* or jy/ju*, нас/nas, вас/vas, их/ih

* jy/ju is used instead of je/je when the verbal JE is present.

Питала *сам те*.	Pitala *sam te*.	I asked *you*.
Да *ли је* Данко дао Стевану књигу?	Da *li je* Danko dao Stevanu knjigu?	*Did* Danko give Steven the book?
Јесте, дао *му jy je*.	Jeste, dao *mu ju je*.	Yes, he gave *it (her)* to *him*.

4. The reflexive form **ce/se**: this enclitic, the short form of the reflexive pronoun себе/sebe (see Section 8.2 Reflexive pronouns), takes last position in the enclitic order:

| Жалили *смо му се* на галаму. | Žalili *smo mu se* na galamu. | We complained *to him* about the noise. |

The verbal enclitic **je/je**, 3rd person singular present tense form of the verb бити/biti (to be) also takes last position in the overall enclitic word order. When it follows the reflexive enclitic **ce/se** it is generally omitted and **ce/se** effectively remains in the last position:

| Упитала *се (је)* да ли ће он да дође. | Upitala *se (je)* da li će on da dođe. | She asked *herself* whether he would come. |
| Жалио *ми се (је)* на галаму. | Žalio *mi se (je)* na galamu. | He complained *to me* about the noise. |

In the above examples, the first word in the sentence was in the past tense, thus requiring the auxiliary verb **je/je**. However, as the enclitic **ce/se** is also included in the sentence, the verbal enclitic **je/je** is omitted:

| Упитала *се* | Upitala *se* | She asked *herself* |

Order and importance of enclitics

after which another clause was introduced with its own set of enclitics:

| да *ли* ће он да дође. | da *li* će on da dođe. | *whether* he *would* come. |

The following rules apply to the use of enclitics:

1. An enclitic can never begin a sentence or an independent clause. In the initial position in the sentence or clause, various elements can stand including the subject, the main verb, a conjunction (in dependent clauses), etc. An enclitic can separate the subject if it consists of more than one word, but it can never separate a preposition from the noun it precedes. Nor can it separate a title from a person's name:

Добра *му је* вила оставила новчић.	Dobra *mu je* vila ostavila novčić.	The good fairy left *him* a coin.
На ручак *су јој* дошле обе сестре.	Na ručak *su joj* došle obe sestre.	For lunch both sisters came (*to her*).
Госпођа Јовановић *му је* дала писмо.	Gospođa Jovanović *mu je* dala pismo.	Mrs Jovanović gave *him* the letter.

2. Enclitics follow interrogatives (где/gde (where), одакле/odakle (from where), како/kako (how), чији/čiji (whose), etc.) and most conjunctions (да/da (that), кад/kad (when), ако/ako (if), јер/jer (because), etc.). Importantly, conjunctions a/a (but, and) and и/i (and) can never take initial position with respect to the enclitic word order. They are either followed by the long or stressed forms or another word has to take initial position before an enclitic can follow:

| Они је воле, *али му* то није драго. | Oni je vole, *ali mu* to nije drago. | They like her, *but he* isn't pleased about it. |
| Они је воле, *а њему* то није драго. | Oni je vole, *a njemu* to nije drago. | They like her, *but he* isn't pleased about it. |

But not:

| Они је воле, *а му* то није драго. | Oni je vole, *a mu* to nije drago. |

Order and importance of enclitics

3   All enclitics which appear in a sentence or clause must be kept together. They are placed as close to the beginning of the sentence (or clause) as possible, and immediately follow the introductory word or phrase in that sentence:

| Да *ли си је се* сетио? | Da *li si je se* setio? | *Did you* remember *her*? |

4   The subject, if expressed, normally follows the enclitics, unless it is the initial word in the sentence:

| Синоћ *га је* Миодраг видео. | Sinoć *ga je* Miodrag video. | Last night Miodrag saw *him*. |
| Миодраг *га је* синоћ видео. | Miodrag *ga je* sinoć video. | Miodrag saw *him* last night. |

5   As a rule, the verbal enclitic form **je/je** does not take precedence over any other enclitic and never precedes pronominal enclitics, other verbal enclitics or **ce/se**.

| Отац *ми је* дошао с пута. | Otac *mi je* došao s puta. | Father has returned from his trip. |
| Нервирао *се (је)* због тога. | Nervirao *se (je)* zbog toga. | He was irritated because of that. |

6   When verbal and pronominal enclitics occur together, the verbal enclitic precedes the pronominal:

| Волела *сам га*. | Volela *sam ga*. | I loved *him*. |
| Сви *смо га* волели. | Svi *smo ga* voleli. | We all loved *him*. |

7   Of the pronominal enclitics, the dative enclitics precede the accusative and genitive enclitics:

| Ја сам *му је* обећао. | Ja sam *mu je* obećao. | I've promised (*it* f) to him. |
| Ми бисмо *јој га* послали да смо имали њену адресу. | Mi bismo *joj ga* poslali da smo imali njenu adresu. | We would have sent (*it* m/n) to her had we had her address. |

8   When the negative past tense is used, the auxiliary verb is no longer considered an enclitic and can take first position in the sentence, followed by an enclitic if there is one:

| Нисмо *му се* јавили. | Nismo *mu se* javili. | We didn't say hello to him. |
| Није *ми* дао да платим. | Nije *mi* dao da platim. | He didn't allow *me* to pay. |

Order of enclitics following the initial word:

Initial position	Verbal enclitics		Pronominal enclitics		Reflexive **се/se**, or verbal **je**
			Dative	*Genitive or Accusative*	
	cам – sam		ми – mi	ме – me	
Да ли/Da li	си – si		ти – ti	те – te	
	смо – smo	(past tense)	му – mu	га – ga	
	сте – ste		joj – joj	je – je* or jy – ju*	ce – se je – je
	су – su		нам – nam	нас – nas	
Ако/Ako	ћу – ću		вам – vam	вас – vas	
	ћеш – ćeš		им – im	их – ih	
Зимус/Zimus	ће – će	(future tense)			
	ћемо – ćemo				
	ћете – ćete				
Данас/Danas	ће – će				
	бих – bih	(aorist tense)			
Јер/jer	би – bi				
	би – bi				
	бисмо – bismo				
	бисте – biste				
	би – bi				

* Her = Jy/ju is used before verbal **je**, if used at all.

Chapter 14
Numerals

Four numeral forms are used:

- Cardinal numbers, један/jedan (one), два/dva (two), etc.;
- Ordinal numbers, први/prvi (first), други/drugi (second), etc.;
- Collective numerals, двоје/dvoje (a group of two mixed gender beings), троје/troje (a group of three mixed gender beings);
- Number nouns, двојица/dvojica (a group of two male human beings), тројица/trojica (a group of three male human beings), etc. There is no special number form for counting females.

14.1 Cardinal numbers and their declension

0	zero	нула nula	
1	one	један jedan	Behaves as adjective
2	two	два dva	Has some case endings
3	three	три tri	
4	four	четири četiri	
5	five	пет pet	
6	six	шест šest	
7	seven	седам sedam	

14 Numerals

8	eight	осам	osam
9	nine	девет	devet
10	ten	десет	deset
11	eleven	једанаест	jedanaest
12	twelve	дванаест	dvanaest
13	thirteen	тринаест	trinaest
14	fourteen	четрнаест	četrnaest
15	fifteen	петнаест	petnaest
16	sixteen	шеснаест	šesnaest
17	seventeen	седамнаест	sedamnaest
18	eighteen	осамнаест	osamnaest
19	nineteen	деветнаест	devetnaest
20	twenty	двадесет	dvadeset
21	twenty-one	двадесет (и) један	dvadeset (i) jedan
22	twenty-two	двадесет (и) два	dvadeset (i) dva
23	twenty-three	двадесет (и) три	dvadeset (i) tri
24	twenty-four	двадесет (и) четири	dvadeset (i) četiri
25	twenty-five	двадесет (и) пет	dvadeset (i) pet

Cardinal numbers

30	thirty	тридесет trideset	
40	forty	четрдесет četrdeset	
50	fifty	педесет pedeset	
60	sixty	шездесет šezdeset	
70	seventy	седамдесет sedamdeset	
80	eighty	осамдесет osamdeset	
90	ninety	деведесет devedeset	
100	one hundred	сто/једна стотина sto/jedna stotina	Is a noun, with number, gender and case
200	two hundred	двеста(двесто)/ две стотине dvesta(dvesto)/ dve stotine	
300	three hundred	триста/три стотине trista/tri stotine	
400	four hundred	четиристо/четири стотине četiristo/četiri stotine	
500	five hundred	петсто/пет стотина petsto/pet stotina	
501	five hundred and one	петсто један petsto jedan	
1,000	one thousand	хиљаду/једна хиљада hiljadu/jedna hiljada	Is a noun, with number, gender and case
1,001	one thousand and one	хиљаду један hiljadu jedan	

14 Numerals

2,000	two thousand	две хиљаде dve hiljade	
5,000	five thousand	пет хиљада pet hiljada	
10,000	ten thousand	десет хиљада deset hiljada	
100,000	one hundred thousand	сто хиљада sto hiljada	
1,000,000	one million	(један) милион (jedan) milion	Is a noun, with number, gender and case
1 + 9 zeros	one thousand million (UK) one billion (USA)	(једна) милијарда (jedna) milijarda	Is a noun, with number, gender and case
1 + 12 zeros	one billion (UK) one trillion (USA)	(један) билион (jedan) bilion	Is a noun, with number, gender and case

14.1.1 Numeral one

Number one, један/jedan, behaves as a true adjective, agreeing with the noun in gender and case:

Један човек	Jedan čovek	One man (nom. m)
Једна жена	Jedna žena	One woman (nom. f)
Једно дете	Jedno dete	One child (nom. n)
Возач једног аутобуса	Vozač jednog autobusa	The driver of one bus (gen. m)
Без једне терасе	Bez jedne terase	Without one terrace (gen. f)
У једном селу	U jednom selu	In one village (loc. n)

The verb following number one is in the singular and has gender (where appropriate):

Један човек је дошао.	Jedan čovek je došao.	One man came.
Једна жена је певала.	Jedna žena je pevala.	One woman sang.

All numbers ending in one (except compound number 11 ending in **неаст/neast**) follow the same rules:

> Cardinal numbers

Двадесет један аутобус *је био* на станици.	Dvadeset jedan autobus *je bio* na stanici.	Twenty-one buses were at the station.
Тридесет једна зграда *је порушена*.	Trideset jedna zgrada *je porušena*.	Thirty-one buildings were demolished.
Осамдесет једно дете *је било* на излету.	Osamdeset jedno dete *je bilo* na izletu.	Eighty-one children were at the picnic.

Number one, **један/jedan**, can also be used in the following ways:

(a) As the indefinite article 'a/an':

Наишли су на *једног* просјака.	Naišli su na *jednog* prosjaka.	They came across *a* beggar.

(b) As an adjective signifying 'equality-sameness', in which instance it can have a plural form:

Све ми је *једно*.	Sve mi je *jedno*.	It's all *the same* to me.
Једних су родитеља.	*Jednih* su roditelja.	They are of *the same* parents.

(c) With nouns in the plural that have a singular meaning (*pluralia tantum*):

Нашао је *једне* црне панталоне.	Našao je *jedne* crne pantalone.	He found *a pair* of black trousers.
Стајали су поред *једних* врата.	Stajali su pored *jednih* vrata.	They stood by *a* door.

(d) As the pronoun 'some', when used independently:

Једни су стајали а *једни* су седели.	*Jedni* su stajali a *jedni* su sedeli.	*Some* were standing and *some* were sitting.

(e) In the expression **један једини/jedan jedini**, the meaning is 'one and only':

То је био *један једини* пут да га је потражила.	To je bio *jedan jedini* put da ga je potražila.	It was *the one and only time* that she looked for him.

(f) As an expression of affection or anger, meaning 'you' and used with the noun in the vocative case (the context and facial expression and intonation will indicate which effect is being expressed):

Будало *једна*! **Budalo** *jedna*! *You fool!*

The negative form of the numeral one, **ниједан**/nijedan, 'not one, not a, none', behaves exactly like **један**/jedan. The verb that follows it must be negated. When used with a preposition, the preposition must come between the prefix **ни**/ni- and the number **један**/jedan.

Ниједан човек није дошао.	*Nijedan* čovek nije došao.	Not *one* man came.
Ни на *једно* пиће није дошао.	Ni na *jedno* piće nije došao.	He didn't come *for* even *one* drink.

14.1.2 Numerals two, three and four and the numeral 'both'

Numbers two, **два**/dva, three, **три**/tri, and four, **четири**/četiri, behave differently from number one and from numerals five, six, seven, etc.

The number two and the numeral 'both' have two forms. One form is used for both masculine and neuter nouns and the other is for feminine nouns:

(a) The ending -**а** is added to the stem of masculine and neuter nouns and adjectives following the number two, **два**/dva, and the numeral 'both', **оба**/oba. This ending is only applied when the numbers are not declined:

дв*а* велик*а* камион*а*	dv*a* velik*a* kamion*a*	two large trucks
дв*а* леп*а* сел*а*	dv*a* lep*a* sel*a*	two pretty villages
дв*а* директн*а* пренос*а*	dv*a* direktn*a* prenos*a*	two live broadcasts
об*а* студент*а*	ob*a* student*a*	both students

(b) The ending -**е**/e is added to the stem of regular feminine nouns and adjectives following the number two, **два**/dva, and the numeral 'both', **оба**/oba, while the ending -**и**/i is added to irregular feminine nouns (those ending in a consonant):

дв*е* велик*е* кућ*е*	dv*e* velik*e* kuć*e*	two large houses
дв*е* леп*е* ноћ*и*	dv*e* lep*e* noć*i*	two beautiful nights
об*е* књиг*е*	ob*e* knjig*e*	both books

Number two, два/dva, and the numeral 'both', оба/oba, decline in the following way:

Cardinal numbers

	Masculine and neuter		Feminine	
Nom.	два камиона/села	оба камиона/села	две жене	обе жене
	dva kamiona/sela	oba kamiona/sela	dve žene	obe žene
Gen.	двају камиона/села	(од) оба камиона/села	двеју жена	(од) обе жене
	dvaju kamiona/sela	обоје камиона/села	dveju žena	обеју жена
		(od) oba kamiona/sela		(od) obe žene
		oboje kamiona/sela		obeju žena
Dat.	двама камионима/селима	обома камионима/селима	двема женама	обема женама
	dvama kamionima/selima	oboma kamionina/selima	dvema ženama	obema ženama
Acc.	два камиона/села	оба камиона/села	две жене	обе жене
	dva kamiona/sela	oba kamiona/sela	dve žene	obe žene
Voc.	два камиона/села	оба камиона/села	две жене	обе жене
	dva kamiona/sela	oba kamiona/sela	dve žene	obe žene
Inst.	двама камионима/селима	обома камионима/селима	двема женама	обема женама
	dvama kamionima/selima	oboma kamionina/selima	dvema ženama	obema ženama

Loc.	двама камионима/ селима	обома камионима/ селима	двема женама	обема женама
	dvama kamionima/ selima	oboma kamionina/ selima	dvema ženama	obema ženama

Although they are frequently used in the spoken language, the forms **обадва/obadva** and **обадве/obadve** for 'both' are considered to be incorrect.

Numbers three, **три/tri** and four, **четири/četiri** remain the same in form as they do not have gender. However, the nouns and adjectives that follow them take the same endings as for numeral two.

(a)	три велик*а* камион*а*	tri velik*a* kamion*a*	three large trucks
	три леп*а* сел*а*	tri lep*a* sel*a*	three pretty villages
	три директн*а* пренос*а*	tri direktn*a* prenos*a*	three live broadcasts
(b)	три велик*е* кућ*е*	tri velik*e* kuć*e*	three large houses
	три леп*е* ноћ*и*	tri lep*e* noć*i*	three beautiful nights

Although numbers three, **три/tri** and four, **четири/četiri** do decline, their declension is replaced by the number in the nominative which is preceded by the appropriate preposition denoting its function in the sentence. In the case of masculine and neuter nouns, they can be replaced by the collective numeral (see Section 14.4 Collective numerals):

Отишла је *са* четири жене.	Otišla je *sa* četiri žene.	She went *with* four women.
Упаковали су их *у* три кутије.	Upakovali su ih *u* tri kutije.	They packed them *in* three boxes.
Писао сам *тројици* мушкараца.	Pisao sam *trojici* muškaraca.	I wrote to (a group of) three men. (coll. num.)

With numbers two, three and four and the numeral 'both', all nouns are followed by verbs in the plural. The gender ending of verbs agrees with the nouns, except in the masculine where the verb ending generally agrees with the ending **-a**, rather than the appropriate gender ending, which when used would not be considered incorrect:

Дв*а*/об*а*/три/четири млад*а* војник*а су* дошл*а*.	Dv*a*/ob*a*/tri/četiri mlad*a* vojnik*a su* došl*a*.	Two/both/three/ four young soldiers came.

Два/оба/три/четири детета су се играла.	Dva/oba/tri/četiri deteta su se igrala.	Two/both/three/four children played.	Cardinal numbers
Две/обе/три/четири младе жене су чекале.	Dve/obe/tri/četiri mlade žene su čekale.	Two/both/three/four young women waited.	
Две/обе/три/четири лепе ноћи су прошле.	Dve/obe/tri/četiri lepe noći su prošle.	Two/both/three/four beautiful nights went by.	

The same applies to all numbers ending in two, three, four (except twelve, thirteen and fourteen which are compound numbers ending in **наест/naest**):

Двадесет четири млада вука су дошла.	Dvadeset četiri mlada vuka su došla.	Twenty-four young wolves came.
Осамдесет три лепе ноћи су прошле.	Osamdeset tri lepe noći su prošle.	Eighty-three beautiful nights went by.

14.1.3 Numerals five, six, seven and onwards

Numerals five, six, seven, eight, nine, ten, eleven to nineteen and all other numerals ending in five, six, seven, eight, nine and zero are followed by adjectives and nouns in the genitive plural:

Пет добрих камиона.	Pet dobrih kamiona.	Five good trucks.
Осам лепих девојака.	Osam lepih devojaka.	Eight beautiful young women.
Двадесет седам малих острва.	Dvedeset sedam malih ostrva.	Twenty-seven small islands.

Although the adjectives and nouns related to these numerals are in the genitive plural, the numerals themselves are considered to be of singular neuter gender because the verb following them is of singular neuter gender:

Пет добрих камиона је стајало.	Pet dobrih kamiona je stajalo.	Five good trucks were standing.
Осам лепих девојака је чекало.	Osam lepih devojaka je čekalo.	Eight beautiful young women were waiting.
Двадесет седам малих острва је насељено.	Dvedeset sedam malih ostrva je naseljeno.	Twenty-seven small islands are populated.

Although used less frequently, for semantic congruency, the verb can also be in the plural, agreeing in gender with the noun:

Пет добр*их* камион*а* с*у* стајал*и*.	**Pet dobr***ih* **kamion***a* **s***u* **stajal***i*.	Five good trucks were standing.
Осам леп*их* девојак*а* с*у* чекал*е*.	**Osam lep***ih* **devojak***a* **s***u* **čekal***e*.	Eight beautiful young women were waiting.
Двадесет седам мал*их* острв*а* с*у* насељен*а*.	**Dvadeset sedam mal***ih* **ostrv***a* **s***u* **naseljen***a*.	Twenty-seven small islands are populated.

Cardinal numbers from eleven to nineteen are formed by adding the suffix -наест/neast to numbers 1–9:

једанаест	**jedanaest**	11
дванаест	**dvanaest**	12
шеснаест	**šesnaest**	16
осамнаест	**osamnaest**	18

A hundred (**стотина**/**stotina** – f), a thousand (**хиљада**/**hiljada** – f), a million (**милион**/**milion** – m) and a billion (**милијарда**/**milijarda** – f) are nouns used to express numbers. As such, they have number, gender and case endings.

Изашла је на демонстрацију *са стотином других* жена.	**Izašla je na demonstraciju *sa stotinom drugih* žena.**	She went to the demonstration with *a hundred* other women. (inst.)
Председник се обратио *милионима*.	**Predsednik se obratio** *milionima*.	The President addressed the *millions*. (dat.)

When used in the singular, the nouns **стотину/stotinu** (a hundred) and **хиљаду/hiljadu** (a thousand) have an -**у/u** ending (as in the feminine accusative):

Прошло је хиљаду ноћи.	**Prošlo je hiljadu noći.**	1,000 nights went by. (Verb neuter singular agreeing with **хиљаду ноћи**)
Прошла је хиљаду и једна ноћ.	**Prošla je hiljadu i jedna noć.**	1,001 nights went by. (Verb feminine singular agreeing **једна ноћ**)

14.2 Ordinal numbers and their declension

All ordinal numbers function as definite adjectives, taking the gender, number and case of the noun they qualify.

With the exception of numbers 1–4, ordinal numbers are derived from cardinal numbers to which the following suffixes are added:

Masculine	Neuter	Feminine
-и/i	-о/o	-а/a
	-е/e for third only	

Пет*и* члан је стигао.	Pet*i* član je stigao.	The *fifth* member arrived.
Десет*о* дете се разболело.	Deset*o* dete se razbolelo.	The *tenth* child fell ill.
Петнаест*а* столица је сломљен*а*.	Petnaest*a* stolica je slomljen*a*.	The *fifteenth* chair was broken.

Ordinal numbers 1–4:

Masculine	Neuter	Feminine	
прв*и*	прв*о*	прв*а*	first
prv*i*	prv*o*	prv*a*	
друг*и*	друг*о*	друг*а*	second
drug*i*	drug*o*	drug*a*	
трећ*и*	трећ*е*	трећ*а*	third
treć*i*	treć*e*	treć*a*	
четврт*и*	четврт*о*	четврт*а*	fourth
četvrt*i*	četvrt*o*	četvrt*a*	

Прв*а* награда је најбољ*а*.	Prv*a* nagrad*a* je najbolj*a*.	The first prize is the best.
Мира је добила трећ*у* награду за цртање.	Mira je dobila treć*u* nagradu za crtanje.	Mira won the third prize for drawing.

In addition to being an ordinal number, други/drugi (second) also means 'another, other/s, someone else'.

Купила је *другу* књигу од истог аутора.	Kupila je *drugu* knjigu od istog autora.	She bought the *second* book by the same author.

Ordinal numbers

| Други су купили исту књигу. | Drugi su kupili istu knjigu. | Others bought the same book. |

Cardinal numbers seven (**седам/sedam**) and eight (**осам/osam**) lose the -a and become **седма/sedma** and **осма/osma** in the feminine, **седми/sedmi** and **осми/osmi** in the masculine, and **седмо/sedmo** and **осмо/osmo** in the neuter.

The ending -e (rather than -o) for the neuter is used only for 'third' – **треће/treće**

With compound numbers, only the last digit has the ordinal form.

| Они станују на двадесет првом спрату. | Oni stanuju na dvadeset prvom spratu. | They live on the twenty-*first* floor. |

The cardinal numbers **сто/sto** (one hundred), **хиљада/hiljada** (a thousand), **милион/milion** (a million) become ordinals **стоти/stoti**, **хиљадити/hiljaditi**, **милионити/milioniti** in the masculine:

| *Стоти* путник се укрцао у авион. | *Stoti* putnik se ukrcao u avion. | The *hundredth* passenger boarded the plane. |

| Сваки *хиљадити* потрошач је добио поклон. | Svaki *hiljaditi* potrošač je dobio poklon. | Every *thousandth* customer received a gift. |

Written in a numerical form, ordinal numbers are followed by a full stop:

2003.

Ordinal numbers are used when expressing dates in answer to the question 'When?' with the noun following in the genitive:

| Рођена је двадесет пет*ог* децембра. | Rođena je dvadeset *petog* decembra. | She was born on 25*th* December. |

The cardinal number one, **један/jedan**, used together with the ordinal number two, **други/drugi** denote a relationship of reciprocity ('one another, each other . . .'):

| *Један другог* су загрлили. | *Jedan drugog* su zagrlili. | They embraced *each other.* (masc.) |

| Помогли су *један другом*. | Pomogli su *jedan drugom*. | (They) helped *one another.* (masc.) |

When using the expression 'For the first, second, third, etc., time . . .', the preposition **по/po** is used with all ordinal numbers except the number one:

Срели су се	Sreli su se *prvi*	They met *for the first time*
први пут	*put* u novembru.	in November.
у новембру.		
По трећи пут	Po treći put mu	I'm telling him *for the third*
му говорим да	govorim da	*time* to close the door.
затвори врата.	zatvori vrata.	

14.3 Fractions and decimal numbers

When the first number of the fraction is one, fractions in Serbian are expressed using a derived noun or ordinal number with an ending to agree with a feminine singular noun in the nominative case:

једна   jedna   one

The remaining part of the fraction is expressed with the ending in **-ина/ina**:

једна половина   jedna polovina   ¹/₂   one-half

When the fraction begins with the numbers two, three or four, the cardinal number ending agrees with a feminine plural noun in the nominative case:

две   dve   two

and the derived noun ends in **-ине/ine**:

две трећине   dve trećine   ²/₃   two-thirds

Fractions beginning with three and four are formed in the same way.

With fractions beginning with five onwards, the ordinal number does not change, while the derived noun that follows it takes on the ending **-ина/ina**:

пет осмина   pet osmina   ⁵/₈   five-eighths

In Serbian full stops are used to indicate when a number has gone into the one thousand and over range, while commas are used to indicate decimal points.

In speaking, commas are expressed with either the word **кома/koma** or **зарез/zarez**:

2,3   два кома три   dva koma tri   2.3   two point three

While zeros are both written and read out:

0,3   нула кома три   nula koma tri   0.3   zero point three

Fractions and decimals

14.4 Collective numerals

Collective numerals are used when referring to a group or collective of persons or animals of mixed gender and/or age.

Collective numerals range from two to ninety-nine. Numerals two, 'both' and three end in **-оје/-oje**, as do all collective numerals ending in numbers two and three, except the number twelve:

двоје	dvoje	a group of	two
оboje	oboje		both
троје	troje		three
осамдесет двоје	osamdeset dvoje		eighty-two

and all others, excluding numerals ending in one, end in **-оро/oro**:

четворо	četvoro	a group of	four
петоро	petoro		five
седморо	sedmoro		seven
десеторо	desetoro		ten
двадесеторо	dvadesetoro		twenty
тридесето петоро	trideset petoro		thirty-five

Collective numerals are also used with collective nouns (see Section 7.1), ending with the suffix **-а** and **-ад/ad** in the nominative singular:

| троје браће | troje braće | (a group of) three brothers |
| седамнаесторо јагњади | sedamnaestoro jagnjadi | (a group of) seventeen lambs |

Note that the collective noun **деца/deca** cannot be used with cardinal numbers, but must be preceded by collective numerals from five onwards, while two to four can be expressed using the genitive singular of **дете/dete**:

| два детета | dva deteta | two children |
| петоро деце | petoro dece | five children |

Although there exists a declension for collective numerals through the cases, the dative and genitive cases are the only cases used where there is *no* appropriate preposition to precede the numeral, otherwise, prepositions are used with the collective in the accusative form followed by the genitive plural of most nouns:

| Књига је *за* двоје студената. | Knjiga je *za* dvoje studenata. | The book is *for* the *two* students. |

| Дао је књигу | Dao je knjigu | (He) gave the book |
| двома студентима. | dvoma studentima. | to the two students. |

When the collective is declined, the noun following it is appropriately declined as well. Generally, smaller numbers are declined, while higher numbers are used only in the nominative and the accusative forms.

Collective numerals are neuter in gender and the verb is in the neuter singular. The noun that follows the collective, or pronoun or determiner (which would also be of neuter gender) that precedes it, is in the genitive plural.

То троје нас је видело.	To troje nas je videlo.	Those three saw us.
Деветоро деце је положило испите.	Devetoro dece je položilo ispite.	(A group of) nine children passed their exams.
Нас осамнаесторо је седело у чамцу.	Nas osamnaestoro je sedelo u čamcu.	We eighteen were sitting in the boat.
Петоро људи се пријавило.	Petoro ljudi se prijavilo.	Five people (of mixed gender) signed up.

As distinguished from:

| Пет људи се пријавило. | Pet ljudi se prijavilo. | Five men signed up. |

14.5 Number nouns

Number nouns apply only to animate nouns of masculine gender. They refer to a group of male human beings, described by the number noun formed with the suffix -ица/ica:

двојица	dvojica	a group of two masculine gender beings
тројица	trojica	a group of three masculine gender beings
петнаесторица	petnaestorica	a group of fifteen masculine gender beings

Number nouns can be formed with all the numbers, excluding the number one and all numbers including it, up to but not including 100. These nouns belong to the third declension. The noun following number nouns is in the genitive plural. The verb is in the plural with the past participle ending in -a (although the masculine и/i ending would not be incorrect).

| двојица другова | dvojica drugova | a group of two friends |
| су дошла | su došla | came |

In addition to the above, other nouns are formed from cardinal and ordinal numbers with the suffixes -ица/ica, -ац/ac, -ка/ka:

седмица	sedmica	a week, a figure of seven
једанаестерац	jedanaesterac	a penalty kick
двојка	dvojka	the figure two

14.6 Multiplicatives

Multiplicatives in Serbian are formed in a similar manner to their English equivalents, 'twofold, threefold, fivefold', etc. – a number and the word 'fold' are linked to form one word. The **струки/struki** ('-fold') adjective follows a collective numeral, where -o links them to the number:

једноструки	jednostruki	singlefold
двоструки	dvostruki	twofold
четвороструки	četvorostruki	fourfold

The word **дупли/dupli** is the equivalent of the English 'double':

| *Дупли* виски | *Dupli* viski | *Double* scotch on ice. |
| са ледом. | sa ledom. | |

тродупли/trodupli (triple) is derived from it.

When functioning as adjectives, they have number and gender, as well as declension:

| трострука превара | trostruka prevara | a *triple (threefold)* deception |

Multiplicatives can also function as adverbs:

| *Троструко* га | *Trostruko* ga | He deceived him |
| је преварио. | je prevario. | *threefold.* |

14.7 Approximatives

Approximatives are numbers indicating an approximate quantity. There are two types of approximatives.

The first relates to quantities described to be in the vicinity of any numeral ending with zero (other than zero on its own) up to 100 – 10, 20, 30, 40, 50, 60, 70, 80, 90 and 100 – as well as numerals in the teens, to which the suffix -ак/ak is added:

Десетак момака је изашло на улицу.	*Desetak* momaka je izašlo na ulicu.	*Approximately ten* young men stepped out into the street.
Петнаестак војника је чекало.	*Petnaestak* vojnika je čekalo.	*Fifteen or so* soldiers waited.

The second type relates to approximate quantities around the single or compound numerals ending in numerals other than zero. This type is formed by adding a hyphen and the next ascending number:

Пет-шест особа се јавило на оглас.	*Pet-šest* osoba se javilo na oglas.	*Five or six* people responded to the advertisement.
Тридесет две-три жене су певале у хору.	*Trideset dve-tri* žene su pevale u horu.	*Thirty-two or three* women sang in the choir.

Nouns following the first type of approximates are in the genitive plural, whereas agreement for the second type follows the same pattern given for cardinal numbers.

14.8 Distributives

The division of something into equal parts is expressed through the use of distributive numbers. Distributive numbers are cardinal numbers in front of which the preposition **по/po** is placed, indicating the number of parts of the whole that were distributed or assigned:

Деца су добила *по два* парчета торте.	Deca su dobila *po dva* parčeta torte.	The children got *two* pieces of cake *each*.
Свако је купио *по један* сладолед.	Svako je kupio *po jedan* sladoled.	Everybody bought *one* ice-cream *each*.

The preposition **по/po** does not change the gender and case of the number and noun before which it is put. The number agrees with the noun in gender and follows the cardinal number agreement rules.

14.9 Frequentatives

Frequentatives in Serbian are formed in a similar manner to their English equivalents, 'two times, three times, four times', etc. – a cardinal or ordinal number and the word 'times' are linked to form one word.

14 Numerals

In Serbian the word **пут/put** (times) follows the cardinal number to form one word:

Двапут сам јој рекла.	**Dvaput sam joj rekla.**	I told her *twice* *(two times)*.

With an ordinal number, the two are separated and the number is often preceded by the preposition **по/po** (following all ordinal numbers except first):

По трећи пут га зовем.	**Po treći put ga zovem.**	I'm calling him *for the third time*.

The same can be expressed with the use of **пута/puta**, although in that formation the number preceding is cardinal and stands on its own:

Два пута сам јој рекла.	**Dva puta sam joj rekla.**	I told her *twice* *(two times)*.
Три пута га зовем.	**Tri puta ga zovem.**	I am calling him *three times*.

Frequentatives behave as adverbs and do not decline.

14.10 Weights and measures

The metric system is used for weights and measures:

Мере за тежину:	**Mere za težinu:**	Weights and measures:
један грам	**jedan gram**	one gram
петсто грама	**petsto grama**	five hundred grams
један килограм	**jedan kilogram**	one kilogram
пола кила	**pola kila**	half a kilo
једно кило	**jedno kilo**	one kilo
два кила	**dva kila**	two kilos
једна тона	**jedna tona**	one ton
Мере за дужину:	**Mere za dužinu:**	Measures of length and distance:
један милиметар	**jedan milimetar**	one millimetre
један сантиметар	**jedan santimetar**	one centimetre

пола метра	pola metra	half a metre
један метар	jedan metar	one metre
два метра	dva metra	two metres
сто метара	sto metara	one hundred metres
један километар	jedan kilometar	one kilometre
два километра	dva kilometra	two kilometres
Мере за течност:	**Mere za tečnost:**	*Measures for liquids:*
један децилитар/ један деци	jedan decilitar/ jedan deci	one decilitre
пола литра	pola litra	half a litre
седам десилитра/ седам деци	sedam decilitra/ sedam deci	seven decilitres
један литар	jedan litar	one litre
два литра	dva litra	two litres

14.11 Age

Asking and telling of age is expressed in several ways:

1	Колико година има Марко?	Koliko godina ima Marko?	How many years does Marko have?
2	Колико је Марко стар?	Koliko je Marko star?	How old is Marko?
3	Колико је Марку година?	Koliko je Marku godina?	How many years is (it to) Marko?

The following replies correspond to the questions:

1	Марко има десет година.	Marko ima deset godina.	Marko has ten years.
2	Марко је стар десет година.	Marko je star deset godina.	Marko is ten years old.
3	Марку је десет година.	Marku je deset godina.	(To) Marko (it) is ten years.

In the first two examples, Marko is in the nominative case. In the last example, Marko is in the dative case.

14 Numerals

Ја имам двадесет три године.	Ja imam dvadeset tri godine.	I am twenty-three years old.
Она је стара дванаест година.	Ona je stara dvanaest godina.	She is twelve years old.
Њему је три године.	Njemu je tri godine.	To him it is three years.

If the person whose age is being inquired about is a friend or is someone of whom it is known that their birthday has just passed or is about to come, then a common form of the question pertains to the number of years one has completed (filled), i.e. lived:

Колико си година напунио?	Koliko si godina napunio?	How many years have you completed?
Колико година пуниш?	Koliko godina puniš?	How many years are you completing?
Напунио сам 18 година.	Napunio sam 18 godina.	I have completed 18 years.
Пуним 18 година.	Punim 18 godina.	I am completing 18 years.

14.12 Days, months and dates

The following are the days of the week. These are not capitalised. Some days are of the masculine and some of the feminine gender:

понедељак	ponedeljak	Monday (m)
уторак	utorak	Tuesday (m)
среда	sreda	Wednesday (f)
четвртак	četvrtak	Thursday (m)
петак	petak	Friday (m)
субота	subota	Saturday (f)
недеља	nedelja	Sunday (f)

A week is referred to as **недеља/nedelja** or **седмица/sedmica**. When referring to only one week, the expression is:

недељу дана	nedelju dana	a week (of days)

When referring to more than a week, the number preceding 'week' is cardinal:

две недеље dve nedelje two weeks

The preposition **у/u** ('in' but in this context the English equivalent is 'on') followed by the accusative is always used in reply to questions relating to the days of the week – 'on what day?':

када...?	kada...?	when (on what day)...?
у понедељак	u ponedeljak	on Monday
у среду	u sredu	on Tuesday
у петак	u petak	on Friday

The following are the months of the year. These are not capitalised:

јануар	januar	January
фебруар	februar	February
март	mart	March
април	april	April
мај	maj	May
јуни	juni	June
јули	juli	July
август	avgust	August
септембар	septembar	September
октобар	oktobar	October
новембар	novembar	November
децембар	decembar	December

All the months are masculine gender and those with a **-бар/bar** ending have a fleeting **a**, reflected through the cases as **-бра/bra, -бру/bru**:

| окто*бра* | okto*bra* | October (gen.) |
| окто*бру* | okto*bru* | October (dat./loc.) |

The months June (**јуни/juni**) and July (**јули/juli**) lose their final **-и/i** when endings are added through the cases:

| првог јуна/јула | prvog juna/jula | (on) 1 June/July (gen.) |
| у јуну/јулу | u junu/julu | in June/July (loc.) |

Days, months and dates

As with weeks, when referring to only one month, the expression is:

месец дана   **mesec dana**   a month (of days)

When referring to more than a month, the number preceding 'month' is cardinal:

два месеца   **dva meseca**   two months

The preposition **y/u** (in) with the locative case is used in reply to when?:

у јануару	**u januaru**	in January
у марту	**u martu**	in March
у јулу	**u julu**	in July

Ordinal numbers, which function as definite adjectives, are used in forming dates (see Section 14.2 Ordinal numbers):

| **први мај** | **prvi maj** | 1 May |
| **пети октобар** | **peti oktobar** | 5 October |

In compound numbers, only the last digit is an ordinal number, while the preceding numbers are cardinal:

двадесет (card.) **први** (ordinal nom.) **мај** (nom.)	**dvadeset** (card.) **prvi** (ordinal nom.) **maj** (nom.)	The twenty-first of May
двадесет (card.) **пети** (ordinal nom.) **октобар** (nom.)	**dvadeset** (card.) **peti** (ordinal nom.) **oktobar** (nom.)	The twenty-fifth of October
тридесет (card.) **први** (ordinal nom.) **децембар** (nom.) **хиљаду*** (acc.) **девет сто** **деведесет** (nom.) **девете** (ord. gen.) **године** (gen. sg.)	**trideset** (card.) **prvi** (ordinal nom.) **decembar** (nom.) **hiljadu*** (acc.) **devet sto** **devedeset** (nom.) **devete** (ord. gen.) **godine** (gen. sg.)	The thirty-first of December one thousand* nine hundred and ninety ninth year
31. децембар 1999.	**31. decembar 1999.**	31st December 1999

тринаести (ord. nom.) јули (nom.) две хиљаде (card.) и друге (ord. gen.) године (gen. sg.)	trinaesti (ord. nom.) juli (nom.) dve hiljade (card.) i druge (ord. gen.) godine (gen. sg.)	The thirteenth of July two thousand and second year	**Days, months and dates**
13. јули 2002.	13. juli 2002.	13th July 2002	

* One thousand хиљаду/hiljadu is in the accusative.

When the date is given in response to the questions:

када . . . ?   kada . . . ?   when . . . ?

којег датума?   kojeg datuma?   on what date?

the genitive case is used:

првог маја	prvog maja	on the first of May
петог октобра	petog oktobra	on the fifth of October
Рођена сам тринаестог (ord. gen.) јула (gen.) хиљаду (acc.) девет стотина (card.) и педесет (card.) четврте (ord. gen.) године (gen. sg.).	Rođena sam trinaestog jula hiljadu devet stotina i pedeset četvrte godine.	I was born on the thirteenth of July one thousand nine hundred and fifty four (one thousand nine hundred and fifty fourth year).

No preposition precedes the date in Serbian:

Били смо у Лондону осмог јануар.	Bili smo u Londonu osmog januara.	We were in London on the eighth of January.
Идемо на скијање дванаестог фебруара.	Idemo na skijanje dvanaestog februara.	We're going skiing on the twelfth of February.
Вратили су се двадесет трећег јула.	Vratili su se dvadeset trećeg jula.	They returned on the twenty-third of July.

In the numerical form, dates are followed by a full stop:

| 2003. година је брзо прошла. | 2003. godina je brzo prošla. | The year 2003 went by quickly. |
| Преселили смо се у Београд 1998. године. | Preselili smo se u Beograd 1998. godine. | We moved to Belgrade in 1998. |

14.13 Time

14.13.1 Telling the time

Time is expressed using a cardinal number and any of the following nouns:

час	čas	hour (used in 24-hour clock)
сат	sat	hour/o'clock
и по	i po	half past
пола*	pola*	30 minutes to/of

* Precedes the cardinal number and refers to half of the next hour and not the one just gone.

| петнаест до* | petnaest do* | 15 minutes to |
| и петнаест | i petnaest | 15 minutes past |

* See above.

The words 'hour' and 'minute' after two, three and four get the ending -a: два сата/dva sata (two hours/o'clock), три сата/tri sata (three hours/o'clock), четири минута/četiri minuta, while five and above follow the genitive plural (excluding compound numbers ending in the numbers one, two, three and four:

један сат/минут	jedan sat/minut	one hour/o'clock/ one minute
два сата/минута	dva sata/minuta	two hours/o'clock/ two minutes
три сата/минута	tri sata/minuta	three hours/o'clock/ three minutes
четири сата/ минута	četiri sata/minuta	four hours/o'clock/ four minutes

Time

пет сати/минутā	pet sati/minutā	five hours/o'clock/ five minutes	
десет сати/минутā	deset sati/minutā	ten hours/o'clock/ ten minutes	

In reply to the question:

Колико је сати?	Koliko je sati?	What is the time?	

one could say:

један сат и пет минутā	jedan sat i pet minutā	five minutes past one	1:05
пет минута прошло један	pet minuta prošlo jedan	five minutes past one	1:05
петнаест минутā прошло осам	petnaest minutā prošlo osam	fifteen minutes past eight	8:15
осам и петнаест	osam i petnaest	quarter past eight	8:15
двадесет три часа и осамнаест минутā	dvedeset tri časa i osamnaest minutā	twenty-three hours and eighteen minutes	23:18
осам сати и петнаест минутā	osam sati i petnaest minutā	eight o'clock and fifteen minutes	8:15
двадесет часова и двадесет пет минутā	dvadeset časova i dvadeset pet minutā	twenty hours and twenty-five minutes	20:25

The word **сат/sat** or **час/čas** (hour) need not always be included, neither need **минута/minuta** (minute):

један и пет	jedan i pet	five past one	1:05
осам и четрдесет пет	osam i četrdeset pet	eight forty-five	8:45
петнаест до девет	petneast do devet	quarter to nine	8:45
два и тридесет	dva i trideset	two thirty	2:30
пола три	pola tri	half past two	2:30

In reply to the question:

У колико сати?	u koliko sati?	at what time?

one could say:

у један сат и пет минута̄	u jedan sat i pet minutā	at five minutes past one
у осам и четрдесет пет	u osam i četrdeset pet	at eight forty-five
у петнаест до девет	u petneast do devet	at a quarter to nine

14.13.2 Time-related words and expressions

Some of the following are time-related adverbs, adverbial expressions and adjectives (adverbs and adverbial expressions do not decline, nor do they have number or gender, while adjectives do):

Adverb	јутрос	jutros	this morning
Adjective	јутрашњи	jutrašnji	this morning's
Adverb	данас	danas	today
Adjective	данашњи	današnji	today's
Adverb	вечерас	večeras	this evening
Adjective	вечерашњи	večerašnji	this evening's
Adverb	ноћас	noćas	night just passed/ tonight
Adjective	ноћашњи	noćašnji	night's just passed/ tonight's
Adverb	ујутро-ујутру	ujutro-ujutru	in the morning
Adjective	јутарњи	jutarnji	morning
Adverb	дању	danju	in the day
Adjective	дневни	dnevni	daily
Adverb	увече	uveče	in the evening
Adjective	вечерњи	večernji	evening
Adverb	прекјуче	prekjuče	day before yesterday
Adjective	прекјучерашњи	prekjučerašnji	day before yesterday's
Adverb	синоћ	sinoć	last night
Adjective	синоћњи	sinoćnji	last night's
Adverb	сутра	sutra	tomorrow
Adjective	сутрашњи	sutrašnji	tomorrow's

Time

Adverb	недеља	nedelja	Sunday/week
Adjective	недељнц	nedeljni	weekly/sunday's
	недељом, понедељком, etc.	nedeljom, ponedeljkom	on Sundays, Mondays, etc. (use of the instrumental to indicate a regular, plural occurrence)

In reply to the question:

када...? kada...? when...?

If replying with 'every...' **сваки/svaki**, 'last...' **прошли/prošli**, 'next...' **идући/iduće**, the genitive case with the appropriate gender ending would be used:

сваког/прошлог/идућег сата	svakog/prošlog/idućeg sata	every/last/next hour
сваког/прошлог/идућег јутра	svakog/prošlog/idućeg jutra	every/last/next morning
сваке/прошле/идуће вечери	svake/prošle/iduće večeri	every/last/next evening
сваке/прошле/идуће ноћи	svake/prošle/iduće noći	every/last/next night
сваког/прошлог/идућег понедељка	svakog/prošlog/idućeg ponedeljka	every/last/next Monday
сваке/прошле/идуће среде	svake/prošle/iduće srede	every/last/next Wednesday
сваког/прошлог/идућег четвртка	svakog/prošlog/idućeg četvrtka	every/last/next Thursday
сваке/прошле/идуће суботе	svake/prošle/iduće subote	every/last/next Saturday
сваке/прошле/идуће недеље	svake/prošle/iduće nedelje	every/last/next Sunday
сваког/прошлог/идућег месеца	svakog/prošlog/idućeg meseca	every/last/next month
сваког/прошлог/идућег јануара	svakog/prošlog/idućeg januara	every/last/next January
сваког/прошлог/идућег априла	svakog/prošlog/idućeg aprila	every/last/next April
сваког/прошлог/идућег двадесет петог у месецу	svakog/prošlog/idućeg dvadeset petog u mesecu	every/last/next twenty-fifth of the month

Chapter 15
Quantifiers

Quantifiers can function as nouns, adjectives or adverbs and they refer to quantity ('many, enough, a little, a bunch of', etc.). Most quantifiers are followed by nouns in the genitive case.

15.1 Types of quantifiers

Quantifiers can be used with nouns representing things or beings that can be counted (**човек/čovek** – 'man', **сто/sto** – 'table', etc.), those that cannot be counted (**киша/kiša** – 'rain', **шећер/šećer** – 'sugar', **брашно/brašno** – 'flour', etc.), as well as collective nouns (**грожђе/grožđe** – 'grapes', **камење/kamenje** – 'stones', **јагњад/jagnjad** – 'lambs', etc.).

15.1.1 Countable quantifiers

The nouns **број/broj** (number) and **део/deo** (part), when preceded by adjectives denoting number or size, can be used to quantify countable nouns. The nouns following these are in the genitive plural (or genitive singular, if describing a part of something), while the verb is in agreement with the original quantifying noun, i.e. **број/broj** – masculine singular – or **део/deo** – neuter singular.

велики/већи/највећи број	veliki/veći/najveći broj	a great/greater/greatest number of
мали/мањи/најмањи број	mali/manji/najmanji broj	a small/smaller/smallest number of
добар број	dobar broj	a good, significant number of

велики/већи/највећи део	veliki/veći/najveći deo	a great/greater/ greatest part of
мали/мањи/најмањи део	mali/manji/najmanji deo	a small/smaller/ smallest part of
добар део	dobar deo	a good, significant part of

Types of quantifiers

The following nouns denote quantity and are followed by countable nouns in the genitive plural. The verb agrees with the original quantifying noun in gender and number.

асортиман	asortiman	an assortment of (m)
букет	buket	a bouquet of (m)
низ	niz	a series of (m)
пар	par	a pair of (m)
група	grupa	a group of (f)
неколицина	nekolicina	(a group of) several (f) (applies to masculine human nouns only. The verb is in the feminine singular.)

Countable quantifiers and the adjectives preceding them decline, while the nouns following them remain in the genitive plural or singular, as the case may be:

Молим вас, покажите ми *онај пар ципела*.	Moli vas, pokažite mi *onaj par cipela*.	Show me that pair of shoes please.
Та група момака је била веома весела.	*Ta grupa momaka* je bila veoma vesela.	That group of youths was quite happy.
Дао је новац *неколицини младића*.	Dao je novac *nekolicini mladića*.	He gave the money to (a group of) several youths.

The quantifier неколико/nekoliko (several) is followed by genitive plural nouns and collective nouns ending in -ад/ad. The verb following it is in the neuter singular.

Its adjectival form, неколики/nekoliki, has all three genders and is followed by plural nouns in the same case as the adjective:

15 Quantifiers

Plural:

	Masculine	Feminine	Neuter
Nom.	неколики nekoliki	неколике nekolike	неколика nekolika
Gen.		неколиких nekolikih	
Dat.		неколиким(а) nekolikim(a)	
Acc.	неколике nekolike	as nom.	as nom.
Voc.		as nom.	
Inst.		as dat.	
Loc.		as dat.	

15.1.2 Uncountable quantifiers

The main quantifiers used with uncountable nouns are the nouns **количина**/količina and **свота**/svota, both translating as 'amount/quantity'. These are preceded by adjectives. Both are feminine nouns and can be used in the singular and in the plural. The nouns following them are in the genitive singular and the verb will agree with the quantifying noun in gender and number.

велика/већа/највећа количина/свота	**velika/veća/najveća količina/svota**	a great/greater/ greatest amount of
мала/мања/најмања количина/свота	**mala/manja/najmanja količina/svota**	a small/smaller/ smallest amount of
значајна количина/свота	**značajna količina/svota**	a significant amount of

Uncountable quantifiers and the adjectives preceding them decline, while the nouns following them remain in the genitive singular:

Девојка је просула велику количину млека.	**Devojka je prosula veliku količinu mleka.**	The girl spilt *a large quantity of milk.*

| У сефу су се налазиле *мале* своте новца. | U sefu su se nalazile *male* svote novca. | There were *small amounts of money* in the safe. |

The following nouns are used to quantify uncountable nouns. The noun following them is in the genitive singular and the verb agrees with the original quantifying noun in number and gender.

комад	komad	a piece of
парче	parče	a piece, part of
флаша	flaša	a bottle of
чаша	čaša	a glass of
векна	vekna	a loaf of
кашика	kašika	a spoonful of
шоља	šolja	a cup of
кило	kilo	a kilo of
литар	litar	a litre of
метар	metar	a metre of

| *Чаша воде* је стајала на столу. | *Čaša vode* je stajala na stolu. | *A glass of water* stood on the table. |
| Дајте јој *парче торте*. | Dajte joj *parče torte*. | Give her *a piece of cake*. |

15.1.3 Countable and uncountable quantifiers

The following quantifiers can be used with both countable and uncountable nouns and are followed by the genitive plural of countable nouns, but by the genitive singular of uncountables:

много	mnogo	many, a great many, a lot of (gen. pl.), much, a lot of (gen. sg.)	Followed by noun in genitive. If partitive, noun takes genitive singular, otherwise genitive plural. The verb takes neuter singular. Also has adverbial function.
више	više	more	Comparative of много/mnogo.
највише	najviše	most	Superlative of много/mnogo.

Types of quantifiers

15 Quantifiers

Cyrillic	Latin	Meaning	Notes
пуно	puno	a lot of, plenty of	As много/mnogo.
мало	malo	a little, some	As много/mnogo.
мање	manje	less	Comparative of мало/malo.
најмање	najmanje	least	Superlative of мало/malo.
мноштво	mnoštvo	a multitude of	Neuter singular noun takes neuter singular verb.
део	deo	a part of	Masculine singular noun takes masculine singular verb.
доста	dosta	enough	As много/mnogo.
довољно	dovoljno	sufficient	As много/mnogo.
нешто	nešto	some	As много/mnogo.
већина	većina	a majority of, the greater part of	Feminine singular noun and feminine singular verb.
мањина	manjina	a minority of, a smaller part of	As већина/većina.

The following adjectives are followed by countable nouns and take the case of the noun:

Cyrillic	Latin	Meaning
безбројни	bezbrojni	countless
бројни	brojni	numerous

Cyrillic	Latin	English
Он пије кафу с много шећера.	On pije kafu s mnogo šećera.	He drinks coffee with *a lot of* sugar.
У соби је било много столова.	U sobi je bilo mnogo stolova.	There were *many* tables in the room.
Имате ли мало кафе?	Imate li *malo* kafe?	Do you have *some* coffee?
Део намештаја је био старомодан.	Deo nameštaja je bio staromodan.	*Part of* the furniture was old fashioned.
Мноштво деце се скупило на плажи.	Mnoštvo dece se skupilo na plaži.	*A multitude of* children gathered on the beach.

Већина навијача	*Većina navijača*	*The majority of fans*	Types of quantifiers
је имала улазнице.	*je imala ulaznice.*	had tickets.	
Безбројне кише	*Bezbројne kiše*	*Countless rains* fell.	
су падале.	*su padale.*		

Много/mnogo has an adjectival form, **многи/mnogi** (many, a lot of). As such, it has all three genders and declines as an adjective. It is used in the singular to quantify countable and uncountable nouns, and in the plural to quantify countable and collective nouns.

Declension of **многи/mnogi** (many, a lot of)

	Singular			Plural		
	Masculine	Neuter	Feminine	Masculine	Neuter	Feminine
Nom.	многи mnogi	много mnogo	многа mnoga	многи mnogi	многа mnoga	многе mnoge
Gen.	многог(а) mnogog(a)	m sg.	многе mnoge		многих mnogih	
Dat.	многом(е/у) mnogom(e/u)	m sg.	многој mnogoj		многим(а) mnogim(a)	
Acc.	as nom. = inanimate gen. = animate	as nom.	многу mnogu	многе mnoge	as nom.	as nom.
Voc.	as nom.	as nom.	as nom.	as nom.	as nom.	as nom.
Inst.	многим mnogim	m sg.	многом mnogom		as dat.	
Loc.	as dat.	as dat.	as dat.		as dat.	

Многа села су	*Mnoga sela su*	*Many villages* were
уништена.	*uništena.*	destroyed.
Многи људи	*Mnogi ljudi vole*	*Many people* like
воле ту музику.	*tu muziku.*	that music.
Многе жене иду	*Mnoge žene idu*	*Many women* go to
код козметичара.	*kod kozmetičara.*	a beautician.
Многи је човек	*Mnogi je čovek*	*Many a man* suffered.
страдао.	*stradao.*	

Chapter 16
Determiners

Determiners are words or phrases that come at the beginning of a noun phrase and signal whether the information is new or familiar. They are elements of noun phrases and include articles (a/an, the), quantifiers (a little, a lot), numbers, possessive adjectives (e.g. my, your, their) and demonstrative adjectives and pronouns (this, that, these, those).

16.1 Possessive determiners

Possessive determiners are also referred to as possessive pronouns. Possessive determiners can stand along other types of determiners and are used to tell to whom a body part, item of clothing, or family member or anything else belongs.

Of special importance in Serbian is the possessive determiner **свој/svoj** (also referred to as the reflexive possessive pronoun – 'one's own'). It is used for all persons, genders and number and declines as the possessive pronoun **мој/moj** (see Section 8.3 Possessive pronouns):

Видела је *њену* **децу.**	**Videla je** *njenu* **decu.**	She saw *her* children.
Видела је *своју* **децу.**	**Videla je** *svoju* **decu.**	She saw *her own* children.

Although **њену децу/njenu decu** (her children) may refer to children belonging to her, it may also mean the children belonging to any previously referred to female. Such ambiguity does not occur with **своју децу/svoju decu** which refers back to the subject, which might be a 1st, 2nd or 3rd person subject, and without which it cannot be used.

The determiner **свој/svoj** is also used with the indefinite pronoun **свако/svako**:

Свако **је узео** *своје* **ствари.**	*Svako* **je uzeo** *svoje* **stvari.**	*Everyone* took *his/her own* things.

Свако гледа *своје*.	*Svako* gleda *svoje*.	*Each* takes care of *his/her own*.

Personal pronouns in the dative case can also function as possessive determiners (see Section 7.3.3 Dative case):

Где *ти* је књига?	Gde *ti* je knjiga?	Where is *your* book?
Мајка *ми* је болесна.	Majka *mi* je bolesna.	*My* mother is ill.

16.2 Demonstrative determiners

Demonstrative determiners are also referred to as demonstrative pronouns (see Section 8.4).

Овог месеца сам одлучио да штедим.	*Ovog* meseca sam odlučio da štedim.	*This* month I've decided to save.
Сећаш ли се кад смо *оне* године продавали честитке на улици?	Sećaš li se kad smo *one* godine prodavali čestitke na ulici?	Do you remember *that* year (in the past) when we sold Christmas cards on the street?

Quantifiers can be used together with demonstrative determiners in a sentence:

Мали *број ове* деце уме да чита.	Mali *broj ove* dece ume da čita.	A small *number of these* children knows how to read.
Ова група деце касни?	*Ova grupa* dece kasni.	*This group* of children is late.

The demonstrative determiners **овакав/ovakav, онакав/onakav, такав/takav** are also used to replace the English equivalent of 'this' and 'that', particularly in a qualitative sense:

Допада ми се *оваква* кућа.	Dopada mi se *ovakva* kuća.	I like *this (kind of)* house.

while the demonstrative determiners **оволики/ovoliki, онолики/onoliki, толики/toliki** are used in a quantitative sense:

Упецали смо *оволику* рибу.	Upecali smo *ovoliku* ribu.	We caught a fish *this big*.

The demonstrative determiner **исти/isti** ('the same') is used in the following manner:

| Он увек *исто* ради. | On uvek *isto* radi. | He is always doing the *same* thing. |
| Ви *исто* мислите. | Vi *isto* mislite. | You think *the same*. |

16.3 Indefinite determiners

Indefinite determiners, the equivalent of 'some, any, anyone, either, both, someone's, somebody's, anyone's, anybody's' in English, have gender, number and case and include the following:

неки	neki	some, any
понеки	poneki	a, an occasional one
покоји	pokoji	some
било који	bilo koji	any
ма који	ma koji	any
који год	koji god	whichever
нечији	nečiji	somebody's, someone's, anybody's, anyone's
ичији	ičiji	anyone's
било чији	bilo čiji	anyone's
ма чији	ma čiji	anyone's
чији год	čiji god	whose ever
некакав	nekakav	some, any
икакав	ikakav	any
било какав	bilo kakav	any
ма какав	ma kakav	any kind
који год	koji god	whose ever
којекакав	kojekakav	any, some sort of
било колики	bilo koliki	however big
ма колики	ma koliki	of any size
колики год	koliki god	however big
један	jedan	a, some

| *Неки* те је човек тражио. | *Neki* te je čovek tražio. | *Some* man was looking for you. |

Сетићеш се нас *једног* дана.	Setićeš se nas *jednog* dana.	You will remember us *one* day.	Negative determiners
Ти си ми лепша од *било какве* лепотице.	Ti si mi lepša od *bilo kakve* lepotice.	You are more beautiful to me than *any* beauty queen.	
Изабери *било коју* од ове три књиге.	Izaberi *bilo koju* od ove tri knjige.	Choose *any one* of these three books.	
Нашао сам *нечије* кључеве.	Našao sam *nečije* ključeve.	I found *someone's* keys.	

The above can be used with the following meanings as well:

И није *неки* филм.	I nije *neki* film.	It's not *a* good film.
Кад бисте му дали *који* динар не би морао да позајмљује.	Kad biste mu dali *koji* dinar ne bi morao da pozajmljuje.	If you gave him *a* dinar he wouldn't have to borrow.

16.4 Interrogative determiners

In addition to the explanation given under interrogative pronouns (see Section 8.6), **који/koji** (which?) and **какав/kakav** (what kind/sort?) also take on the meaning of 'what?':

Који си намештај одлучила да купиш?	*Koji* si nameštaj odlučila da kupiš?	*What* furniture have you decided to buy?
Какав је он идиот!	*Kakav* je on idiot!	*What* an idiot he is!

16.5 Negative determiners

The negative determiners decline like the original determiner/pronoun from which the negative was formed by the addition of the prefix **-ни/ni**:

ничији	ničiji	no-one's, nobody's
никакав	nikakav	no (kind)
ниједан	nijedan	neither, no, no-one
Немамо *никаквог* уља.	Nemamo *nikakvog* ulja.	We don't have *any* kind of oil.

Ниједан се кувар није јавио на оглас.	*Nijedan* se kuvar nije javio na oglas.	*No* chef replied to the advertisement.
Не занима ме *ничије* мишљење.	Ne zanima me *ničije* mišljenje.	*Nobody's* opinion interests me.
Ниједно од ова два одела ми се не допада.	*Nijedno* od ova dva odela mi se ne dopada.	I don't like *either* one of these two suits.

Negative determiners have gender, number and case, and are used with negative verbs.

Chapter 17
Particles, conjunctions and exclamations

The following are the most frequently used particles, conjunctions and exclamations:

a	**a**	and, but	Cannot be followed by enclitic
ако	**ako**	if	
али	**ali**	but	Interchangeable with **a** but not **и/i**
бар/барем	**bar/barem**	at least	
баш	**baš**	exactly, really	Emphatic: **Баш си паметан!/** **Baš si pametan!** You're really clever!
без сумње	**bez sumnje**	without doubt	
вероватно	**verovatno**	probably	
ваљда	**valjda**	hopefully	
да	**da**	yes, that	
да ли	**da li**		Interrogative: **Да ли знате** **колико је сати?** **Da li znate koliko je sati?** Do you know what the time is?
дакако	**dakako**	indeed	
ево	**evo**	here (you) are/is	

17 Particles, conjunctions and exclamations

ето	eto	there (you) are/is	
заиста	zaista	really, truthfully	
зар?	zar?	still, really?	Interrogative and emphatic: **Зар је морао да га удари?** **Zar je morao da ga udari?** Did he have to hit him?
зато што	zato što	because	+ noun/verb (complete clause)
зато	zato	that's why	+ noun (usually complete clause)
зашто?	zašto?	why?	
због	zbog	because of	+ genitive
због тога што	zbog toga što	because (of the fact that)	+ noun/verb (complete clause)
и	i	and, too, also	Cannot be followed by enclitic
или	ili	or	
ипак	ipak	anyhow, anyway, still	
јасно је (да)	jasno je (da)	obviously, it's clear that	
једино	jedino	only, except	
јер	jer	since, because, as, really?!	
као и	kao i	as, as well as	Cannot be followed by enclitic
као	kao	as, like (comparison)	Cannot be followed by enclitic
ли	li		Interrogative particle (enclitic): **Има ли новца у кући?** **Ima li novca u kući?** Is there money in the house?

			With the construction **не би ли/ne bi li** also used to indicate intention or hope (often with sarcastic/humorous overtones): **Иде у лов не би ли нешто уловио. Ide u lov ne bi li nešto ulovio.** He's going hunting in the hope of catching something.
међутим	međutim	meanwhile, in the meantime, however	Cannot be followed by an enclitic
можда	možda	perhaps	
не	ne	no	Cannot be followed by an enclitic
нема никаквог спора (да)	nema nikakvog spora (da)	there is no doubt (that)	
нема сумње (да)	nema sumnje (da)	there is no doubt (that)	
несумњиво	nesumnjivo	undoubtedly	
ни	ni	neither, nor, either	Also used to emphasise negation: **Није хтео ни да је види! Nije hteo ni da je vidi!** He didn't even want to see her! Cannot be followed by an enclitic
нипошто	nipošto	under no circumstances	Followed by negative verb
нити	niti	neither, nor	

Particles, conjunctions and exclamations

17 Particles, conjunctions and exclamations

но	no	but, however	Interchangeable with **a** and **али/ali** but not **и/i**.
па	pa	so, and, then	
пак	pak	however	
по	po	each (distributive)	Cannot be followed by an enclitic
разуме се	razume se	obviously	
само	samo	only, except	
свакако	svakako	certainly	
свега	svega	only, in all	
такође	takođe	also	
што	što	that	

Part IV
Sentence elements and structure

Chapter 18
Sentences

A sentence generally consists of a subject and a predicate. A subject often tells us what the predicate (everything in the sentence or clause that comes after the subject) is about. The subject is usually a noun or a noun phrase. Noun phrases can consist of one word – a noun or pronoun – or of several words connected to and including the main noun. The predicate contains the verb and everything describing and following it. In Serbian, all the elements in a sentence need to be in agreement with respect to person, gender and number, wherever applicable.

18.1 Elements of a sentence

1   A sentence will usually contain at least a subject and a verb or verb phrase. The subject is in the nominative case. The subject and the verb need to be in agreement with respect to gender (with appropriate tense) and number:

   Миланка пева.
   Milanka peva.
   Milanka is singing.

   Subject   Verb

   Миланка је стајала и смејала се.
   Milanka je stajala i smejala se.
   Milanka was standing and laughing.

   Subject   Verb phrase

2   The verb may further dictate whether a direct or an indirect object will follow. The direct object is in the accusative case, while the indirect object is generally in the dative case:

Миланка пева песму.
Milanka peva pesmu.
Milanka is singing a song.

    S   V   Direct Object

Миланка пева песму сину.
Milanka peva pesmu sinu.
Milanka is singing a song to her son.

    S   V   DO   Indirect Object

3   A sentence may also include a complement, which tells something about the subject, and usually follows verbs such as 'to be', 'to appear', 'to feel'*, 'to seem', 'to become', 'to look', 'to think', etc. A complement can be:

    (a)   A noun phrase:

           Миланка је добра певачица.
           Milanka je dobra pevačica.
           Milanka is a good singer.

           S   V   Noun Phrase

    (b)   An adjective or adjective phrase:

           Миланка је лепа.
           Milanka je lepa.
           Milanka is pretty.

           S   V Adjective

    (c)   A prepositional phrase:

           Миланка је била под притиском.
           Milanka je bila pod pritiskom.
           Milanka was under pressure.

           S   V   Prepositional Phrase.

           * The verb 'to feel' – **осећати се/osećati se** – is followed by the instrumental:

           Миланка се осећала глупом.
           Milanka se osećala glupom.
           Milanka felt stupid.

4   A sentence may also contain adverbials. Adverbials tell something about the verb.

An adverbial can be:

(a) A noun phrase:

> После вечере смо појели *јагоде са шлагом*.
> Posle večere smo pojeli *jagode sa šlagom*.
> After dinner we ate strawberries and cream.
>
>   S   V   Noun Phrase

(b) An adverb phrase:

> *Често* се свађају.
> *Često* se svađaju.
> They argue often.
>
>   V   Adverb

(c) A prepositional phrase:

> Он ради *у својој соби*.
> On radi *u svojoj sobi*.
> He is working in his room.
>
> S   V   Prepositional Phrase

The equivalent of the English definite and indefinite articles, 'the' and 'a/an', does not exist in Serbian and their meaning is conveyed through the use of other words. Generally, the words closer to the beginning of the sentence, after the enclitic word order, are definite in nature, while the later in a sentence they appear, the more indefinite their character.

The number one, **један/jedan**, when used as a modifier (a word modifying a noun; it can be an adjective, noun, adverb-adjective), gives the meaning of the indefinite article 'a/an':

| Помогао нам је *један* војник. | Pomogao nam je *jedan* vojnik. | A soldier helped us. |

The aspect of the verb can also indicate whether the noun is definite or indefinite:

| Она *пише* писмо. | Ona *piše* pismo. | She is writing *a* letter. |
| Она је *написала* писмо. | Ona je *napisala* pismo. | She wrote *the* letter. |

18.2 Types of clauses

A clause is part of a sentence and it consists of a group of words containing a subject and a verb. There are two types of clauses: a main clause and a subordinate clause. A main clause, when on its own, is a

18 Sentences

complete simple sentence. A subordinate clause gives additional information about the main clause. It contains a subject and a verb and is generally linked to the rest of the sentence (possibly another clause) by a conjunction. Main clauses are considered to be independent, while subordinate clauses are dependent. A sentence may contain a main clause and a subordinate clause:

Посетићемо вас *ако нас будете позвали*.
Posetićemo vas *ako nas budete pozvali*.
We will visit you if you call us.

Clause 1   conj. Clause 2

The main clause contains the main idea of a sentence and can stand on its own:

Посетићемо вас.   **Posetićemo vas.**   We will visit you.

A subordinate clause tells more about the main clause and is attached to it.

Деца су била радосна *кад су стигла на плажу*.
Deca su bila radnosna *kad su stigla na plažu*.
The children were joyous *when they got to the beach*.

Main Clause   Subordinate Clause

There are different types of subordinate clauses, including:

1   Relative clauses, beginning with 'who' or 'which':

Нашла сам књигу *коју сам тражила*.
Našla sam knjigu *koju sam tražila*.
I found the book *(which) I was looking for*.

Main Clause   Subordinate Clause

Ово је жена *која чува нашу децу*.
Ovo je žena *koja čuva našu decu*.
This is the woman *who takes care of our children*.

Main Clause   Subordinate Clause

2   Interrogative clauses:

Питам вас, *кога сте видели*?
Pitam vas, *koga ste videli*?
I ask you, *whom did you see?*

Main Clause   Subordinate Clause

Chapter 19
Sentence structure

19.1 Word order

Word order is Serbian is very flexible with the exception of enclitics and the order they must follow (see Chapter 13 Enclitics):

| Наша школа се налази у центру града. | Naša škola se nalazi u centru grada. | Our school is located in the centre of town. |
| У центру града се налази наша школа. | U centru grada se nalazi naša škola. | In the centre of town is located our school. |

19.2 Punctuation

Punctuation is generally as in English, with some differences.

1. A full stop is used in the following instances:
   - (a) At the end of a sentence;
   - (b) After abbreviations:

о.м. – овог месеца	o.m. – ovog meseca	this month
т.г. – текуће године	t.g. – tekuće godine	current year
в.д. – вршилац дужности	v.d. – vršilac dužnosti	acting (chief/head, etc.)
бр. – број	br. – broj	number
стр. – страница	str. – stranica	page

и др. – и друго	i dr. – i drugo	and other
и сл. – и слично	i sl. – i slično	and so on
итд. – и тако даље	itd. – i tako dalje	etc.
тзв. – такозвани/а/о	tzv. – takozvani/a/o	so-called
тј. – то јест	tj. – to jest	that is, i.e.
нпр. – на пример	npr. – na primer	for example, e.g.
ул. – улица	ul. – ulica	street
проф. – професор	prof. – profesor	professor
г. – господин	g. – gospodin	mister, Mr
Бгд. – Београд	Bgd. – Beograd	Belgrade
инж. – инжењер	inž. – inženjer	engineer
мед. – медицински/а/о	med. – medicinski/a/o	medical
срп. – српски	srp. – srpski	Serbian

(c) Following ordinal numbers;
(d) Following numbers and Roman numerals when listing by number or letter:

I. Увод   **I. Uvod**   I. Introduction

а. Именице   **a. Imenice**   a. Nouns

(e) Dividing large numbers – where in English a comma is used:

1.000   **1.000**   1,000

100.000   **100.000**   100,000

A full stop is omitted in the following instances:

(a) Following certain titles:

др	dr	Doctor
мг	mg	Magistrate
гђа	gđa	Mrs, madam
гђица	gđica	Miss

(b) Following most abbreviations with capital letters:

НАТО	NATO	NATO
УН	UN	UN
ЕУ	EU	EU

(c) Following cardinal numbers

2   A comma is used in the following instances:

(a) to divide a sentence into parts, to include or exclude something;

(b) to separate expressions or discourse markers:

| А *поред тога*, касно је. | A *pored toga*, kasno. | Besides, it's late. |
| Ми ћемо, *без сумње*, вама помоћи. | Mi ćemo, *bez sumnje*, vama pomoći. | We will, *without doubt*, help you. |

(c) Following appositions to the subject:

| Гђа Влашић, *наша комшиница*, је вегетеријанка. | Gđa Vlašić, *naša komšinica*, je vegeterijanka. | Mrs Vlašić, *our neighbour*, is a vegetarian. |

(d) Preceding subordinate clauses;

(e) Usually after the conjunctions: **а/a**, **али/ali**, both meaning 'but';

(f) Separating parts of a sentence containing verbal adverbs;

(g) Preceding non-restrictive relative clauses:

| Њихова сестра, *која ради у болници*, је наша пријатељица. | Njihova sestra, *koja radi u bolnici*, je naša prijateljica. | Their sister, *who works in a hospital*, is our friend. |

A comma is omitted when preceding coordinating conjunctions: **и/i** (and), **a/a** (and).

3   Quotation marks:

(a) Are used in the same way as in English with the difference that the initial set of inverted commas lies on the base line and is not suspended:

| „Ти си добар човак", рекао је Џон. | „Ti si dobar čovek", rekao je Džon. | "You're a good man", John said. |

(b) Are used when referring to names and titles of things:

| хотел „Југославија" | hotel „Jugoslavija" | Hotel "Jugoslavija" |
| часопис „Астрологус" | časopis „Astrologus" | the magazine *Astrologus* |

19.3 Simple sentences

A simple sentence expresses a complete thought, containing a subject and a predicate:

Оља воли Милоша. **Olja voli Miloša.** Olja loves Miloš.

Simple sentences are incomplete when either is missing. The reflexive pronoun **се/se** is generally used to form an impersonal sentence, where there is no given subject, equivalent to the use of the English 'one':

Путује се. **Putuje se.** One travels.

A simple sentence will have one predicate.

19.4 Complex sentences

Complex sentences are made up of clauses:

| **Купила сам колач** | **Kupila sam kolač** | I bought the cake (main clause) |
| **који волите.** | **koji volite.** | which you like. (subord. clause) |

A complex sentence can contain two or more simple sentences, or independent clauses, or it can contain two or more simple sentences, or clauses, of which one at least is independent, while the other can be a dependent clause. Two dependent clauses cannot exist together to form a complex sentence.

A complex sentence can have two or more predicates.

Chapter 20
Word formation

Words are formed in response to a need to express something. The majority of words in Serbian were generally formed from an original, independent word, which was taken as the root for the new word, and to which prefixes, infixes or suffixes were added. The new word is related in meaning to the original word through its root, and it is possible to trace the origin of most words. Many, however, are taken as the original.

As such, there are three types of words, depending on how they were formed.

In the examples:

киша	kiša	rain – noun
кишан	kišan	rainy – adjective
кишобран	kišobran	umbrella (rain-guard) – noun formed from two words

Киша/kiša (rain) is a noun which can stand on its own. It can be used as the root to form other words.

Кишан/kišan (rainy) is an adjective derived from the original noun, to which an **н/n** suffix has been added.

Кишобран/kišobran (umbrella) is a noun formed from two separate words: **киш/kiš** from **киша/kiša**, and **бран/bran**, derived from the verb **бранити/braniti** (to guard), linked together by the letter **o**.

Similarly:

бранити	braniti	to guard, protect, defend
бранилац	branilac	defender
браник	branik	(car) bumper
бранилачки	branilački	defending (adj.)

with the addition of the suffix **-лац/lac**, or the suffix **-ик/ik**, to the root of the verb **бранити/braniti**, a new word is formed.

20 Word formation

These elements used to form new words, be they prefixes, infixes or suffixes, are referred to as being productive because their form is still valid and can be used to this day to make new words. Some words are formed from several elements:

стан	stan	flat
стан-ар	stan-ar	tenant
стан-ар-ина	stan-ar-ina	rent

20.1 Prefixes

Words formed with the following prefixes acquire new meanings:

до/do-
(i) up to, to, as far as
(ii) conveys the idea of successful completion of the action

донети/doneti (to bring to)

дочекати/dočekati (to receive or meet that or whom one had been waiting for)

за/za-
(i) gives special emphasis to the starting of the action
(ii) conveys a meaning of 'at the back of, or behind'

започети/započeti (to start)

заплакати/zaplakati (to start crying)

завући/zavući (to pull, hide behind something)

у/u-
in, into

убацити/ubaciti (to throw, put into)

од/od-
from, to reciprocate or return an action

одбацити/odbaciti (to reject, cast aside – to throw away)

из/iz-
(i) from, from out of
(ii) conveys an idea of an action being carried out to its end or in fullness

изаћи/izaći (to come out from)

изморити/izmoriti (to tire out)

Prefixes

при/pri-	(i)	conveys the idea of adding to something, or the attachment of a smaller body to a larger body
	(ii)	conveys the idea of bringing an action to a head

придружити/pridružiti (to join)

присилити/prisiliti (to force)

под/pod-		conveys the meaning of under

подвући/podvući (to underline)

потписати/potpisati (to sign – under the text or line)

на/na-	(i)	conveys idea of bringing the action to an end or to its fulfilment
	(ii)	conveys a meaning of on, onto

научити/naučiti (to learn)

набацати/nabacati (to throw on or onto)

о/o-, об/ob-		around

обићи/obići (to tour, to pay a visit, to go around)

описати/opisati (to describe, talk around something giving its description)

с/s-, са/sa-	(i)	conveys a sense of cooperation, togetherness
	(ii)	conveys a meaning of off

сарађивати/sarađivati (to cooperate)

скренути/skrenuti (to turn off the main path, road, direction, etc.)

уз/uz-	(i)	alongside
	(ii)	to carry out an action with an upward or 'begin to' meaning

уздржати се/uzdržati se (to control oneself)

узбудити/uzbuditi (to excite)

про/pro-	(i)	through
	(ii)	to carry out or perform an action thoroughly, in detail

проћи/proći (to pass through)

проучити/proučiti (to study)

20 Word formation

пре/pre-		across, over
	прегледати/pregledati (to examine, look over)	
раз/raz-		conveys the idea of an action bringing about the distribution of the subject into different directions, or parts
	разгледати/razgledati (to look around, in all directions)	
	разместити/razmestiti (to arrange in different positions)	
	разбити/razbiti (to break into pieces)	

20.2 Suffixes

20.2.1 Nouns

Nouns can be formed from verbal roots, adjectival roots or from other nouns or they can be compounded from two words.

1   Nouns formed from verbal roots with the following suffixes indicate:

(a) The person carrying out the action:

-ац/ac	пис*ац*	pis*ac*	a writer
			писати/pisati – to write
-лац/lac	спаси*лац*	spasi*lac*	a saviour
			спасити/spasiti – to save
-ач/ač	пев*ач*	pev*ač*	a singer
			певати/pevati – to sing
-ар/ar	чув*ар*	čuv*ar*	a watchman
			чувати/čuvati – to keep, to guard
-лица/lica	лута*лица*	luta*lica*	a wanderer
			лутати/lutati – to wander

-ља/lja	праља	pra**lj**a	a laundress (usually of feminine gender)
			прати/prati – to wash

(b) An event or condition produced by the action:

-ај/aj	догађај	događ**aj**	an event
			догодити се/ dogoditi se – to happen
-ба/ba	изложба	izlož**ba**	exhibition
			изложити/izložiti – to exhibit
-ва/va	жетва	žet**va**	harvest
			жети/žeti – to reap
-(љ)је/(l)je	славље	slav**lje**	celebration
			славити/slaviti – to celebrate
-ња/nja	штедња	šted**nja**	savings
			штедети/štedeti – to save

2 Nouns formed from adjectival roots with the following suffixes usually indicate:

(a) The person carrying the traits described by the adjective or passive past participle (of masculine gender):

-ац/ac	белац	bel**ac**	a white man
			бео/beo (white)
-ак/ak	лудак	lud**ak**	a mad man
			луд/lud (mad)
-ик/ik	ученик	učen**ik**	a pupil
			учен/učen (taught)
-јак/jak	учењак	učen**jak**	a learned person

(b) A noun denoting the trait described by the adjective:

-ина/ina	брзина	brzina	speed брз/brz – fast
-је/je	ослобођење	oslobođenje	liberty ослобођен/oslobođen – liberated
-оћа/oća	самоћа	samoća	loneliness сам/sam – alone
-ота/ota	лепота	lepota	beauty леп/lep – pretty
-ост/ost	храброст	hrabrost	courage храбар/hrabar – brave
-ство/stvo	богатство	bogatstvo	wealth богат/bogat – wealthy

3   Nouns formed from other nouns with the following suffixes usually indicate:

(a) A place:

-ана/ana	кафана	kafana	coffee shop/pub
-ара/ara	месара	mesara	the butcher's
-иште/ište	паркиралиште	parkiralište	parking area
-ница/nica	посластичарница	poslastičarnica	sweetshop
-њак/njak	воћњак	voćnjak	orchard

(b) A person involved, usually professionally, with the underlying noun:

-ар/ar	месо	meso	meat
	месар	mesar	a butcher

	посластица	poslastica	dessert
	посластич*ар*	poslastič*ar*	a sweetshop attendant

(c) A person originating from the place represented by the noun:

Of masculine gender:

-ац/ac	Ирац	Ir*ac*	an Irishman
-анац/anac	Мексиканац	Meksik*anac*	a Mexican
-анин/anin	Ирачанин	Irač*anin*	an Iraqi man
-ин/in	Србин	Srb*in*	a Serbian man

Of feminine gender:

-ица/ica	Немица	Nem*ica*	a German woman
-иња/inja	Иркиња	Irk*inja*	an Irish woman
-ка/ka	Ирачанка	Irač*anka*	an Iraqi woman
-киња/kinja	Српкиња	Srp*kinja*	a Serbian woman

(d) A young offspring of human or animal species:

-ић/ić	синчић	sinčić	little son
-че/če	слонче	slonče	little elephant, the young of an elephant

(e) Diminutives, either real or affectionate:

For masculine gender:

-(ч)ић/(č)ić	ланчић	lančić	necklace chain
	ланац	lanac	a chain

For feminine gender:

-ица/ica	бакица	bak*ica*	granny
	бака	baka	a grandmother

For neuter gender:

-це/ce	језерце	jezerce	a small lake
	језеро	jezero	a lake

Suffixes

(f) Pejoratives for all genders:

-ина/ina	бабетина	babetina	a fat old woman
	баба	baba	an old woman
	баруштина	baruština	a big puddle
	бара	bara	a puddle

4 Nouns (and adjectives) compounded from two words, each of which has its own meaning, are linked by the vowel o or e:

јγгозапад	jugozapad	southwest
јγг + о + запад	jug + o + zapad	south + o + west
североисток	severoistok	northeast
север + о + исток	sever + o + istok	north + o + east
једнособан	jednosoban	one-bedroom
једн + о + соба + ан	jedn + o + soba + an	one + o + room + adjective forming suffix
многобожац	mnogobožac	polytheist
много + о + бог + ац	mnogo + o + bog + ac	many + o + God + (m noun forming suffix = English -ist)

20.2.2 Adjectives

1 Most adjectives are formed with **-к/k** and **-н/n** suffixes (for masculine gender, with an a ending for feminine gender, replaced by an o for neuter gender – see Chapter 9 Adjectives):

тежак	težak	heavy (m)
тешка	teška	(f)
тешко	teško	(n)
паметан	pametan	clever, smart (m)
паметна	pametna	(f)
паметно	pametno	(n)

2   Adjectives with the following suffixes indicate possession:

-ин/in	мам*ин*	mam*in*	mother's
-ји/ji	свачи*ји*	svači*ji*	everybody's
-њи/nji	вечер*њи*	večer*nji*	evening's
-шњи/šnji	јучера*шњи*	jučera*šnji*	yesterday's
-ски/ski	британ*ски*	britan*ski*	British
-чки/čki	балти*чки*	balti*čki*	Baltic
-шки/ški	че*шки*	če*ški*	Czech
-ов/ov	брат*ов*	brat*ov*	brother's
-ев/ev	оч*ев*	oč*ev*	father's

3   Adjectives formed with **-ав/av**, **-ат/at** and **-овит/ovit** are characterised by (a lot of) the underlying noun, usually giving an augmentative force to the adjective:

крв*ав*	krv*av*	bloody, of something having (a lot of) blood on it
брад*ат*	brad*at*	bearded, having a (prominent) beard
песк*овит*	pesk*ovit*	sandy, having (a lot of) sand on it

Bibliography

Benson, M., *Englesko-Srpskohrvatski Rečnik*, Prosveta, Beograd, 1986.
Ćupić, D., Fekete, E. and Terzić, B., *Slovo o jeziku*, Partenon, Beograd, 2002.
Dešić, M., *Pravopis srpskog jezika*, P.S. Grmeč – Privredni pregled, Beograd, 1995.
Đorđević, R., *Engleski i srpskohrvatski jezik*, Naučna Knjiga, Beograd, 1989.
Drvodelić, M., *Hrvatsko ili srpsko engleski jezik, Rečnik*, Školska knjiga, Zagreb, 1989.
Krajišnik, V., *Naučimo padeže*, Filološki fakultet, Beograd, 2000.
Magner, T.F., *Introduction to the Croatian and Serbian Language*, The Pennsylvania State University Press, University Park, PA, 1991.
Major, R.A., *The History of Serbian Culture*, Porthill Publishers, Edgware, Middlesex, 1995.
Partridge, M., *Serbo-Croat, Practical Grammar and Reader*, Prosveta, Beograd, 1991.
Pravopis Srpskohrvatskog jezika, Matica Srpska, Marica Hrvatska, Novi Sad – Zagreb, 1989.
Sljivic-Simsic, B., *Serbo-Croatian Just for You*, The Ohio State University, Columbus, OH, 1985.
Stanojčić, Ž., Popović, L., *Gramatika srpskog jezika*, Zavod za udžbenike i nastavna sredstva, Beograd, 2000.
Stevanovič, M., *Gramatika srpskohrvatskog jezika*, Obod, Cetinje, 1971.

Index

Bold indicates main entry

active participle of past action *see* adverbs, verbal
active past participle *see* adjectives, verbal
adjectives 24, 27, 96, 116, 121, 147, 178, **201–3**, 224, 226, 230, 232, 247, 258, 260, 264, 270, 276, 280, 282, 283, 286, 287, 300, 307, 311, 312, 314; classification **203–5**; comparative 26, 202, 203, 209, **214–16**, 226; declension 138, 151, 204, 207, 209, 212; definite 138, 139, 142, 145, 146, 151, 189, 191, 196, 202–4, 205, **207–9**, 211; descriptive 202, 204, 214, 216; indefinite 189, 191, 194, 197, 202–4, **205–7**, 208; possessive 29, 118, 188, 208, **210–12**, 288; superlative 202, 203, 209, **216–17**, 226; verbal 24, 26, 65–7, 82, 84, 85, 93, **217–22**, 224
adverbs 96, 129, 143, 216, **223–32**, 272, 280, 282; adjectival **226**; pronominal **226–8**; substantival **224–5**; verbal 229, 305; verbal past **231–2**; verbal present **229–31**
age 273–4
alphabet **13**; cyrillic 6, **13–16**; latin 8, 13, 14, **16**
aorist tense 36, 40, 64, **75–81**, 83, 85–7, 93, 96; formation and use 76–80, 86; interrogative 80; negative 80; negative interrogative 81
approximatives 270

biti – *бити/biti* **61–4**, 66, 67, 69, 70, 76, 82, 84, 85, 87, 92, 96, 98, 99, 120, 129, 198; present perfective of 58, 82, 83, 93, **99**
više – *више/više* **215–17**

cases of nouns 105, **112–51**, 152, 153; accusative 28, 90, 113, 115, **133–9**, 145, 147, 168, 183, 184, 185, 186, 187, 188, 206, 208, 238, 251, 253, 265, 268, 269, 275, 277, 299; dative 23, 28, 92, 103, 111, 113, 115, **126–32**, 149, 163, 174, 181, 183, 184, 185, 204, 208, 235, 238, 247, 251, 253, 273, 289, 299; genitive 23–5, 28, 97, 105, 111, 113, 115, **117–26**, 129, 133, 137, 144, 145, 149, 152, 153, 156, 162, 164, 169, 174, 175, 177, 181, 183–6, 235, 236, 251, 253, 264, 266, 268, 269, 271, 277, 281–5, 294; instrumental 23, 26, 30, 113, 115, **142–6**, 155, 169, 174, 181, 204, 224, 239; locative 28, 113, 115, **146–52**, 163, 174, 183, 204, 208, 239, 276; nominative 23–5, 28, 105, 111–13, **115–17**, 118, 121, 136–42, 152, 153, 155, 168, 175, 183, 188, 189, 204–6, 208, 226,

Index

234, 267, 269, 273, 299; vocative 27, 113, 115, **140–2**, 154, 163, 181, 188, 234
change of л/l to o 23, **24–5**, 68, 153, 154, 169
čije – чији/čije 117, 124, 130, 138, 150, 152, 188, 195, 196, 198, 200, 210
clause types 72, **82–5**, 99, 189, 195, 240, 242, 243, 246, 250, 252, 253, 301, 305, 306
conditional 76, **82–6**, 93, 96
conjugation **36–7**; type I 36, 37, 39, **41**, 43, 59, 88; type II 36, 37, 39, **42–8**, 59, 89; type III 36, 37, 39, **48–50**, 60, 89
conjunctions 38, 58, 63, 64, 70, 73–5, 80, 81, 84, 87–9, 93–5, 99, 101, 104, 122, 137, 183, 185, 215, 233, **240–8**, 250, 252, **293–6**, 305; coordinating 37, 55, 58, 73, 83, 87, 93, 95, 99, 101, 102, 104, 183, 185, **240–3**, 305; subordinating 55, 58, 81, 83–5, 87–9, 99, **243–6**
consonants 8, **17–19**, 29, 219, 221, 232; assimilations **21–2**, 38, 47; change of л/l to o **23–5**, 68, 153, 154, 169; contractions **22**, 23; effects of e/e and и/i on к/k, r/g and x/h 27, 28, 47, 78, 132, 140, 150, 153; fleeting a 22, **23**, 25, 47, 67, 68, 125, 137, 144, 153, 164, 206, 214, 216, 219, 275; ʲ changes 25, 26, 46, 78, 169, 214; soft and hard **20–1**, 25, 29, 30, 43, **52–4**, 139, 140, 141, 153–5, 158–61, 173, 189, 203–6, 208, 216; voiced and unvoiced **19–21**

dates **274–80**
days **274–80**
decimals 267
declension **152–3**; 1st A **153–61**; 2nd E **162–7**, 181; 3rd И/I **168–72**; adjectives 138, 151, 204, 207, 209, 212; cardinal numbers **255**, 261, **262**; nouns 105, **152**, 208; nouns (irregular) 105, **173–7**; ordinal numbers 209, 265; personal pronouns 151, **181–4**; pronominal **182**; quantifiers 287
determiners 268, **288–92**; demonstrative **289**; indefinite **290**; interrogative **291**; negative **291**; possessive **288**
dialects **9–10**
distributives 271

effects of e/e and и/i on к/k, r/g and x/h 27, 28, 47, 78, 132, 140, 150, 153
enclitics 62, 64, 72, 74, 80, 81, 84, 92, 181, **249–54**, **293–6**, 301; order and importance 62, 64, 67, 70, 90, 94, 95, 184, 185, 250
exclamations 38, 58, 63, 64, 70, 73–5, 80, 81, 84, 87–9, 93–5, 99, 101, 104, 122, 137, 183, 185, 215, 233, **240–8**, 250, 252, **293–6**, 305
expressions of greetings *see* greeting expressions

fleeting *a* 22, **23**, 25, 47, 67, 68, 125, 137, 144, 153, 164, 206, 214, 216, 219, 275
fractions 267
frequentatives 271
future II 36, **81–2**, 83, 84, 93, 99; formation and use **81–2**
future tense 36–8, 55, 63, **71–5**, 84, 93, 97, 99, 102–4, 218; formation and use **71–3**, 82, 83; interrogative 74; negative 73, 98; negative interrogative 75

greeting expressions **135**; manner 142, 143; means 142, 147, 148; place 142, 147, 148; time 135, 142, 147

hteti – хтети/hteti 63, 71, 73, 74, 79, 86, 92, 93, 96, 98, 99, 121

Index

ići – ићи/*ići* 57, 68, 82, 99, 133

imati – имати/*imati* 41, 63, 79, 96, 97, 120
imperative 29, **87**, **88**
infinitive 36, 37, 38, **45–8**, 55, 65, 67, 72, 74, 75, 78, 93, 110, 175, 218, 219, 220, 222, 232; classification 35, **37–9**, 71, 72, 77, 104, 110; stem 36, 38, **39–40**, 47, 58–61, 67, 78, 111
interrogative formation 63, 70, 74, 80, 87–90, **93–5**, 250

J changes 25, 26, 46, 78, 169, 214

kakav – какав/*kakav* 117, 124, 130, 150, 195, 197, 198, 200, 205, 291
kći – ћи/*kći* 111, 112, 132, 142, 151, 152, 153, **168–72**, 268
ko – ко/*ko* 116, 124, 130, 133, 150, 178, 195, 196, 198
koji – који/*koji* 117, 124, 130, 138, 150, 152, 195, 196, 198, 207, 246, 291, 302
koliki – колики/*koliki* 117, 124, 130, 150, 195, 197, 198

mati – мати/*mati* 111, 112, 132, 137, 141, 151–3, **162–7**, 205
manje – мање/*manje* **215–17**
moći – моћи/*moći* 104
modal verbs (*need to, should, ought to*) 37, 86, 95, **101–4**, 121
months **274–8**
morati – морати/*morati* 38, 41
multiplicates **270**

negative formation 63, 69, 70, 73, 80, 87–90, 93, **95–8**, 120, 253, 260, 291
nemati – немати/*nemati* 41
nouns 24, 26, 27, 96, **105**, 122, 145, 147, 148, 175, 178, 195, 201, 208, 222, 224, 233, 252, 258, 259, 260, 262, 264, 265, 267, 269, 271, 282–7, 307, 310, 312–15; cases 105, **112–15**, 152, 153; declension 105, **173–7**; ending in -*a* 111, 112, 132, 137, 141, 151–3, **162–7**, 205; ending in consonant or -*o*, -*oct/ost*, -*ад/ad* 111, 112, 132, 142, 151, 152, 153, **168–72**, 268; gender 24, 25, 105, **111–12**; masculine and neuter nouns 111, 137, **153–61**, 204; numbers 255, **269–70**; types **105–11**, 141, 155, 162, 163, 164, 168, 176, 210, 211, 268, 282; ћи/*kći* 111, 112, 132, 142, 151, 152, 153, **168–72**, 268
numbers 178, **255–81**, 288, 304; 1 (one) 206, **258–60**, 266, 268; 2, 3, 4 and the numeral both 119, 177, 206, **260–3**; 5, 6, 7 and onwards 118, 119, 177, **263–4**; cardinal **255–8**, 265, 266, 268, 271, 272, 275, 276, 305; collective 255, **268–70**; nouns 255, **269–70**; ordinal 209, 255, **265–7**, 271, 276, 304
numerals *see* numbers

otac – отац/*otac* 18, 22

particles 38, 58, 63, 64, 70, 73–5, 80, 81, 84, 87–9, 93–5, 99, 101, 104, 122, 137, 183, 185, 215, 233, **240–8**, 250, 252, **293–6**, 305
passive participle *see* adjectives, verbal
passive past participle *see* adjectives, verbal
past adjectival participle *see* adjectives, verbal
past participle *see* adjectives, verbal
past tense *see* perfect tense
past verbal adverb *see* adverbs, verbal
perfect tense 23, 36, 41, 44, 47, 49, 50, 51, 55, **64–71**, 75, 84, 85, 92, 96, 97, 100–4, 120, 218, 253; formation and use 47, **64–9**; interrogative 70, 94; negative **69**, 98; negative interrogative 70

Index

prefixes 20, 22, 45, 56, 95, 96, 98, 100, 121, 127, 203, 215, 216, 224, 226, 291, 308

prepositions 23, 32, 123, 124, 126, 130, 133, 134, 142–9, 169, 183, 184, 185, 187, 224, 233, 249, 271, 272, 275–7, 308; accentuation 235, 249; compound 123, 124, 145, 233, **235**; simple 118, 123, 124, 134, 142–9, 233, **234**; through the cases **236**

present participle *see* adverbs, verbal

present tense 27, 36, 42, 43, 45–8, 51, 55, 58–64, 71, 74, 75, 84, 93, 95–7, 99–102, 100, 104, 219, 230, 251; formation and use **58–62**; interrogative **64**, 94; negative **63**, 94, 95; negative interrogative **70**; personal endings **58–60**; stems 35, 36, **39–40**, 47, 58–61, 67, 78

present verbal adverb *see* adverbs, verbal

pronouns 116, 178, 224, 226, 233, 259, 269, 288; declension 151, **181–4**; demonstrative 138, 139, 152, **192–5**, 289; indefinite 178, 179, 288; interrogative 94, 116, 117, 124, 138, 139, 152, **197**, 247, 291; negative **178–80**; personal 112, 129, **180–6**, 249, 250, 251, 253, 289; possessive 118, 138, 138, 152, **188–92**, 189, 190, 191, 288; reflexive 90, 129, 181, **186–8**, 251, 288, 306; relative 116, 117, 124, 130, 133, 138, 145, 150, 152, **195–8**; stressed **183**; universal **199–200**; unstressed **184**, **185**

pronunciation 9, 17, 29, 31, 219

punctuation 230, 303

quantifiers **282–7**; countable 119, 120, **282–4**, 285; types **282**; uncountable 119, 120, **284–5**, 285

sentence 72, **299–302**; complex **306**; elements 112, 116, 181, 299;

simple **306**; structure 249, 250, 252, 253, 288, **303–6**; types of clauses 72, 82–5, 99, 189, 195, 240, 242, 243, 246, 250, 252, 253, 301, 305, 306; word order **303**

šta – шта/šta 116, 124, 130, 133, 150, 178, 195, 196, 198, 246, 302

stress 29, **31**; sentence **32**; shift **32**; words and tone **31**, 235

suffixes 20, 22, 25, 26, 30, 38, 51–3, 105–11, 202, 203, 206, 210, 214, 229, 265, 268–70, 307, 308, **310–15**

svako – свако/svako **199–200**, 288

sve – све/sve **199–200**

svi – сви/svi **199–200**

svoj – свој/svoj **189–91**, 288

time **278–81**; expressions **280**; telling **278**

trebati – требати/trebati 38, 41, 86, 87, **102–3**, 121

verbs 35–7, 121, 126–9, 135, 136, 147, 148, 193, 198, 205, 224, 229, 230, 232, 258, 262, 264, 265, 269, 283, 292, 299, 300, 307; auxiliary 36, 64, 66, 67, 71, 72, 74, 82–5, **92**, **93**, 97, 103, 129, 250, 251, 253; conjugation **37**; durative **51**; gender **36–7**; imperfective 35, 36, 38, **51–8**, 93, 218, 230, 231; impersonal 17, **91–2**, 128, 129; infinitive 36, 37, 45–8, 55, 65, 67, 72, 74, 75, 78, 93, 110, 175, 218, 219, 220, 222, 232; intransitive 35, **50**, **51**, 90, 122, 218; iterative **51**; motion (of) 127, 133, 134, 147; perfective 35, 36, 38, **55–8**, 93, 218; reflexive 90, 91, 122, 128, 251; transitive 35, **50**, **51**, 90, 122, 133, 218, 220; types of and aspects **50**, 58

voleti – волети/voleti 86

vowels 9, 10, 18, 29, 31, 32, 232

weights and measures **272–3**
words: formation 141, 307; order
  303; prefixes 20, 22, 45, 56, 95,
  96, 98, 100, 121, 127, 203, 215,
  216, 224, 226, 291, 308; suffixes
  20, 22, 25, 26, 30, 38, 51–3,
  105–11, 202, 203, 206, 210,
  214, 229, 265, 268–70, 307, 308,
  310–14

žao – жао/žao **122**
zar – зар/zar 64, 70, 75, 81, 87, 94, 95

eBooks – at www.eBookstore.tandf.co.uk

A library at your fingertips!

eBooks are electronic versions of printed books. You can store them on your PC/laptop or browse them online.

They have advantages for anyone needing rapid access to a wide variety of published, copyright information.

eBooks can help your research by enabling you to bookmark chapters, annotate text and use instant searches to find specific words or phrases. Several eBook files would fit on even a small laptop or PDA.

NEW: Save money by eSubscribing: cheap, online access to any eBook for as long as you need it.

Annual subscription packages

We now offer special low-cost bulk subscriptions to packages of eBooks in certain subject areas. These are available to libraries or to individuals.

For more information please contact webmaster.ebooks@tandf.co.uk

We're continually developing the eBook concept, so keep up to date by visiting the website.

www.eBookstore.tandf.co.uk